WEST of
Imagining

AN ANTHOLOGY EDITED BY

North Point Press

the WEST

California

LEONARD MICHAELS

DAVID REID

RAQUEL SCHERR

San Francisco   1989

The editors extend affectionate thanks to our editor at North Point, Jennie
McDonald, for her wise council, good humor, extraordinary diligence, and
unfailing patience.

LIBRARY OF CONGRESS CATALOGING-IN-PUBLICATION DATA
West of the West / edited by Leonard Michaels, David Reid, Raquel Scherr
    p.   cm.
  ISBN: 0-86547-403-6
  1. California—Civilization. 2. California—Literary collections.
  I. Michaels, Leonard, 1933– . II. Reid, David, 1946– . III. Scherr,
  Raquel L.
F861.5.W4   1989
979.4'05—dc19   89-31123

Contents

Preface

In 1940 California was the fifth most populous state (after New York, Pennsylvania, Illinois, and Ohio). There were blue laws in Hollywood. The telephone exchanges in San Francisco were named China, Klondike, Seabright, Skyline, and Evergreen. The only Californian ever to become president was Herbert Hoover. As I write, California's population exceeds that of all other states, its economy is the sixth largest in the world, and Los Angeles County alone will soon claim one million more inhabitants (legal and other) than New York City's five boroughs. The latest Californian president gave social Darwinism a human face. As an unlooked-for consequence of our defeat in Indochina, the state is more Asian than it has been since the 1850s, when the world looked upon San Francisco as a Chinese city.

Though we sometimes stray as far back as the nineteenth century, when California was the exotic colony on the Pacific Coast of the imperial United States, most of the writing in this book was done after 1945 and reflects the great transformation that began during the Second World War. The excerpts and other selections in this book are neither strictly literary nor strictly documentary, if it is still permissible to make the distinction. Rather, the book moves promiscuously between the two. It contains crime reporting, meditations, travelers' tales, autobiography, new journalism, sociology, curious learning, diaries, diverse apocalypses, a jeremiad; writing by native Californians, born-again Californians, exiles and émigrés, Beat poets, and French savants; the reflections of a student revolutionary, a Trinidadian journalist, a Mexican poet, an Italian semiotician. This side of perversity, we have preferred the new or neglected to the familiar and frequently anthologized. Here you will not find "The Outcasts of Poker Flat," Raymond Chandler's description of a Santa Ana in "Red Wind," the lyrics of "California Dreaming" by the Mamas and the Papas, or "Hotel California" by the Eagles. Nothing about Aimee Semple McPherson, the Black Dahlia case, lifeguards at Zuma Beach, SoMa, Steve Jobs, or the acquisitions budget of the Getty Museum. You will find dispatches that regard sexual politics in Berkeley, mass murder, Altamont, Castro Street before the fall, community in East Oakland, mah-jongg in the Sunset district, graveyards in Glendale, two different versions of "hyperreality," the San Francisco poetry renaissance, Aryan migrations to the sea, writers "running down like clocks" on the beach at Big Sur, and Jonestown.

The book moves from south to north, pausing where pressure of history or spirit of place has impelled the most interesting writing. It reflects, obviously, the biases and eccentricities and limitations of our own tastes and reading. It describes a journey.

In California postmodernity exists against a primeval landscape suffused with golden light. Landscape and light have defined the complex body of fate which, incubuslike, shapes our lives on the Coast. Accordingly, the fiction, poetry, reportage, and controversy in this book are suspended between two great aerial views—Carey McWilliams's of Southern California and Aldous Huxley's of the desert. Against this background, in this live air and brilliant light, emerge the perennial California themes: youth, money, and the movies; asceticism and sensuality; the city, the coast, and the lowlands; apocalypse and renewal; mortuaries and mysticism; death and transfiguration.

DAVID REID
Berkeley, California

When I am in California, I am not in the west,
I am west of the west.   THEODORE ROOSEVELT

California is a queer place—in a way, it has
turned its back on the world, and looks into
the void Pacific.   D. H. LAWRENCE

WEST
of the
WEST

Atmospheres

There is an island called California, on the right hand of the Indies, very near the Earthly Paradise. . . .

ORDÓÑEZ DE MONTALVO

Carey McWilliams

South of Tehachapi

Southern California is the land "south of Tehachapi"—south, that is, of the transverse Tehachapi range which knifes across to the ocean just north of Santa Barbara. Once this range has been crossed, as Max Miller has said, "even the ocean, as well as the land structure, as well as the people, change noticeably." In the political parlance of the state, Northern California candidates have always "come down to the Tehachapi" with a certain majority. In the vast and sprawling state of California, most statewide religious, political, social, fraternal, and commercial organizations are divided into northern and southern sections at the Tehachapi line. When sales territories are parceled out, when political campaigns are organized, when offices are being allocated, the same line always prevails. The Tehachapi range has long symbolized the division of California into two major regions: north and south. While other states have an east-west or a north-south division, in no state in the Union is the schism as sharp as in California. So sharp is the demarcation in California that, when statewide meetings are held, they are usually convened in Fresno, long the "neutral territory" for conventions, conferences, and gatherings of all sort.

1. The Region

From San Francisco south, the coastline extends in a north-south direction until Point Conception is reached at latitude 34.30 degrees; then the line swerves abruptly east and the shoreline begins to face almost due south. Once Point Conception has been rounded in an ocean liner, once the Tehachapi range has been crossed by train or car, even the most obtuse observer, the rankest neophyte, can *feel* that he has entered a new and distinct province of the state. If Southern California is entered from the east, through El Cajon Pass or San Gorgonio Pass, the impression is even more vividly sensed. On the Pacific side, the coast range turns east. The mountains no longer shut off the interior from the sea. The air is softer, the ocean is bluer, and the skies have a lazy and radiant warmth. South of Point Conception, a new Pacific Ocean emerges: an ocean in which you can actually bathe and swim, an ocean that sparkles with sunlight, an ocean of many and brilliant colors. Here is California del Sur, the Cow Counties, subtropical California, the land south of Tehachapi.

Physically the region is as distinct, as unlike any other part of the state, as though it were another country. But this separateness is not accurately reflected in county boundaries. Southern California, properly speaking, is one of the smallest geographic regions in America. It includes part of Santa Barbara County (the portion south of Tehachapi), all of Ventura, Los Angeles, and Orange counties, and those portions of San Bernardino, Riverside, and San Diego counties west of the mountains. It does *not* include Imperial County, for Imperial Valley belongs, geographically and otherwise, to the Colorado River basin. Southern California is a coastal strip of land—"the fortunate coast" as Hamlin Garland once called it—275 miles in length and with a depth that ranges from a few miles to nearly a hundred miles from the mountains to the sea. The land area itself embraces approximately 11,729 square miles.

As a region, Southern California is rescued from the desert by the San Bernardino and San Jacinto mountains on the east and is walled off from the great Central Valley by the transverse Tehachapi range which, running in an east-west direction, unites the Sierra Nevada and the coast ranges. Not only do these towering mountain ranges serve to keep out the heat and dust of the desert, but they are high enough to snatch moisture from the ocean winds and to form clouds. The land itself faces west, toward the Pacific, from which the winds blow with great regularity. It is this combination of mountain ranges, ocean breezes, and semidesert terrain that makes the climate, and the climate in turn makes the land.

Offshore are the Channel Islands, definitely a part of the region although traditionally detached from its social life. At one time several of the islands were thickly populated with Indians, but the Spaniards removed the Indians to the mainland, leaving the islands as deserted as they are today (with the exception of resort-ridden Santa Catalina). To the north, near Point Conception, are the islands of the Santa Barbara group: perennially fogbound San Miguel, the Anacapas, Santa Rosa, Santa Cruz, and San Nicolas well offshore. About a hundred miles south of Santa Barbara are the Catalina Islands: Santa Catalina and San Clemente; while still further south, near San Diego, are the islands of the Los Coronados group.

In all of Southern California, there are no fully mature soils. Stretching from the Sierras to the sea, the lowlands are covered with huge coalescing alluvian fans formed of materials washed down from the mountains. The coastal plains are broken, here and there, by branches of the Sierra Madre range and by three of the driest rivers in America: the Los Angeles, the San Gabriel, and the Santa Ana. It was surely of these rivers that Mark Twain spoke when he said that he had fallen into a California river and "come out all dusty." Today the three rivers carry only a limited amount of surface and drainage waters, although each has an excellent underground flow. Here, in Southern California, as J. Russell Smith has observed, "rain makes possible the homes of man where otherwise there would be only jack rabbits, pastures, a little extensive farming, and a few small irrigated oases."

Basically the region is a paradox: a desert that faces an ocean. Since it is desert or semidesert country, maximum sunshine prevails most of the year. The sunshine makes up for what the soils lack—a discovery that both Anglo and Hispano settlers were slow to make. Before man completely changed the ecology of the region, the natural landscape was not particularly prepossessing. The native vegetation consisted of chaparral on the moist mountain slopes and bunch grass on the lowlands. The real richness of the land is not to be found in the soils but in the combination of sky and air and ocean breezes. The wisecrack that Los Angeles is half wind and half water describes a real condition. As a region, Southern California lacks nearly everything: good soils; natural harbors (San Diego has the one natural harbor); forest and mineral resources; rivers, streams, and lakes; adaptable flora and fauna; and a sustaining hinterland. Yet the region has progressed amazingly by a succession of swift, revolutionary changes, from one level of development to another, offsetting natural limitations with an inventive technology. Its one great natural asset, in fact, is its climate.

The climate of Southern California is palpable: a commodity that can be labeled, priced, and marketed. It is not something that you talk about, complain about, or guess about. On the contrary, it is the most consistent, the least paradoxical factor in the environment. Unlike climates the world over, it is predictable to the point of monotony. In its air-conditioned equability, it might well be called artificial. The climate is the region. It has attracted unlimited resources of manpower and wealth, made possible intensive agricultural development, and located specialized industries, such as motion pictures. It has given the region its rare beauty. For the charm of Southern California is largely to be found in the air and the light. Light and air are really one element: indivisible, mutually interacting, thoroughly interpenetrated. Without the ocean breezes, the sunlight would be intolerable; without the sunlight and imported water, virtually nothing would grow in the region.

When the sunlight is not screened and filtered by the moisture-laden air, the land is revealed in all its semiarid poverty. The bald, sculptured mountains stand forth in a harsh and glaring light. But let the light turn soft with ocean mist, and miraculous changes occur. The bare mountain ranges, appallingly harsh in contour, suddenly become wrapped in an entrancing ever-changing loveliness of light and shadow; the most commonplace objects assume a matchless perfection of form; and the land itself becomes a thing of beauty. The color of the land is in the light and the light is somehow artificial and controlled. Things are not killed by the sunlight, as in a desert; they merely dry up. A desert light brings out the sharpness of points, angles, and forms. But this is not a desert light nor is it tropical for it has neutral tones. It is Southern California light and it has no counterpart in the world.

The geographers say that the quality of Southern California's climate is pure Mediterranean—the only specimen of Mediterranean climate in the United States. But such words as "Mediterranean" and "subtropical" are most misleading when applied to Southern California. Unlike the Mediterranean coast, Southern California has no sultry summer air, no mosquito-ridden malarial marshes, no mistral winds. A freak of nature—a cool and semimoist desert—Southern California is climatically insulated, shut off from the rest of the continent. As Helen Hunt Jackson once said, and it is the best description of the region yet coined, "It is a sort of island on the land." It is an island, however, of sharp contrasts. To William Rose Benet, the land suggests "a flowing life circle cut into contrasting angles . . . hills change over a week from garish green to golden brown; days are hot in the sun and cool in the shade; dense fog and spotless sky; giant trees or bare slopes; burnt sand or riotous flowers."

Traveling west from Chicago, the transition from one landscape to another, although often abrupt, is altogether logical. The rich, black Mississippi bottom lands shade off imperceptibly into the Kansas wheat lands; the Kansas plains lead naturally up to the foothills of the Rocky Mountains; once over the mountains, stretches of desert alternate with high piñon-covered plateaus; and, across the Colorado River, the desert climbs slowly to the last mountain range.

Up to this point, the contrasting landscapes have seemed pleasing and appropriate; the eye has not been offended nor the emotions shocked. But, once the final descent has been made from the desert, through Cajon Pass to the floor of the coastal plain at San Bernardino, one has entered a new world, an island tenuously attached to the rest of the continent. "My first impression," wrote L. P. Jacks, "was such as one might receive on arriving in a City of Refuge, or alternatively on entering the atmosphere of a religious retreat. Here, it seems, is the place where harassed Americans come to recover the joy and serenity which their manner of life denies them elsewhere, the place, in short, to study America in flight from herself." Logically Southern California should be several miles offshore, so that one might be prepared for the transition from the desert and the intermountain West. But, if the long train trip is thought of, as it should be, as an ocean crossing, then the island-like character of the region is properly revealed.

Southern California is the land of the "sun-down sea," where the sun suddenly plummets into the ocean, disappearing "like a lost and bloody cause." It is a land where "the Sun's rim dips—at one stride comes the Dark." Of landward rolling mists, but not of clouds; of luminous nights, but not of stars; of evanescent light, but not of sunsets; of rounded rolling hills and mountains without trees. Here the sun glares out of a high blue sky—a sun that can beat all sense from your brains, that can be "destructive of all you have known and believed": a relentless, pounding, merciless sun. But when the mists roll in at evening, the skies brighten with "blue daylight" and the air is like "a damp cloth on the forehead of the hills." Cool and fragrant and alive, the nights engulf the glaring pavements, the white stucco homes, the red-tiled roofs, the harsh and barren hills. From Mount Wilson, late at night, one can look down on a vast pulsating blaze of lights, quivering like diamonds in the dark. Here, as Frank Fenton notes, the land does not hug the sky; it is the sky that is solid and real and the land that seems to float. At times you feel as though you were far away "on the underside of the earth."

2. The Seasons

Most people believe that there are only two seasons in Southern California: "the wet" and "the dry." But this crude description fails to take account of the imperceptible changes that occur within the two major seasons. Actually, Southern California has two springs, two summers, and a season of rain. The first spring—the premature spring—follows closely upon the early rains in the late fall. In November the days shorten, the nights become cooler, the atmosphere clears (except when brush fires are burning in the hills), the air is stilled, and the land is silent. By November people have begun to *listen* for rain. The land is dry and parched and the leaves of the trees are thick with dust. The dry season has now begun to fray nerves, to irritate nostrils, and to bear down on the people. When the wind blows, it is full of particles of dust and dry leaves, of sand and heat.

And then come the first rains, drifting in long graceful veils, washing the land, clearing the atmosphere: the gentlest baptism imaginable. The people have known to a moral certainty that these rains would come; they have been expecting them; and yet they are forever delighted and surprised when they appear. The earth is reborn, the year starts anew with the rains. James Rorty has perfectly captured the elation aroused by the first rains:

> Faultless in wisdom, at my window-pane
> Compassionate sweet laughter of the rain.
> The cowled hills, rising, met and kissed
> The grey-eyed daughters of the mist;
> Above the flawed and driven tide
> The white gulls flapped wet wings and cried;
> High on the slope the cattle lowed and ran,
> On every hill the meadow-larks began
> Their confident loud chime of Spring's rebirth;
> Iris and tooth-wort stirred the fragrant earth . . .
>
> I, too, who let the blown rain whip my face,
> Received my portion of the season's grace.

After these first rains—which fall gently, never in torrents—the sun is softer: it no longer burns, the air is cool and fragrant, and the hills begin to change. In a miraculously short period—a matter of days—the country is green and fresh. It is not the "green-dense and dim-delicious" green of the poets of the English countryside. Rather the land is clothed in a freakish greenery, a green so bright that, at times, it is almost sickening. "It is a bright emerald hue," as one observer has noted, "and has a sheen upon it which is like that upon the rind of green fruit, but much stronger. This appearance is very rank, and looks as though it would come off on your hands."

The first spring has now arrived: "the little spring" that only lasts a few weeks. A premonition of spring, it tricks the senses of the people and deludes the plants and flowers which start to bud and blossom out of season. Often called the false spring, it deceives the gullible semitropical plants which sometimes bloom weeks, and even months, in advance of their regular schedule. Jasmine, bougainvillea, privet, hibiscus, oleanders, and trumpet vines, usually dormant at this time of the year, suddenly start to bloom. Under the illusion that spring has arrived, bare-root roses blossom and the buds of peach and apricot trees begin to swell. But this is not spring, only a conceit of nature, a lovely winter mirage.

And then in January, February, and March come the real rains: heavy, torrential, soggy. These rains do not slant in from the sea, but, like emptied buckets of water, fall straight and level on the earth. The arroyos race with rain waters; the dry river beds overflow; the floods have arrived. The earth now smells wet and the chaparral begins to brighten. The last rains come in April— "grasshopper rains" they were once called—showers and squalls, fitful and intermittent. Before the last rains have fallen, the real spring has arrived. There is a sudden blaze of color on the land. The green has changed from its early vividness to the heavier dense green of the rains, and, as the season advances, the green begins to bleach and fade. This second spring is really an aborted summer.

The second spring ends with the first desert winds, which usually come in May and last for several days. The ocean breezes suddenly cease, as the hot dry desert winds come whirling down the canyons, through the passes, and rush out across the valleys. Harsh and burning winds, they rip off palm leaves, snap branches, topple over eucalyptus trees, and occasionally carry off a flimsy roof. The desert winds bring dust and heat. The mountains stand out in the sharpest possible outline, so clear that you can see the rocks and boulders, so close that you can almost touch them. These are the winds once called "northers," but which the Spanish called "santannas." Doña Magdalena Murrillo, born on the Las Bolsas Rancho in 1848, said that the winds were called "Santa Anas" because they came down the Santa Ana Canyon. They were always very hot, she said, and stirred up a *polvareda grande*. When the Santa Anas came, no one dared light a fire, even in a stove. Don Jesus Aguilar, of San Juan Capistrano, said the wind was called *El Viento del Norte*; but Willa Cather, referring to hot desert winds in New Mexico, called them "santannas." The desert winds often precede the last rain of the season.

After the desert winds comes June: cool and gray, with day-long mists and overcast. The summer flowers are at their loveliest; the lawns are damp and fragrant; and the leaves of the camphor tree, brightest and gayest of all the trees in Southern California, shimmer and dance in the air. But by late May it is already fall—in the hills, away from the fountains and the sprinklers. The hills are tawny and the black shade of the live oaks is dense and heavy. The full blaze of summer color has gone by July and the summer that follows is the long summer of the dry season, when the hills are brown as umber. August is "only the long-lingering afternoon of a long-lingering summer day." In late August the sea breeze dies and once again the desert winds sweep across the land. This is the hottest spell of the year: baking hot, desert-hot, oppressive. Brush fires break out in the foothills just as they often do when the Santa Anas come in May. Heat from the brush fires, smoking and blazing in the foothills, makes the inland districts writhe and burn.

"Where had been a lush thicket of ferns," writes Steward Edward White, "now the earth lay naked and baked, displaying unexpected simplicities of contour that had before been mysteriously veiled. So hard and trodden looked this earth that it seemed incredible that any green thing had ever, or could ever again, pierce its steel-like shell. The land was stripped bare. In the trees the wind rustled dryly. In the sky the sun shone glaringly." The fog banks, however, prevent the summers from being oppressive throughout the season. Forming beyond the islands, they can be seen moving in toward the coast "in long attenuated streamers and banners, as night comes on, filling up the valleys of the coast with great tumultuous seas." With the morning sunlight, the mists obligingly roll out to sea. Throughout the summer, one can see this fog bank, about a thousand feet thick, lying offshore on the water. It has the strange feature, wrote Van Dyke, "of moving in against a breeze—the land-breeze—and moving out against another—the sea-breeze."

Toward the end of the long summer, when the unirrigated sections of the land are a gray, sunbaked tan, one can see, as James M. Cain has observed, that "the naked earth shows through everything that grows on it." It is then that one notices the sparseness of leafage in relation to the land. The earth is naked and exposed in Southern California. It is like the skin of a suntanned body with the few indigenous trees standing out sharply, like the hairs on the body, and not, as in other areas, like a thick mat of hair on the head. There is no carpet on the earth. Everywhere exposed, the earth is brown and gray and only seldom green. Today the appearance of the region is deceitful and illusory, for essentially it is a barren, a semiarid land.

Julián Marías

California
as Paradise

The usual word for California, the one that first rises to the lips, is that it is a paradise. And that is true. Arriving in California from the East, you gain the impression of entering into the land of Paradise. And not only if you arrive in winter: for the contrast between the ice, snow, glacial winds, and bare trees of the rest of the country and California's warm air, blue sky, greenery, and lazy ocean is too obvious and therefore not particularly significant. It is the same impression as that induced by a move from one hemisphere to another when a plane takes us in a few hours from winter to summer. No, an arrival in California takes on more interest when the circumstances are more equal; when, for instance, the sun shines forth with as great intensity in the East and Middle West and in the Rocky Mountains as on the shores of the Pacific; when the whole land is covered with green and the entire sky is heavenly blue; when all that beauty is absolutely true. Then one still feels (and this time without tricks or playing false with the seasons) that one has entered Paradise.

What is Paradise? A garden, as was the Garden of Eden. Few places in the United States are garden spots. There are wild, untrammelled, and rugged forest lands in the North Atlantic states and along the Canadian border; there is utilitarian land, good for growing wheat and corn, on the endless plains of Illinois and Ohio; bleak prairies and wastelands in Wyoming or Utah; deserts in

Arizona and New Mexico. California is another matter, truly an oasis—especially Southern California—a colossal oasis nourished by irrigation and the Pacific Ocean, where the hand of man is felt close by. And even in the wildest areas, where nature has taken charge of everything, there is a strange kind of carefulness, a peculiar composition of forms, a kind of order—_kósmos_—that is reminiscent of a garden. Thus it is even in the redwood forests, among the sequoias that border the city of San Francisco, trees two thousand years old, straight and tall and all nicely arranged. A whole family of deer may start up from among them, and at dusk there is an air of mystery that descends; but it is a literary mystery, out of a child's book, that has to do with a gigantic garden, a paradise from _Gulliver's Travels_, the wonders of Alice, and the magic world of Bambi and Falina.

And the cities? They too belong in Paradise. White stucco houses, often capriciously incongruous, that look like toys or, better, like a stage setting. And gardens that in some places, such as Pasadena, dominate the whole scene. And an air of constant fiesta or vacation; nowhere else in the world is effort less visible, less apparent, less exhibited. Thus Adam cultivated the Garden of Eden—without painful effort, without toiling, without suffering. Even in the least prosperous or well-to-do sections which are, if one looks carefully, very sordid and depressingly ugly (East Los Angeles, for example) the ever-present ghastly billboards with enormous letters of all colors, the paper or plastic streamers surrounding the lots where hundreds of used automobiles are stockpiled for sale, the transient air of the flimsy frame houses, almost shanties, all lend an atmosphere of fair or carnival, a party disguise, to those shoddy remnants of Paradise. (Where there is no Paradise at all is in the old town, the downtown center of Los Angeles, today mostly a Mexican quarter, because there the city is decaying under the sordidness that crept over it; it has "fallen away"—quite the opposite description from Paradise; Paradise Lost, if you prefer.)

This paradisaical character of California makes all the more surprising the discovery, only a few miles from Los Angeles, of enormous oil fields, of refineries working around the clock, of Navy arsenals where colossal pyramids of underwater mines are stockpiled. This presents a brusquely unexpected transition from Paradise to the City of Enoch, but the first stage remains so "natural," so alive and so powerful that perhaps the oil wells therefore spring up from a foreground of blazing flowers. And nearby is a cemetery for dogs, with small monuments and even a Conestoga wagon: again we get the impression of a plaything, a child's tale, a fable, unreality.

Paradise is the absence of limitation, the lack of difficulty. The first condition may be found in many places, in all lands with space to spare where history is scarce; the second condition is more improbable. It cannot obtain where nature is rugged, violent, or immoderate, where heat and cold are oppressors, where there is an everyday battle against inclemency; nor can it flourish where man is inferior to his environment, where he is in need of everything or of many things—nor even where he lacks superfluous but vital luxury.

For this reason many gentle lands are not Paradise, and for the same reason California is; for that is the place where a well-nigh miraculous technology, an unprecedented amount of wealth, and the perfect structuring of man's cities have together achieved the height of pure implausibility.

Certainly, California is a paradise. The complimentary cliché is right. But even as I admit that, I am inclined to turn the statement into a reproach. In a sense, together with all its joys, that is the defect that California presents; because Paradise is an impossibility for men to construct on earth, and the Californian is no exception to the rule. Furthermore, the excellences of Paradise are in the long run deficiencies in the "real world," which is of necessity constituted of possibilities and limitations, facilities and difficulties, urgency and constraint. To live in the world means to be always between the swordpoint and the wall, to have to make the right choice with every moment, to have infinite resources at one's disposition but a counted number of days, to be born and to die.

Yes, also to die, of course; the world is a place where death does exist. And California (especially the most indubitably Californian part of the state, Los Angeles) tries to make death disintegrate and vanish. Not by denying death—that would be too naive—but quite to the contrary, by infusing its presence everywhere, making it part of everyday trivia, removing its sting, despoiling death thus of its inevitability. This is why ads for funeral homes and cemeteries are as common as those praising automobiles, beer, or perfume—and similar in tone. This is why one "manages" with such complete naturalness everything "that has to do with" death, an ingenious manner of eliminating death itself. This is also why, finally, Forest Lawn cemetery, one of California's most representative creations, is established on the basis of two kinds of life: that of those who stroll through the gates, bathed by the sun and caressed by the breezes of the Pacific only a short distance from Hollywood; and the happy afterlife of those with property rights therein, whether lying horizontally or encased in an urn of ashes. This avoids the elementary fact that the latter are *dead*, that in order to enter Forest Lawn and that blessed life thereafter, they had to cross through the narrow door we call death—the one thing that is missing in any paradise, the thing that appears on the horizon when one leaves Paradise and enters irrevocably into the human world.

Vincent Bugliosi (with Curt Gentry)

Saturday, August 9, 1969

It was so quiet, one of the killers would later say, you could almost hear the sound of ice rattling in cocktail shakers in the homes way down the canyon.

The canyons above Hollywood and Beverly Hills play tricks with sounds. A noise clearly audible a mile away may be indistinguishable at a few hundred feet.

It was hot that night, but not as hot as the night before, when the temperature hadn't dropped below 92 degrees. The three-day heat wave had begun to break a couple of hours before, about 10 P.M. on Friday—to the psychological as well as the physical relief of those Angelenos who recalled that on such a night, just four years ago, Watts had exploded in violence. Though the coastal fog was now rolling in from the Pacific Ocean, Los Angeles itself remained hot and muggy, sweltering in its own emissions, but here, high above most of the city, and usually even above the smog, it was at least ten degrees cooler. Still, it remained warm enough so that many residents of the area slept with their windows open, in hopes of catching a vagrant breeze.

All things considered, it's surprising that more people didn't hear something. But then it was late, just after midnight, and 10050 Cielo Drive was secluded. Being secluded, it was also vulnerable.

Cielo Drive is a narrow street that abruptly winds upward from Benedict Canyon Road. One of its cul-de-sacs, easily missed though directly opposite Bella Drive, comes to a dead end at the high gate of 10050. Looking through the gate, you could see neither the main residence nor the guest house some distance beyond it, but you could see, toward the end of the paved parking area, a corner of the garage and, a little farther on, a split-rail fence which, though it was only August, was strung with Christmas-tree lights.

The lights, which could be seen most of the way from the Sunset Strip, had been put up by actress Candice Bergen when she was living with the previous tenant of 10050 Cielo Drive, TV and record producer Terry Melcher. When Melcher, the son of Doris Day, moved to his mother's beach house in Malibu, the new tenants left the lights up. They were on this night, as they were every night, adding a year-round holiday touch to Benedict Canyon.

From the front door of the main house to the gate was over a hundred feet. From the gate to the nearest neighbor on Cielo, 10070, was almost a hundred yards.

At 10070 Cielo, Mr. and Mrs. Seymour Kott had already gone to bed, their dinner guests having left about midnight, when Mrs. Kott heard, in close sequence, what sounded like three or four gunshots. They seemed to have come from the direction of the gate of 10050. She did not check the time but later guessed it to be between 12:30 and 1 A.M. Hearing nothing further, Mrs. Kott went to sleep.

About three-quarters of a mile directly south and downhill from 10050 Cielo Drive, Tim Ireland was one of five counselors supervising an overnight camp-out for some thirty-five children at the Westlake School for Girls. The other counselors had gone to sleep, but Ireland had volunteered to stay up through the night. At approximately 12:40 A.M. he heard from what seemed a long distance away, to the north or northeast, a solitary male voice. The man was screaming, "*Oh, God, no, please don't! Oh, God, no, don't, don't, don't. . .*"

The scream lasted ten to fifteen seconds, then stopped, the abrupt silence almost as chilling as the cry itself. Ireland quickly checked the camp, but all the children were asleep. He awoke his supervisor, Rich Sparks, who had bedded down inside the school, and, telling him what he had heard, got his permission to drive around the area to see if anyone needed help. Ireland took a circuitous route from North Faring Road, where the school was located, south on Benedict Canyon Road to Sunset Boulevard, west to Beverly Glen, and northward back to the school. He observed nothing unusual, though he did hear a number of dogs barking.

There were other sounds in the hours before dawn that Saturday.

Emmett Steele, 9951 Beverly Grove Drive, was awakened by the barking of his two hunting dogs. The pair usually ignored ordinary sounds but went wild when they heard gunshots. Steele went out to look around but, finding nothing out of place, returned to bed. He estimated the time as between 2 and 3 A.M.

Robert Bullington, an employee of the Bel Air Patrol, a private security force used by many of the homeowners in the affluent area, was parked in front of 2175 Summit Ridge Drive, with his window down, when he heard what sounded like three shots, spaced a few seconds apart. Bullington called in; Eric Karlson, who was working the desk at patrol headquarters, logged the call at 4:11 A.M. Karlson in turn called the West Los Angeles Division of the Los Angeles Police Department (LAPD), and passed on the report. The officer who took the call remarked, "I hope we don't have a murder; we just had a woman-screaming call in that area."

Los Angeles Times delivery boy Steve Shannon heard nothing unusual when he pedaled his bike up Cielo Drive between 4:30 and 4:45 A.M. But as he put the paper in the mailbox of 10050, he did notice what looked like a telephone wire hanging over the gate. He also observed, through the gate and some distance away, that the yellow bug light on the side of the garage was still on.

Seymour Kott also noticed the light and the fallen wire when he went out to get his paper about 7:30 A.M.

About 8 A.M., Winifred Chapman got off the bus at the intersection of Santa Monica and Canyon Drive. A light-skinned black in her mid fifties, Mrs. Chapman was the housekeeper at 10050 Cielo, and she was upset because, thanks to L.A.'s terrible bus service, she was going to be late to work. Luck seemed with her, however; just as she was about to look for a taxi, she saw a man she had once worked with, and he gave her a ride almost to the gate.

She noticed the wire immediately, and it worried her.

In front and to the left of the gate, not hidden but not conspicuous either, was a metal pole on the top of which was the gate-control mechanism. When the button was pushed, the gate swung open. There was a similar mechanism inside the grounds, both being positioned so a driver could reach the button without having to get out of the car.

Because of the wire, Mrs. Chapman thought the electricity might be off, but when she pushed the button, the gate swung open. Taking the *Times* out of the mailbox, she walked hurriedly onto the property, noticing an unfamiliar automobile in the driveway, a white Rambler, parked at an odd angle. But she passed it, and several other cars nearer the garage, without much thought. Overnight guests weren't that uncommon. Someone had left the outside light on all night, and she went to the switch at the corner of the garage and turned it off.

At the end of the paved parking area was a flagstone walkway that made a half circle to the front door of the main house. She turned right before coming to the walk, however, going to the service porch entrance at the back of the residence. The key was secreted on a rafter above the door. Taking it down, she unlocked the door and went inside, walking directly to the kitchen, where she picked up the extension phone. It was dead.

Thinking that she should alert someone that the line was down, she proceeded through the dining room toward the living room. Then she stopped suddenly, her progress impeded by two large blue steamer trunks, which hadn't been there when she had left the previous afternoon—and by what she saw.

There appeared to be blood on the trunks, on the floor next to them, and on two towels in the entryway. She couldn't see the entire living room—a long couch cut off the area in front of the fireplace—but everywhere she could see she saw the red splashes. The front door was ajar. Looking out, she saw several pools of blood on the flagstone porch. And, farther on, on the lawn, she saw a body.

Screaming, she turned and ran back through the house, leaving the same way she had come in but, on running down the driveway, changing her course so as to reach the gate-control button. In so doing, she passed on the opposite side of the white Rambler, seeing for the first time that there was a body inside the car too.

Once outside the gate, she ran down the hill to the first house, 10070, ringing the bell and pounding on the door. When the Kotts didn't answer, she ran to the next house, 10090, banging on that door and screaming, "*Murder, death, bodies, blood!*"

Fifteen-year-old Jim Asin was outside, warming up the family car. It was Saturday and, a member of Law Enforcement Unit 800 of the Boy Scouts of America, he was waiting for his father, Ray Asin, to drive him to the West Los Angeles Division of LAPD, where he was scheduled to work on the desk. By the time he got to the porch, his parents had opened the door. While they were trying to calm the hysterical Mrs. Chapman, Jim dialed the police emergency number. Trained by the Scouts to be exact, he noted the time: 8:33.

While waiting for the police, the father and son walked as far as the gate. The white Rambler was some thirty feet inside the property, too far away to make out anything inside it, but they did see that not one but several wires were down. They appeared to have been cut.

Returning home, Jim called the police a second time and, some minutes later, a third.

There is some confusion as to exactly what happened to the calls. The official police report only states, "At 0914 hours, West Los Angeles Units 8L5 and 8L62 were given a radio call, 'Code 2, possible homicide, 10050 Cielo Drive.' "

The units were one-man patrol cars. Officer Jerry Joe DeRosa, driving 8L5, arrived first, light flashing and siren blaring. DeRosa began interviewing Mrs. Chapman, but had a difficult time of it. Not only was she still hysterical, she was vague as to what she had seen—"blood, bodies everyplace"—and it was hard to get the names and relationships straight. Polanski. Altobelli. Frykowski.

Ray Asin, who knew the residents of 10050 Cielo, stepped in. The house was owned by Rudi Altobelli. He was in Europe, but had hired a caretaker, a young man named William Garretson, to look after the place. Garretson lived in the guest house to the back of the property. Altobelli had rented the main residence to Roman Polanski, the movie director, and his wife. The Polanskis had gone to Europe, however, in March, and while they were away, two of their friends, Abigail Folger and Voytek Frykowski, had moved in. Mrs. Polanski had returned less than a month ago, and Frykowski and Folger were staying on with her until her husband returned. Mrs. Polanski was a movie actress. Her name was Sharon Tate.

Hollywood

Los Angeles had been on fire for three days. As I took a taxi from the studio I asked the driver, "How's the fire doing?" "You mean," said the Hollywoodian, "the holocaust." The style, you see, must come as easily and naturally as that.   GORE VIDAL

David Thomson

Driving in a Back Projection

Try to imagine a traveling enquiry in which the view changes according to what may be our most commonplace magic, driving in the city, handling the wheel and being rewarded with a stream of effortless, unexpected sights.

As far back as the eye can see, the air and place of American movies are California. I am thinking of elements in the picture that we take for granted: the adrenaline light, some sediment of haze and sight's limits that stand for distance, the prickly hump of hill behind John Wayne, the square of receding street seen through the back of a car in which Cagney's fierce but defeated eyes are fixed on "getaway"—fierce because he wants to go, but defeated because this car never moves, no matter how persistently the background assures his escape.

The story's hoodlums did break out, into death or glory. But the actors resided in Bel Air; and if they lasted long enough they noticed that the city's light was growing brown and bitter from the crowd and all the ways it used up freshness.

That perfect light is always there on the screen, even in day-for-night where it makes nocturnal meetings hot and sweaty; it is one of the abundant natural facilities that made California the home of picture-making. The hill has been patient in countless shoot-outs, never once winking at the camera to say,

"Don't you *know* who's going to win?" And the street scene was kept in a can for years, available to be unwound behind every rocking but tethered car, a back projection as serviceable as the length of red carpet that travels with the British royal family to ensure that their steps are hallowed.

These are real commodities. Three hundred days of sunshine a year in Southern California are no more fraudulent or less photogenic than half that number from New Jersey. The most heavily used back lot may have been trampled flat by the design staffs who erected Shanghai there last week, and Casablanca this, but it can be measured in square feet and property values. Today, pictures can go to Casablanca and Shanghai; they are ablaze with the real thing. But they miss the point, the imperial, storytelling confidence that staged faraway places in Los Angeles. Obviously that had to do with cheerful indifference to the real China or North Africa. But if we scold that too much we may miss seeing a concomitant insight—that L.A. could be anything, because L.A. was not quite a solid "here" or "there," not quite an item in geography.

The back-projection street that goes with Cagney is a stock item, like "excitement" music that could be poured over every "getaway" scene, or like the close-up of Jimmy, so head-on that it must make driving so much more difficult than the idea of being driven. Still, the street behind was, let us say, Wilshire between Vermont and Western on a Thursday morning in October 1934, and there, fifty yards behind Cagney, was Mrs. Koslovsky, going to the market. She turned back to her dawdling boy, Max, just as Jimmy snarled to the air and an audience yet to be, "I'm crashing out for *good*." Max and his mother were scraps of life in the snapshot, unaware that their midmorning "Come along, slowcoach" would go unheard, but marginally apprehended in fifty Warner Brothers tributes to crime on the streets.

The compliant sunshine, the studio props department, and the Koslovskys were all Californian; and just because they were all bundled together in the same eighty-eight-minute fabrication doesn't mean that the historian, or anyone interested, should dismiss the evidence they offer. As evidence, I think, it is all the more appealing in that it is so casual, so devoid of intent. Movies full of entertaining lies that are stiff with intent and controlled telling are also spilling over with helpless, neglected phenomena, and the least doctored of those, the most available, are visible background, the presence of California. Examine studio records, and you might ascertain that between ten and eleven on that second-unit's morning on Wilshire, it was sunny. Look closer, with a magnifying glass, perhaps, freezing the frames that want to melt away, and you might see a police car bundling past Cagney (when surely it should be after him), giving dreamy Max a scare and disappearing toward downtown where—further research discovers—a jeweler's at Third and Miramar had been broken into by toughs who had seen a Cagney picture the night before, for hints and courage.

Suppose a bystander was killed in the incident at Third and Miramar: imagine your own rage and loathing if you had seen the real thing. Now consider the wicked enthusiasm with which you are urging Cagney on in the screen. Los Angeles was a factory city that manufactured lifelike fancies in which our relationship to reality was drastically altered. It may be a more potent invention than any Bomb.

We do not have enough historians to check out where everyone in that back projection was going. But we do agree that, more or less, in the ordinary way of hope, every one of them thought he or she was the center of the universe. My "Max Koslovsky" is an invention. Still, it seems to me a routine ethnic name, two words a child actor might learn and speak as Cagney's character, rounding a corner, ruffled the child's hair and said, "Hey, kid, what's your name?" But children do amble across momentous streets, and in Los Angeles no one in the last seventy years has ever been sure that a camera isn't watching. Isn't that the drugstore where Lana Turner was discovered? Or is that whole "access to fame" line a conspiracy among small corner stores, inviting us in because we might be discovered? Is that what the video cameras in the top corners of banks and markets are all about? Mrs. Koslovsky may have been setting out to get a nice piece of fish for Maxie, but in Los Angeles she would never have given up loftier dreams for her boy. "Hey, Maxie, do you know what the mailman said? He said you reminded him of that Leo Gorcey"—one of the Bowery Boys, whose exploits were struck in silver salts in Burbank, Culver City, or Gower Gulch.

There are films more deserving of a California historian's attention. When Eric von Stroheim went to San Francisco and Oakland to make *Greed* in the early 1920s, the cities were linked only by ferries. There are moments in *Greed* when you can see and feel the importance of the Ferry Building, though now it is dwarfed and patronized by the Bay Bridge. And there are scenes in which McTeague, the dentist, and Trina, his love, sit on the beach with only pale, desolate water behind them. Their images are lonelier, larger, and more poignant because the progressive spans of bridge do not yet contain them. You can feel how in 1923 the Bay Area was not an area but only a number of separate communities and the daunting space of water.

It seems that Robert Altman made his *The Long Goodbye* only yesterday, instead of in 1973; but that is the farewell fallacy. Think yourself forward to, say, 2019, when the true Los Angeles might meet the studio prognostication of *Blade Runner*, a dense plastic and neon burden of metropolis presiding over alley-streets where Asiatics serve hot snacks, animals jostle the hustlers, and rain makes an undergrowth of trash; and where the burned-out lights of the Bradbury Building give entrance to a deserted cathedral of somber wrought iron, allegedly built for commerce but always more mindful of being available for *film noir*.

In that world, Altman's *Long Goodbye* could seem like an elegy to the deserted village that once was Paradise. Do you remember when people lived at Malibu, the Sunday beach parties, and those plate-glass facades in which, after dark, you might record in your mind's movie, but not have to notice, the reflected image of your husband, drunk, staggering bravely into the waves to kill himself? Remember suicide, and drugs, and those gorgeous cars and the way they seemed to leave an unbroken smear of acid color on the freeways? Do you remember the freeways and the supermarkets, and the morning fog you knew would burn off by eleven? God, the light then, the ease, the jokes. Why, the central character in *The Long Goodbye* teases people all the time, and that's really all he does, imitating actors in movies, and stoically enduring his own failure less than thirty years later to keep up the glamor of Bogart's Philip Marlowe. So he kids himself, and us, for watching. You won't know about kidding in 2019, maybe, but there was a lot of it in L.A. in the 1970s.

I am imagining that teasing will have gone out of our lives, or that it will have become such an orthodoxy, so full a scheme of lying, that there will be no charm or edge left to it. After all, teasing is a moment in our relationship with reality when we know both the real thing and its awful or delicious shadows, and when, in play, we flit from one to the other to show our grace and our spirit of traveling. It is the irony that can see Cagney going hell-for-leather from a fictitious crime, while real police cars charge in the opposite, "wrong" direction toward an authentic outrage. And it is wondering whether the jewel heist was inspired by a Cagney picture. Even in a fireball explosion, "Made it, Ma, top of the world" is hardly a warning or the urging of civil order. It is the payoff in a joke, for only movie stars truly know the exhilaration of screen gangsters.

How far does the irony cut? Does it make everyone his own actor, and every place just a backdrop? Well, California remains a stirring reality, even if its ecology struggles to keep up with the mythology. It is wild still in many places; its beauty is robust, not yet tamed by being photographed. It is the desert, the Sierras, the sparkling gray stretch of Los Angeles like glitter in rubber, the model of pride and danger in the hills of San Francisco, the redwood forests, the coast between Big Sur and Carmel, a valley named Death, the vegetable patch around Salinas, the flower festival at Santa Barbara, the cosiness of small fishing ports up the coast from San Francisco, the mansions on Sunset Boulevard, the rancid border with Mexico, the strange and sinister aqueduct bringing water to Los Angeles.

After two and a half years in California I have seen most of those real things and had some sense of how early filmmakers must have hugged themselves. "It's all here, desert as well as milk and honey, box canyons for Westerns, beaches and cliffs for smuggling pictures, wide streets for car chases." And so on. But I had known them all before I arrived in the West. I had seen the desert in *Greed* and *Zabriskie Point*, perpetual moral reminder and harbinger of nothingness to the busy city ants. In *High Sierra*, I had watched Bogart strive to escape into the peaks; in *10*, there was an exquisite view of Los Angeles spread out beneath Mulholland Drive, and the fear that Dudley Moore could fall all the way down. From *Vertigo* I had a premonition of everyone's first alarm at steepness in San Francisco, and in the same film I had seen Kim Novak in the gloom of the redwoods, remembering, or pretending to remember, her past as she looked at the rings on a cut tree. For me, Salinas is James Dean watching the beans grow in *East of Eden*, and Santa Barbara is *Cutter's Way*, where death grins through the flowers. I learned how to beware of relaxation at Bodega Bay in *The Birds*; I expect Norma Desmond in every other mansion set back on Sunset; I believe in the border because I have been on Orson Welles's camera in *Touch of Evil*, tracking across it; and I know the additive of corruption in L.A.'s water—I've seen *Chinatown*, and I know there's no sense in protesting.

Wherever I might have come from, there's no place I could have seen more of in advance than California. It is the most extensive emporium this world has known, a shop of moods and scenes.

We are all Koslovskys who have come running to a catalogue of real splendor, the biggest back lot in history, top of the world. California was made for movies. Which is a way of saying that, hypothetically, it offers as rich an imagined experience of life as anywhere in the world. Gold and movies started here. They transformed the place into legend. They made the state the most radiant advertisement for the pursuit of happiness: getaways going in every direction; good earth, air and water, space; a stage, a state of mind and becoming, as potent and present in the domestic interiors of *Leave It to Beaver* as in the luxuriant sweep of the Carmel coast where Clint Eastwood played "Misty" for the me in all of us.

Misty indeed, a place forever in and out of focus, our perception always couched in the language of photography. It is the frontier where we step from reality into story. But we are the golden age in a golden state, still aware and fond of the trick, still teasing. The movies are the throwaway art, the souvenir postcards, of that teasing. Camp, but our culture, the fitting, eloquent junk of a place named after appearance, or as Ed Ruscha has it in a twenty-eight by forty-inch painting, blackberry juice on moiré, refined and absurd, "A BLVD. CALLED SUNSET."

Sometimes on the freeway, you do find yourself inextricably placed between a glossy block-long semi and a blonde in a convertible. You cannot escape the impacted trio. The road has its speed, a sort of twenty-four feet per second that cannot be varied. You are being driven by the road: the thought brings an unexpected calm, and begins to explain the stunned peace in the blonde's eyes. The culture of the back projection is here already, no matter that to stray leftwards more than a foot and a half would be to squeal to death against the sheer, silver wall of semi.

There is a shared assumption that Hollywood's L.A. is an affliction, a place where idiots or worse make rubbish for staggering salaries; a place of smog, deceit, vanity, cultural cancellation, death of the soul, et cetera.

These are all among the reasons I try to explain whenever people wonder why I like L.A. Not that I want to offer myself as just a masochist or a necrophile. Those traits are there, and I cannot deny the wounded nostalgia that L.A. furnishes for me, like a fragrance close to decay. But I also enjoy the weather, the beaches, and the driving, as well as the restaurants, the museums, the Lakers, and the people in L.A. nowadays.

My fascination with Los Angeles has been that while the city is evidently so "advanced," so "modern," so "new," so state-of-the-urban-art, it is also a museum of itself and of the process it has given us in which reality, substance, and the thing itself are revealed as gestures caught in a riddle-like intrigue with image, illusion, and lie. Los Angeles has so many characteristics of an anthology of sets, a backdrop, a figment of our imagination. Whenever I call L.A. Lies Allowed, I do not mean to stress the lies in moralistic reproach. It is the condition of being allowed that most interests and stimulates me.

For it is exactly in the absence of classical structure, center, stability, tradition, and integrity that Los Angeles appeals. There is no need to preach any moral advantage in being fixed or in being unstable. I do not mean to propose Los Angeles for its virtuous novelty any more than I can honestly regret its departure from conventional ground plan, neighborhoods, neighborliness and traditional ways of interaction. Rather, it is that Los Angeles is what it is, changing before your eyes—not out of forced, degraded habit, but from nature—slippery, imagistic, and imagined.

What Christopher Isherwood calls "impermanence," it seems to me, is a volatility that waits for metamorphosis. The buildings are as solid as warmth requires, but so are sets solid. Every column of stone in a Tudor set today knows that it was Arabic last week, and Tuscan the week before. And it is happy about this in a stone-faced way, not filled with a sense of exploitation or corruption.

This is not meant to excuse the villainy, the crassness, or the dishonesty of movie people. But I believe there is a way in which all those small, local sins (not really greater than mendacity anywhere) pale in the light that begins to dispense with truth altogether.

It is in L.A. that we may see how far the light itself has acquired the character of a trick, or a service that can be employed and colored for fiction. Whereas painting celebrates light, in a more or less sacred spirit, photography steers it, plays with it and shatters its integrity. Similarly, in L.A. the city manifests itself as the game of so many million art directors—no longer the grim, visionary consistency of planners, architects, and those qualified in urban appearance, but available for every whim and fantasy. Of course it looks awful and trashy, if you compare it with Bath, Florence, or New York. But the look of L.A. should be compared with other things—a studio back lot full of sets is one example, but something fresher and more intriguing may be multichannel TV.

In other words, it can be anything: if you don't like where you are, travel, change the channel. And if real travel is wearisome, impractical, or slow—then let traveling come in the flick of a switch, the work of a cut in the back projection. Let the scene come to you; be the happy client of the Max Koslovsky who grew up to be a maker of TV commercials and atmosphere videos.

It may be that our "great" and "characteristic" works no longer require genius. That was always an implication of the movies that alarmed the Hechts and Vidals—that millions might be moved or tickled, without the divine inspiration of a Mozart or a Tolstoy being responsible. But it has always been a massive dilemma of art and its adherents as to what would happen in an age of universal education and opportunity, when art no longer leaned on forms of advantage and superiority. That's one reason why popular movies (and an unpopular movie is not a movie, it's cinema) frightened the elite in the 20s, 30s, and 40s. That's one reason why some people hate to concede the pleasure there is in L.A. and its tumult of fictional forms, styles, and views. It is the first place which has given up the truth and not been swallowed by the earth or a furious god. I know, the earthquake *is* there, an ongoing coming attraction. Meanwhile, Lies *Allowed*.

Artist, Friend, and Moneymaker

The telegram he delivered on this spring day in 1925 came from the unknown Scythian wastes of Hollywood, California. It read, "Will you accept three hundred per week to work for Paramount Pictures. All expenses paid. The three hundred is peanuts. Millions are to be grabbed out here and your only competition is idiots. Don't let this get around.—Herman Mankiewicz."

Enter, the Movies

For many years I looked on movie writing as an amiable chore. It was a source of easy money and pleasant friendships. There was small responsibility. Your name as writer was buried in a flock of "credits." Your literary pride was never involved. What critics said about the movie you had written never bothered you. They were usually criticizing something you couldn't remember. Once when I was a guest on a radio quiz show called *Information Please*, the plot of a movie I had written a year before and that was playing on Broadway then was recited to me in full. I was unable to identify it.

For many years Hollywood held this double lure for me, tremendous sums of money for work that required no more effort than a game of pinochle. Of the sixty movies I wrote, more than half were written in two weeks or less. I received for each script, whether written in two or (never more than) eight weeks, from fifty thousand to a hundred and twenty-five thousand dollars. I worked also by the week. My salary ran from five thousand dollars a week up. Metro-Goldwyn-Mayer in 1949 paid me ten thousand a week. David Selznick once paid me thirty-five hundred a day.

Walking at dawn in the deserted Hollywood streets in 1951 with David, I listened to my favorite movie boss topple the town he had helped to build. The movies, said David, were over and done with. Hollywood was already a ghost town making foolish efforts to seem alive.

"Hollywood's like Egypt," said David. "Full of crumbled pyramids. It'll never come back. It'll just keep on crumbling until finally the wind blows the last studio prop across the sands."

And now that the tumult was gone, what had the movies been? A flood of claptrap, he insisted, that had helped bitch up the world and that had consumed the fine talents of thousands of men like ourselves.

"A few good movies," said David. "Thirty years—and one good movie in three years is the record. Ten out of ten thousand. There might have been good movies if there had been no movie industry. Hollywood might have become the center of a new human expression if it hadn't been grabbed by a little group of bookkeepers and turned into a junk industry."

"I'm writing a book about myself," I said, "and I keep wondering what I should write about the movies, which are, in a way, part of me."

"Write the truth," said David, "before you start bragging about your fancy Hollywood exploits, put down the truth. Nobody has ever done that!"

I doubt if the truth about Hollywood is as novel as my friend, in his new disillusion, believed. It is novel enough, however, and I shall try to put down as much of it as I know.

What the Movies Are

The movies are one of the bad habits that corrupted our century. Of their many sins, I offer as the worst their effect on the intellectual side of the nation. It is chiefly from that viewpoint I write of them—as an eruption of trash that has lamed the American mind and retarded Americans from becoming a cultured people.

The American of 1953 is a cliché-strangled citizen whose like was never before in the Republic. Compared to the pre-movieized American of 1910–1920, he is an enfeebled intellect. I concede the movies alone did not undo the American mind. A number of forces worked away at that project. But always, well up in front and never faltering at their frowsy task, were the movies.

In pre-movie days, the business of peddling lies about life was spotty and unorganized. It was carried on by the cheaper magazines, dime novels, the hinterland preachers, and whooping politicians. These combined to unload a rash of infantile parables on the land. A goodly part of the population was infected, but there remained large healthy areas in the Republic's thought. There remained, in fact, an intellectual class of sorts—a tribe of citizens who never read dime novels, cheap magazines, or submitted themselves to political and religious howlers.

It was this tribe that the movies scalped. Cultured people who would have blushed with shame to be found with a dime novel in their hands took to flocking shamelessly to watch the picturization of such tripe on the screen.

For forty years the movies have drummed away on the American character. They have fed it naïveté and buncombe in doses never before administered to any people. They have slapped into the American mind more human misinformation in one evening than the Dark Ages could muster in a decade. One basic plot only has appeared daily in their fifteen thousand theaters—the triumph of virtue and the overthrow of wickedness.

Two generations of Americans have been informed nightly that a woman who betrayed her husband (or a husband his wife) could never find happiness; that sex was no fun without a mother-in-law and a rubber plant around; that women who fornicated just for pleasure ended up as harlots or washerwomen; that any man who was sexually active in his youth later lost the one girl he truly loved; that a man who indulged in sharp practices to get ahead in the world ended in poverty and with even his own children turning on him; that any man who broke the laws, man's or God's, must always die, or go to jail, or become a monk, or restore the money he stole before wandering off into the desert; that anyone who didn't believe in God (and said so out loud) was set right by seeing either an angel or witnessing some feat of levitation by one of the characters; that an honest heart must always recover from a train wreck or a score of bullets and win the girl it loved; that the most potent and brilliant of villains are powerless before little children, parish priests or young virgins with large boobies; that injustice could cause a heap of trouble but it must always slink out of town in Reel Nine; that there are no problems of labor, politics, domestic life, or sexual abnormality but can be solved happily by a simple Christian phrase or a fine American motto.

Not only was the plot the same, but the characters in it never varied. These characters must always be good or bad (and never human) in order not to confuse the plot of Virtue Triumphing. This denouement could be best achieved by stereotypes a fraction removed from those in the comic strips.

The effect on the American mind of this forty-year barrage of Mother Goose platitudes and primitive valentines is proved by the fact that the movies became for a generation the favorite entertainment of all American classes.

There are millions of Americans who belong by nature in movie theaters as they belong at political rallies or in fortune-teller parlors and on the shoot-the-chutes. To these millions the movies are a sort of boon—a gaudier version of religion. All the parables of right living are paraded before them tricked out in gang feuds, earthquakes, and a thousand-and-one near rapes. The move from cheap books to cheap movie seats has not affected them for the worse.

But beside these grass-root fans of platitude sit the once intellectual members of the community. They are the citizens whose good taste and criticism of claptrap were once a large part of our nation's superiority. There is little more in them today than the giggle of the movie fan. Watching the movies, they forget that they have taste, that their intelligence is being violated, that they are being booted back into the nursery. They forget even that they are bored.

In the movie theaters, all fifteen thousand of them, the U.S.A. presents a single backward front.

There is a revolution brewing and movie audiences are beginning to thin out. I shall take up this revolt later and mention here only that it is not an intellectual uprising. It is a revolt downward.

The Captive Muse

The persistent banality of the movies is due to the "vision" of their manufacturers. I do not mean, by "manufacturers," writers or directors. These harassed toilers are no more than the lowest of *Unteroffizieren* in movieland. The orders come from the tents of a dozen invisible generals. The "vision" is theirs. They keep a visionary eye glued to the fact that the lower in class an entertainment product is, the more people will buy it.

Since their start, the movies have been practically in the hands of the same dozen. A few have died, to be replaced by men of identical indifference to every phase of entertainment save one—its profits.

These dozen Tops of the industry have nothing to do with the making of movies. They have to do only with the *sort* of movies that are to be made—commercial ones. There is no murmur of revolt. Only hosannas rise from the movie slave pens.

In no industry into which I have peered have I seen the wanton boss flattery that is normal in movieland. Proud and wealthy men of intelligence are not ashamed to prostrate themselves publicly before the hollow-headed big boss—the Owner. They will gasp with wonder over his dullest droppings and see in his fumbling efforts to understand what is going on the constant mark of genius. No workman I have ever seen is as afraid of a boss, no servant as aquiver before a master as are the movie factotums who come near to the golden throne of the movie-company Owner.

The fear that inspires this kowtowing is as deep as religious fear. It rises from the same source—guilt. Nearly all who work in the making and even selling of movies are guilty of distorting, constantly, their minds and in one way or another of violating their tastes and their instincts.

The only movie figure exempt from such guilt is the company Owner. He is usually a man who has no taste to be violated or intelligence to be distorted. He admires with his whole soul the drivel his underlings produce in his factory.

This boss fear-adulation is the chief color of movieland. My contacts with the studio Owners and their viziers who ran the studios for them informed me early in my movie service that most of them were nitwits on a par with the lower run of politicians I had known as a reporter. Yet they all moved in an aura of greatness, and the reports of their genius would have embarrassed Michelangelo.

In addition to the guilt of violating their culture, which brought these courtiers to heel, there was a money guilt. The greater were the sums these underlings received, the more fearful of the boss they grew. When you overpay small people you frighten them. They know that their merits or activities entitle them to no such sums as they are receiving. As a result their boss soars out of economic into magic significance. He becomes a source of blessings rather than wages. Criticism is sacrilege, doubt is heresy.

In the court of the movie Owner, none criticized, none doubted. And none dared speak of art. In the Owner's mind art was a synonym for bankruptcy. An artist was a saboteur to be uprooted as quickly from the company's pay roll as a Communist with a pamphlet.

Whenever the movie-company Owner found himself with three or more employees at his feet he made a pronouncement. "I'm a Showman," he said, "and as long as I remain a Showman all you geniuses who work in my studio don't have to worry. You will have jobs—and big wages."

The movie-company Owner was and is no more Showman than he is a pilgrim bound for Mecca. His single objective as Owner is to see that his movies make profits. He asks nothing else of them. He has no more instinct to gamble with the contents of his product than have the makers of Flit. What the public wants, he proclaims, is "solid entertainment, and for God's sake, Ben, don't stick those ideas of yours into this film. You want to help make a successful film, don't you? A picture people will be glad to see? All right then—don't insult the things they believe in. Make 'em realize how wonderful life is, and what a fine fella this hero of yours is, so that everybody will be glad to have him elected senator."

The movie Owners are the only troupe in the history of entertainment that has never been seduced by the adventure of the entertainment world—by the dream of diverting people with something a "little better," or a "little different." Their fixation on peddling trash has many causes. For one thing, they are further removed from the creation of their product than any showmen have ever been before.

Showmen in the theater read manuscripts, interview actors, select out of their tastes the product on which they put their names. The gypsy aroma of entertainment goes to their heads, however hard they are. And however greedy they are, the tinkle of show bells becomes as winsome to them as the tinkle of money. The movie showmen, however, read no scripts, consort with no actors. They have no ideas to offer. They stick no finger in the pie. Thus they have no spiritual or mental stake in their product. No show bells tinkle in their counting rooms.

Their product, also, is a more expensive one than any heretofore peddled by showmen. Millions of dollars and not mere thousands are involved. Men who manipulate the spending of millions must put aside enthusiasm for anything but money. The artists they employ may bask in press notices. The Owners can afford to bask only in box-office returns.

The fame of the movie-company Owners is small in the public eye. It is even small in movieland, where the movies are made. In my years in and out of the Hollywood studios I have not managed to learn all the names of my true bosses—the "men of vision" who dictated my work. I have encountered some of them. L. B. Mayer, Howard Hughes, the Schencks, the Cohens, the Warners, the Balabans. There are others as unknown to me as to any outsider.

The major triumph of the movie-company Owners lies in this fact: The barrage of movie trash has conditioned the public to the acceptance of trash only. A "different" movie is usually scorned by Americans. They will sneer and cat-call during its showing, and leave the theater with cries of having been cheated.

Yet the movie Owner's victory is not a solid one, and here I come to the little revolution that stirs among the sixty million movie fans. The movie industry is beginning to wobble. The sound track is beginning to echo cavernously in its theaters. Although the American will still run from a "different" movie as from a smallpox sign, he has shown a mounting aversion to the hog feed he has hitherto gobbled. The studios continue to manufacture this mush with undiminished cunning and largess. No sum is too vast for the making of a Great Epic of Roman History, or of the Indian Wars, or of the Song-Publishing Business.

Nevertheless the movie fan has begun to stay away from the movie palaces that cater fiercely to his love of trash.

Surveying their sagging box-office charts, the movie Owners point wildly to television as the villain responsible. I have a notion that my old bosses are wrong.

Put a squirrel on a treadmill and he will run gayly and happily for hours on end. But there comes an hour when the squirrel's soul feels the falseness and insufficiency of the treadmill as a road for travel. The squirrel begins, then, to twitch, to roll its eyes, to chatter frenziedly. And if not removed from the treadmill the bewildered little animal will fall dead.

The American moviegoer, experiencing these squirrel-like twitches, is removing himself from the movie-trash treadmill. Confronted by the double problem of being unable to enjoy any longer the dime novel movie, and of disliking angrily still any departure from it, the American has retreated into his parlor to stare at another national eruption of trash on his television set. And acquire another set of twitches.

Money Is the Root

As a writer in Hollywood, I spent more time arguing than writing—until the last four years when the British boycott left me without much bargaining power. My chief memory of movieland is one of asking in the producer's office why must I change the script, eviscerate it, cripple and hamstring it? Why must I strip the hero of his few semi-intelligent remarks and why must I tack on a corny ending that makes the stomach shudder? Half of all the movie writers argue in this fashion. The other half writhe in silence, and the psychoanalyst's couch or the liquor bottle claim them both.

Before it might seem that I am writing about a tribe of Shelleys in chains, I should make it clear that the movie writers "ruined" by the movies are for the most part a run of greedy hacks and incompetent thickheads. Out of the thousand writers huffing and puffing through movieland there are scarcely fifty men and women of wit or talent. The rest of the fraternity is deadwood. Yet, in a curious way, there is not much difference between the product of a good writer and a bad one. They both have to toe the same mark.

Nor are the bad writers better off spiritually. Their way is just as thorny. Minus talent or competence, the need for self-expression churns foolishly in them and their hearts throw themselves in a wild pitch for fame. And no less than the literary elite of Hollywood they feel the sting of its knout. However cynical, overpaid, or inept you are, it is impossible to create entertainment without feeling the urges that haunt creative work. The artist's ego, even the ego of the Hollywood hack, must always jerk around a bit under restraint.

The studio bosses are not too inconvenienced by this bit of struggle. Experience has proved that the Hollywood artist in revolt is usually to be brought to heel by a raise in salary. My own discontent with what I was asked to do in Hollywood was so loud that I finally received a hundred and twenty-five thousand dollars for four weeks of script writing.

Apuleius' Golden Stooge

I have taken part in at least a thousand story conferences. I was present always as the writer. Others present were the "producer," the director, and sometimes the head of the studio and a small tense group of his admirers.

The producer's place in movie making is a matter that, in Hollywood, has not yet been cleared up. I shall try to bring some clarity to it.

The big factory where movies are made is run by a super-producer called Head of the Studio who sits in the Front Office and is as difficult of access as the Grand Lama. He is the boss, appointed by the studio Owner himself. Thus, despite the veneration in which he is held by the thousand studio underlings, he is actually the greatest of the movieland stooges. He must bend his entire spirit to the philosophy of the movie Owner—"make money." He must translate this greedy cry of the Owner into a program for his studio. He must examine every idea, plot or venture submitted to him from the single point of view of whether it is trite enough to appeal to the masses.

If he fails in this task, he is summoned from his always teetering studio throne to the movie Owner's New York Office, in which nothing ever teeters. Here he receives a drubbing which the lowest of his slaves would not tolerate. He is shown pages of box-office returns. He is shoved into the presence of homicidal theater Owners snarling of empty seats. Proof is hurled at his head that he has betrayed his great trust, that he is ruining the movie industry, and that he is either an idiot or a scoundrel.

Shaken and traumatized, he returns to his throne in the studio. Here he must wiggle himself into the Purple again and be ready to flash his eyes and terrorize his underlings with his Olympian whims.

His immediate underlings are the producers. He has hired them to do the actual moviemaking for him. After all, no one man can weigh, discuss, and manipulate fifty movie plots at one time. He has to have lieutenants, men who will keep their heads in the noisy presence of writers and directors and not be carried away by art in any of its subversive guises.

Illustrations by Doré (Gustave)

There are different kinds of producers in the studios, ranging from out-and-out illiterates to philosophers and aesthetes. But all of them have the same function. Their task is to guard against the unusual. They are the trusted loyalists of cliché. Writers and directors can be carried away by a "strange" characterization or a new point of view; a producer, never. The producer is the shadow cast by the studio's Owner. It falls across the entire studio product.

I discovered early in my movie work that a movie is never any better than the stupidest man connected with it. There are times when this distinction may be given to the writer or director. Most often it belongs to the producer.

The job of turning good writers into movie hacks is the producer's chief task. These sinister fellows were always my bosses. Though I was paid often five and ten times more money than they for my working time, they were my judges. It was their minds I had to please.

I can recall a few bright ones among them, and fifty nitwits. The pain of having to collaborate with such dullards and to submit myself to their approvals was always acute. Years of experience failed to help. I never became reconciled to taking literary orders from them. I often prepared myself for a producer conference by swallowing two sleeping pills in advance.

I have always considered that half of the large sum paid me for writing a movie script was in payment for listening to the producer and obeying him. I am not being facetious. The movies pay as much for obedience as for creative work. An able writer is paid a larger sum than a man of small talent. But he is paid this added money *not* to use his superior talents.

I often won my battle with producers. I was able to convince them that their suggestions were too stale or too infantile. But I won such battles only as long as I remained on the grounds. The minute I left the studio my victory vanished. Every sour syllable of producer invention went back into the script and every limping foot of it appeared on the screen.

Months later, watching "my" movie in a theater, I realized that not much damage actually had been done. A movie is basically so trite and glib that the addition of a half dozen miserable inanities does not cripple it. It blares along barking out its inevitable clichés, and only its writer can know that it is a shade worse than it had to be.

Michael Wood

America in the Movies

Hollywood movies, from the end of the 1930s to the beginning of the 1960s, from *Gone With the Wind*, say, to *Cleopatra* (1963), were a *world* in the sense that the novels of Balzac were a world. They were a system of assumptions and beliefs and preoccupations, a fund of often interchangeable plots, characters, patches of dialogue, and sets. Literally interchangeable at times. "Much of Shangri-La," Reyner Banham says in his book on Los Angeles, "had to be built in three dimensions, the spiral ramps of the production numbers of Busby Berkeley musical spectaculars had to support the weight of a hundred girls in silver top hats, and so on. . . . The movies were thus a peerless school for building fantasy as fact, and the facts often survived one movie to live again in another, and another and others still to come."

Lawrence Alloway remarks that the house of *The Magnificent Ambersons* (1942) shows up again in *The Fallen Sparrow* (1943), and Charles Higham points out that *Citizen Kane* (1941) contains clips from *The Hunchback of Notre Dame* (1939) and *Mary of Scotland* (1936), as well as a door left over from *Gunga Din* (1939) and some bats borrowed from *Son of Kong* (1933). *Julius Caesar* (1953), Bob Thomas suggests in his biography of Brando, was made so cheaply because it inherited a lot of scenery and costumes from *Quo Vadis?* (1951); and George N. Fenin and William K. Everson, in their book on westerns, remind us that *Geronimo* (1939) has footage from *The Plainsman* (1936), *Wells Fargo* (1937), and *The Thundering Herd* (1934); while *Laramie* (1950) uses all the big scenes from John Ford's *Stagecoach* (1939). . . . Not only were successful films remade all too frequently, they were often remade in disguise, with their plots transferred from India or the African desert to the American West; from Ireland to the American ghetto.

But even apart from such literal repetitions, the world of Hollywood movies clearly has a moral and physical geography of its own: a definite landscape. However little of it we have seen, we have seen a lot already. Wherever we came in, this is where we came in. "I thought they burned that," Groucho Marx says, looking at a child's sled called Rosebud. "Haven't we met someplace before?" Cary Grant asks Ralph Bellamy in *His Girl Friday* (1940). They have, three years before, in similar roles, in *The Awful Truth* (1937). Such allusions in Hollywood movies do not seem fussy or excessively self-conscious, as they would (and do) in novels, because they simply refer openly to what we all know: that the movies *are* a world, a country of familiar faces, a mythology made up of a limited number of stories.

Novels, with a few famous exceptions, usually pretend that we have never read a novel before in our lives, and may never read another after this one. Movies, on the other hand, tend to assume that we spend every waking moment at the pictures, that anyone who has found his or her way to the cinema is a moviegoer, a regular, an addict. "When I was twelve or thirteen," Fellini told Lillian Ross in an interview, "I went to movies all the time—American movies. But I did not know there were directors of movies. I always thought the actors did everything." We can't all sustain such innocence, any more than Fellini did, and we probably shouldn't try too hard. But Fellini's reminiscence confirms the sense of a world: we see movies as more or less continuous with each other. Movies rely on our experience of other movies, on a living tradition of the kind that literary critics always used to be mourning for, because it died in the seventeenth century or fizzled out with D. H. Lawrence. The movie tradition, of course, specializes in light comedy, well-made thrillers, frothy musicals, and weepy melodramas, rather than in such works as Donne's *Holy Sonnets* or George Eliot's *Middlemarch*; and we shouldn't listen too seriously to the siren voices of those critics who claim big things for Hollywood movies as art. But there *is* a tradition. We have in our heads as we sit in the cinema a sense of all the films we have seen, a range of common reference which is the Greek and Latin of the movies, our classical education. The classics here being the public's classics, rather than the critics': Fred Astaire rather than Flaherty; Lubitsch rather than von Stroheim. . . .

All movies mirror reality in some way or other. There are no escapes, even in the most escapist pictures. In *Night and Day* (1946), for example—a sloppy film biography of Cole Porter starring Cary Grant and aimed at soothing us all into a stupor—the *Lusitania* sinks, and Grant composes "Begin the Beguine" at the front, to the sound of falling bombshells and the "beat-beat-beat of the tom-toms" (wrong song, but no matter) of a French African regiment.

The business of films is the business of dreams, as Nathanael West said, but then dreams are scrambled messages from waking life, and there is truth in lies, too, as Lamar Trotti wrote in the screenplay of *The Ox-Bow Incident* (1943), if you get enough of them. We are not likely to read too much into the usually rosy mirror world of the movies, because we are unable to *not* see our world in the mirror. We always translate and interpret and transfer from films back to life, but we do it instantly and intuitively, working at a level of awareness somewhere just below full consciousness. Much of our experience of popular films—and of popular culture generally: jokes, plays, novels, songs, nightclub acts, television shows and series—resides in the place we usually call the back of the mind, the place where we keep all those worries that won't come out into the open and won't go away either, that nag at us from the edges of consciousness. Movies bring out these worries without letting them loose and without forcing us to look at them too closely. They trot around the park in the half-light and the exercise does us all good. Barbara Deming, in her fascinating (and sometimes irritating) *Running Away from Myself*, speaks of the "real magic" of the Hollywood film: "not only does it bring to the question the right answer; it brings the right answer without letting the audience become fully aware of what the question is." This is very perceptive, and I would add only that frequently there is not even a question, merely a hazy area of preoccupation, and that it doesn't appear to be necessary for a movie to solve anything, however fictitiously. It seems to be enough for us if a movie simply dramatizes our semisecret concerns and contradictions in a story, allows them their brief, thinly disguised parade. Life goes on in the movie, scarcely shaken by the muffled incursion of our troubles, and the movie, by sympathetic magic, may induce life to go on outside it. What is the function of Sidney Poitier in a whole series of films, starting with *Edge of the City* (1957), if not to allude to our anxieties about race without really stirring them up? The allusion will not dispel our fears, but it will keep them quiet until we can get to see Poitier in another reassuring movie.

But movies are entertainment, aren't they? What is this talk of anxiety and sympathetic magic? They *are* entertainment, but the definition is not as comforting or as final as it looks. Why should we be entertained by *these* stories rather than by others? Why is pure escapism so difficult in movies? Why does the *Lusitania* keep sinking in films that really have no call for it? Or, to descend again on the unfortunate Poitier, whose dignity has somehow survived all those smiling, servile roles—even if it is true that Poitier is altogether too presentable, too much the black for people who don't like blacks—why bring up the question of race at all in the movies, if you just want to make money and keep people happy?

It seems that entertainment is not, as we often think, a full-scale flight from our problems, not a means of forgetting them completely, but rather a rearrangement of our problems into shapes which tame them, which disperse them to the margins of our attention. *For Me and My Gal* shows us a newspaper headline, dated 1916: GERMANS NEARING PARIS. But Gene Kelly, who is holding the paper, is not reading this. We are. He is looking for his name on another page. Later, another headline appears: LUSITANIA SUNK. But again, we are the ones who read this, because Kelly is asleep, with the newspaper covering his face. This seems to me almost a paradigm of the way entertainment so often works: The world of death and war and menace and disaster is really there, gets a mention, but then is rendered irrelevant by the story or the star or the music. The *Lusitania* sinks but Gene Kelly is asleep; the battle rages (in *Night and Day*) but Cary Grant is jotting down "Begin the Beguine."

"Leopards break into the temple," Kafka wrote, "and drink to the dregs what is in the sacrificial pitchers; this is repeated over and over again; finally it can be calculated in advance, and it becomes part of the ceremony." The parable describes many situations, both public and private, with uncomfortable precision. For the moment, though, we can see it as describing popular culture at work; and especially the movies. The leopards are all those alarms and preoccupations which we can't acknowledge and can't ignore, and the temple is the fiction which is supposed to entertain us. We can't do anything about the leopards breaking in, and still less can we do anything, it seems, about the actual existence of leopards in the world outside the temple. But while they are in the temple, we can surround them with a consoling or attenuating interpretation of their activity. They still drink the pitchers dry, and they are still, no doubt, dangerous. But they are no longer wild and meaningless; no longer stray, vicious animals haunting the borders of our mind. They are part of the ceremony.

All this makes the movies sound like the instrument of social prevention that many writers have seen in them: a means of keeping the discontented masses quiet, the new opium of the people. (David Robinson reflects a familiar view when he says, "The American studios were dedicated to the manufacture of dreams to keep the nation content through stressful times.") Certainly the movies characteristically offer us packs of lies, but we would not consume these lies so avidly unless we needed them; thus, the target of our attack, if we are disposed to attack this state of affairs, should surely be the world which creates the need for such stories, rather than the stories themselves. There is something too conspiratorial and too literary about many Marxist views of popular culture—from those of Adorno and Horkheimer to those of Roland Barthes. The lies themselves are not the problem, and nothing will be gained by our unmasking them as lies if the world that made us need them remains unchanged. Demystification is an idle task if we still clamor for new mystifications at the end of it.

In any case, things are not often so drastic in the movies. No one is prevented from rushing to the barricades by seeing *Marty* (1955), not even by a lifetime of seeing films like *Marty*. What happens is that we don't worry about the leopards as often as we otherwise might—and there are all kinds of leopards anyway, large and small, major and minor. Movies preserve our moral slumber in the way that dreams are said to preserve our sleep, and only someone who stays awake twenty-four moral hours a day is in any real position to complain. Or to change the metaphor, movies are not our opium, they are only our placebo; our beer and skittles, and our pies in the sky. If they didn't exist, we would have to invent them.

Myra Breckinridge

I can hardly bear it another moment! I am reborn or in the process of rebirth like Robert Montgomery in *Here Comes Mr. Jordan*.

I am seated in front of a French café in a Montmartre street on the back lot at Metro. Last year's fire destroyed many of the studio's permanent outdoor sets—those streets and castles I knew so much better than ever I knew the Chelsea area of Manhattan where Myron and I used to exist. I deeply regret the fire, mourn all that was lost, particularly the famous New York City street of brownstones and the charming village in Normandy. But, thank Heaven, this café still stands. Over a metal framework, cheap wood has been so arranged and painted as to suggest with astonishing accuracy a Paris bistro, complete with signs for Byrrh, while a striped awning shades metal tables and chairs set out on the "sidewalk." Any minute now, I expect to see Parisians. I would certainly like to see a waiter and order a Pernod.

I can hardly believe that I am sitting at the same table where Leslie Caron once awaited Gene Kelly so many years ago, and I can almost re-create for myself the lights, the camera, the sound boom, the technicians, all converged upon this one table where, in a blaze of artificial sunlight, Leslie—much too thin but a lovely face with eyes like mine—sits and waits for her screen lover while a man from makeup delicately dusts those famous features with powder.

From the angle where I sit I can see part of the street in Carvel where Andy Hardy lived. The street is beautifully kept up as the shrine it is, a last memorial to all that was touching and—yes—good in the American past, an era whose end was marked by two mushroom shapes set like terminal punctuation marks against the Asian sky.

A few minutes ago I saw Judge Hardy's house with its neatly tended green lawn and windows covered with muslin behind which there is nothing at all. It is quite eerie the way in which the houses look entirely real from every angle on the slightly curving street with its tall green trees and flowering bushes. Yet when one walks around to the back of the houses, one sees the rusted metal framework, the unpainted wood which has begun to rot, the dirty glass of the windows and the muslin curtains soiled and torn. Time withers all things human; although yesterday evening when I saw Ann Rutherford, stopped in her car at a red light, I recognized immediately the great black eyes and the mobile face. She at least endures gallantly, and I could not have been more thrilled! Must find where Lewis Stone is buried.

This is the happiest moment of my life, sitting here alone on the back lot with no one in sight, for I was able to escape the studio guide by telling him that I wanted to lie down in an empty office of the Thalberg Building; then of course I flew straight here to the back lot which is separated from the main studio by a public road.

If only Myron could have seen this! Of course he would have been saddened by the signs of decay. The spirit of what used to be has fled. Most dreadful of all, NO FILM is currently being made on the lot; and that means that the twenty-seven huge sound stages which saw the creation of so many miracles: Gable, Garbo, Hepburn (Katharine), Powell, Loy, Garland, Tracy, and James Craig are now empty except for a few crews making television commercials.

Yet I must write the absolute truth for I am not Myron Breckinridge but myself and despite the intensely symbiotic relationship my husband and I enjoyed during his brief life and despite the fact that I do entirely support his thesis that the films of 1935 to 1945 inclusive were the high point of Western culture, completing what began that day in the theatre of Dionysos when Aeschylus first spoke to the Athenians, I must confess that I part company with Myron on the subject of TV. Even before Marshall McLuhan, I was drawn to the gray shadows of the cathode tube. In fact, I was sufficiently avant-garde in 1959 to recognize the fact that it was no longer the movies but the television commercial that engaged the passionate attention of the world's best artists and technicians. And now the result of their extraordinary artistry is this new world, like it or not, we are living in: post-Gutenberg and pre-Apocalypse. For almost twenty years the minds of our children have been filled with dreams that will stay with them forever, the way those maddening jingles do (as I write, I have begun softly to whistle "Rinso White," a theme far more meaningful culturally than all of Stravinsky or even John Cage). I submitted a piece on this subject to the *Partisan Review* in the summer of 1960. I believe, without false modesty, that I proved conclusively that the relationship between consumer and advertiser is the last demonstration of *necessary* love in the West, and its principal form of expression is the television commercial. I never heard from *PR* but I kept a carbon of the piece and will incorporate it into the book on Parker Tyler, perhaps as an appendix.

For almost an hour I watched a television commercial being made on the same stage where Bette Davis acted in *The Catered Affair*—that predictably unhappy result of the movies attempting to take over the television drama when what they should have taken over was the *spirit* of the commercials. Then I was given lunch in the commissary which is much changed since the great days when people in extraordinary costumes wandered about, creating the impression that one was inside a time machine gone berserk. Now television executives and technicians occupy all the tables and order what used to be Louis B. Mayer Chicken Soup, only the name of Mayer has been, my guide told me, stricken from the menu. So much for greatness! Even more poignant as reminders of human transiency are the empty offices on the second floor of the Thalberg Building. I was particularly upset to see that the adjoining suites of Pandro S. Berman and the late Sam Zimbalist were both vacant. Zimbalist (immortal because of *Boom Town*) died in Rome while producing *Ben Hur* which saved the studio's bacon, and Pandro S. Berman (*Dragon Seed*, *The Picture of Dorian Gray*, *The Seventh Cross*) has gone into what the local trade papers refer to as "indie production." How tragic! MGM without Pandro S. Berman is like the American flag without its stars.

No doubt about it, an era has indeed ended and I am its chronicler. Farewell the classic films, hail the television commercial! Yet nothing human that is great can entirely end. It is merely transmuted—in the way that the wharf where Jeanette MacDonald arrived in New Orleans (*Naughty Marietta*, 1935) has been used over and over again for a hundred other films even though it will always remain, to those who have a sense of history, Jeanette's wharf. Speaking of history, there was something curiously godlike about Nelson Eddy's recent death before a nightclub audience at Miami. In the middle of a song, he suddenly forgot the words. And so, in that plangent baritone which long ago earned him a permanent place in the pantheon of superstars, he turned to his accompanist and said, "Play 'Dardanella,' and maybe I'll remember the words." Then he collapsed and died.

Play "Dardanella"! Play on! In any case, one must be thankful for those strips of celluloid which still endure to remind us that once there were gods and goddesses in our midst and Metro-Goldwyn-Mayer (where I now sit) preserved their shadows for all time! Could the actual Christ have possessed a fraction of the radiance and the mystery of H. B. Warner in the first *King of Kings* or revealed, even on the cross, so much as a shadow of the moonstruck Nemi-agony of Jeffrey Hunter in the second *King of Kings*, that astonishing creation of Nicholas Ray?

Stephen Bach

Final Cut

"Fellas, this book is a piece of *shit!*"

Chris Mankiewicz's considerable bulk rolled behind the statement, imploring the rest of us to agree. He flung his palms outward toward the room, as if the evidence were smeared there to observe. After a moment he dropped one hand into the pile of sweet rolls on the coffee table before him, piled high with danish and dirty coffee cups.

"Everybody knows that, Chris." Rissner sighed. "It's not about whether it's a piece of shit or it's not a piece of shit. It's about whether we want to make a goddamn deal."

"On this unmitigated, irredeemable piece of *shit?*"

Rissner borrowed matches from someone, lit a cigarette, pointedly ignoring the redundancy. "What's the minimum bid we could make, you think?" he said to the room in general. "A million? A million five?" His voice seemed casual, but his manner suggested constraint as he bent and rebent the borrowed book of matches. He looked up at the circle seated in mismatched chairs around the glass and chrome coffee table in his Culver City office. There was the chairman of the board, down from San Francisco for the morning, looking on with a kibitzer's curiosity, his expression acknowledging nothing more than respectful interest; the president of the company, his mouth a tight line, owl-like eyes swiveling from one face to another behind his huge spectacles, glinting in the early-morning sunlight like windshields; there were the heads of domestic and ancillary distribution, ignoring Mankiewicz's outburst and Rissner's question by burrowing into their synopses of the book in question, readers' reports they were supposed to have read the previous night or on the plane from New York but clearly hadn't. There was Mankiewicz, exasperated beyond belief that his opinion was having no apparent effect on anyone else; there was David Field, looking thoughtful and tactful; and I—I was *confused*. Who cared what the distribution guys thought? I wondered. Why? When? What did they know?

I knew, so I answered Rissner. "My guess is that the least they'll listen to is a million five and a gross percentage, and that won't make a deal. If we're not prepared to go that high, we shouldn't make an offer at all because the agent will decide he's been insulted and our relationship with the agency is weak enough as it is. This *is* the first major submission from them in months, right?"

"Right." Rissner nodded.

"The first major submission because they're trying to hype what even *they* know is a piece of illiterate *shit!*"

"Chris, *please.*"

Albeck looked simultaneously alarmed and annoyed. Why didn't Mankiewicz shut up? He had clearly been given more than a cue by his superior. Or could the book really be all *that* bad? He asked the question of Rissner.

"Andy, the guy's last two books were huge best-sellers. The movie of the first one became one of the top-grossing pictures of all time. The movie of the second one, which was only routine, did forty million dollars. It's not about quality; it's about money and track record."

"Don't talk to me about track record," retorted Mankiewicz. "My old man won four Academy Awards in two years and then went out and made *The Honey Pot*. I know all *about* track record."

Rissner ignored this and turned to me for an opinion. "How would I know?" I waffled. "I turned down the first book. I thought who in Nebraska knows from sharks?"

"But what about the *offer?*"

"Well," I said, grateful for a money discussion to get me off the hook of commenting on a book I didn't like any more than Mankiewicz did, "if you want to make an offer"—I couched it in Rissner's direction with the second-person pronoun—"it should be as preemptive as possible. Otherwise, we look like pikers. What's he want—an auction, what?"

"One offer, all terms, sealed bids. He's submitted the book five places—"

"He *says*." Mankiewicz now seemed to be talking to himself since no one else was apparently listening, except maybe Harvey, but it was hard to tell.

Rissner ignored him again. "—five places, expects five bids by the close of business today, and top bid takes it. So the offer has to be the best and farthest we're willing to go. If we go."

Andy looked up, puzzled and impatient. "Are we obligated to make an offer?"

"No," said Rissner, anticipating resistance.

He was rescued by the musings of domestic distribution. "Forty million?"

"Domestic or worldwide?" asked his ancillary.

"Domestic, I *think*."

Albeck shot sharply: "That was because of big boobies in wet T-shirts. Does this book have boobies?"

Jim Harvey's placidity seemed suddenly jarred, by the subject matter or Andy's terminology one couldn't tell.

"It has boobies and rapes and S and M, and not one word of it has any resemblance to human behavior as we know it!" Mankiewicz chimed in.

Rissner looked bored. "Yes, Andy. It has boobies. Wet ones."

While Andy mulled this over, frowning, I asked where else the book had been submitted.

"You have to assume to the producers of the first picture and the second picture, if only as courtesy submissions. They would be buying for Universal or Columbia. Then there's us, probably Fox and . . . maybe Paramount. Or Warner's."

"Danny, you're close to Warner's," said Andy. "Can you ask them what they think?"

"Why would I do that?" said Rissner, appalled. "What difference would it make? Who cares if they like it or hate it? The point is, what do *we* do? Do we make an offer or not, and if we do, what's the goddamn offer?"

"I got it," said Albeck, chastised, gloomy, but instructed.

We voted. Andy agreed; Harvey said nothing.

An offer was framed, approved, and made, as Mankiewicz fumed in uncharacteristic silence. The offer came to slightly more than two million for the movie rights, based on a floor price which escalated with performance of the book on best-seller lists, in book clubs, and so on; a gross percentage of box-office receipts was added to make the offer unbeatable.

It was beaten.

The producers of the movie made from the author's first book secured the rights for something closer, it was believed, to two and a half million. Losing the book was almost a relief. We had demonstrated we had the money, were willing to spend it, would be again, and it hadn't cost a penny.

Two and a half years later, when the movie based on the book was released and landed with a critical and financial thud, I had lunch with Mankiewicz, who had been long gone from UA.

"I told you it was a piece of shit." He laughed without a trace of a sneer.

"That was never the point, Chris," I said.

"It should have been." He smiled.

Irene Oppenheim

Hollywood Hustle

I'd been living in Los Angeles just under a year when, in the spring of 1983, I answered an ad in the *Hollywood Reporter* for a receptionist ("Lite Typing") and got the job. The pay wasn't much, but the work was in "the Business"—an apt L.A. euphemism for the entertainment industry. The location was within bicycling distance of my home, and they only wanted someone to work mornings. I'd get off by 1 P.M., which I thought would leave me plenty of time to do my own writing. I was wrong about that. The place was so frantic I'd come out wired and need the rest of the day to simply calm down. When, after about two weeks, I realized my afternoons were being spent in activities equivalent to running around the block twenty or thirty times, I asked to be put on full-time. Since I wasn't getting anything else done, why not, I figured, jump in for the total experience.

The (still thriving) company I found myself a part of possessed the unlikely name of Breakdown Services, Ltd. During the six months I worked there, I learned to savor all of that phrase's more cynical reverberations, but in terms of the job it dealt with the dismantling or breakdown of television and film scripts. Scripts gathered from producers or studios would be regurgitated by Breakdown in the form of plot summaries, character descriptions, number of scenes per character, and the number of dialogue lines each speaks. These compilations were then xeroxed and distributed to hundreds of subscribing actors' agents who proceeded to submit their clients for likely parts. It was a process, as I was to discover by way of vituperative phone calls when "breakdowns" arrived late or not at all, that the agents regarded with a reverence others might reserve for morning prayer.

Breakdown Services, Ltd. was the brainchild of a personable, autocratic, ambitious young man named Gary Marsh. Gary was twenty-eight when I met him, but he'd founded Breakdown when he was eighteen and was considered something of an entrepreneurial prodigy. His mother was an agent and he'd observed the piles of scripts she and her agent pals had to plow through in order to match a given role with the talent they represented. He'd also observed how much they hated the reading part of their jobs and had cleverly devised breakdowns as a way of extracting the material they needed.

By the time I arrived, five full-time breakdown writers worked in a desk-lined back room overlooking a parking lot. I've heard the current crew has now advanced to computers, but when I was there typewriters were the norm, and you could sometimes get a whiff of white-out from the furthest end of the hallway. When they weren't typing, the writers would curl up on the office's worn stuffed couch and, with a script propped against one arm, fill legal-sized yellow pads with dialogue line numbers and comments which they'd then type up. It could be a complex job. For example, the breakdown for a film originally called *Teenage Gambler* lists over forty characters, ranging from the teenaged gambling lead to five waiters who sing "Happy Birthday" at a surprise party ("1 song, 1 scene").

Perhaps because of the patience involved in this sort of extraction, women seemed to dominate the ranks of the breakdowners (during my tenure the ratio was four to one). Although Gary knew I'd done a bit of writing, I was relegated to the front office and never received an invitation to try my hand at breakdowns. It wasn't something I really wanted to do. For one thing, the writers were a youthful bunch. The back room senior was in her early thirties, but none of the others had hit twenty-five. And I think Gary rightly surmised I'd be too openly cynical for the job or try to embellish too much. Breakdowns were produced anonymously and offered no artistic evaluations of the scripts. The writers might talk among themselves about a piece they felt was particularly good or bad, but such editorializing was not allowed to make its way into the final product. That this restriction was frustrating is indicated by the fact that two of the writers began venting opinions as moonlighting theater critics for small local papers.

For Gary, the most problematical aspect of the breakdown business was its limited market. This had nothing to do with his operating methodology; he did what he could to exploit the possibilities. Each weekday a hardy crew made predawn deliveries of breakdowns to agents' homes or offices, while a post-dawn quartet of pager-equipped Breakdown field workers haunted the big studios ready to pounce on an available script. For these studio prowlers speed was of the essence, not only because Hollywood tends to be crisis-prone and wants everything done quickly, but because a rival, spawned by the success of Breakdown Services, Ltd. and infuriatingly named BreakThrough Productions, Ltd., was also on the hunt.

Breakdown Services unquestionably dominated the field, but the field itself had immutable perimeters. Breakdown's subscribers had to be accredited agents, though there were some exceptions to this rule. For instance, specialized media organizations, such as the competitive, vulture-like companies that insured movie productions, could keep tabs on the industry by subscribing to the weekly Breakdown summaries. But the whole Breakdown operation was hard to monitor. When I was there, a Breakdown subscription was expensive, something like $500 a year. And though breakdowns were copyrighted and unauthorized reproduction was clearly prohibited, xerox machines are notoriously bad at picking up such distinctions and among the larger agencies breakdowns were undoubtedly duplicated and passed around.

Gary's response to these built-in economic dilemmas was to diversify. A separate department for commercials, for example, appeared as part of the Breakdown menu. (Although Breakdown staffers were supposed to refrain from giving tips to potential talent, I did once tell a friend—who hoped to finance the college educations of her five-year-old identical twins by getting them on a commercial—that a juice company had put out a call for identical twin girls. Their agent submitted them, but they didn't get the job.) The nightly Breakdown delivery system expanded to an all-day messenger service. Gary also made available an assortment of directories and mailing labels listing casting directors, talent agents, and literary agents in Los Angeles and New York. The current Breakdown brochure adds yet another Breakdown amenity; for fifteen dollars you can receive an "actors' relaxation" cassette tape "designed to maximize your abilities and stimulate your creative senses."

Breakdown's directory labels were particularly popular items. But the profit margin was slim and more discerning customers soon discovered that, besides some inevitable deadwood, a goodly number of the labels were addressed back to Breakdown itself. This was especially true for casting directors who frequently preferred to ignore the massive number of solicitations sent to them by work-hungry performers. And among my daily jobs was the task of seeing that the incoming cards, notes, and photos from performers were filed away in the trio of dusty cardboard boxes occupying designated floor space under one of the desks. Every few months a casting director would appear to collect his or her accumulation or call and ask us to throw it away. But just as often the stuff just sat there for months. Eventually a file would get unwieldy and we'd mail it off to the CD and begin again.

After sales for the directory labels slowed, Gary launched a computer-selling sideline. Indeed, one of the reasons I was hired was that I knew some computer basics. At my first interview, Gary told me I'd be able to earn a fifty-dollar bonus for every $5000 computer/printer unit I sold, but that never happened. The computer brand they were peddling was obscure and patrons were scarce. That never seemed too mystifying since, as a consumer, I think I'd balk at buying a piece of expensive equipment from a firm which featured "break-down" so prominently in its name. Gary and Peter (his partner in this endeavor) did, however, pull in a few customers through an advertising campaign which at one point involved a mime demonstration and at another, Gary's pet Persian cats decoratively draped over the machinery.

I had more to do with another Breakdown adjunct called Theaterline. Run by an ex-San Francisco musician, Julio Martinez, Theaterline supplied small or independent theater companies with publicity services. Often this meant publicizing vanity productions financed by the slender savings of anxious actors who, if young, deemed themselves overlooked, and if old, felt they'd been forgotten. It was a bunch with delicate egos. And a goodly portion of my work days were spent coping with performers who not infrequently came equipped with hyphenated names, long resumes, and the capability of throwing madly dramatic tantrums when things went awry. Breakdown and Theaterline parted ways shortly after I left (Julio keeps it going independently), and Gary filled the Theaterline vacuum almost immediately with a new venture called Story, Inc. The idea was to create a kind of creative magazine and newspaper clipping service that would ferret out possible film or TV ideas, package them in newsletter form, and make them available to subscribing writers and producers. It seemed, however, that those targeted preferred to pursue their own creative material. According to Julio, Story, Inc. proved to be one of Gary's quicker fizzles.

Breakdown's offices occupied the entire second floor (just above the Uvasun of Hollywood tanning salon) of a small, newish L.A. building. Office hours were 10 A.M. to 6 P.M., although Gary, whoever was preparing the breakdowns for distribution, and at least one of the writers always stayed later. I arrived at around 9:30 A.M. in order to put on the coffee and water the plants before the phones began ringing and things got truly hectic. Often I'd take a perverse delight in the phone salutation, "Good morning, Breakdown." Equally often, however, it came too close to being the absolute truth.

My jobs varied. Beyond the major task of helping to answer Breakdown's multiple phone lines, I updated labels and directories, filed completed break-downs, prepared Theaterline press kits, and helped mail out the billing (which was done under an archaic system so arduous my chest ached at the prospect). There were usually new employees to train since most Breakdown workers re-garded the job as a transient stepping stone to somewhere else. Besides Gary, Peter, and Gary's wife Susan (who did the accounting), only three of the other dozen or so employees I knew are there now. The guy I started with got a po-sition interviewing potential TV quiz contestants, while the young woman who eventually replaced me went on to become an assistant casting director. Almost everyone in the office had an alternate career—in Hollywood, as one local playwright sardonically put it, the artists are the ones who tell you that what they do is not what they *really* do. Two of the actor/field workers, for in-stance, were involved in founding an avant-garde theater in a downtown L.A. warehouse. During virtually all the months I worked at Breakdown, this duo was scrounging folding chairs or collecting cardboard egg cartons which they planned to spray black and nail to the walls of their "theater" as soundproofing.

I had my own "artistic" ambitions which, chimerical as they proved to be, provided the catalyst for my departure from Breakdown. I'd written a screen-play. But despite mighty efforts, I'd so far been unable to acquire the literary agent I needed to get it read by the major studios. This, at least, was the case un-til one Saturday evening (an odd time, which should have warned me some-thing peculiar was afoot), I received a call from an agent willing to take me on. The following Monday, I took a couple of hours off from Breakdown, buckled my helmet, hopped on my bicycle, and pedaled down to the agent's office.

The address I'd been given (in one of the seedier sections of downtown Los Angeles) was hardly auspicious. When I finally found it, the building turned out to be a rundown, clunky affair of 1930s vintage which, from its creaking el-evator to the frosted glass on the office doors, seemed as though it could have easily served as the set for a Raymond Chandler film. The office itself, however, was pure Monty Python. The floor was chaotically carpeted by thigh-high piles of scripts; the only decorative touches were a couple of grimy plastic plants, and the place smelled as though about 10,000 cigarettes had been consumed since the last time a window had been opened. From behind a paper-strewn desk, where the dominant feature was an overflowing ashtray of hubcap pro-portions, sat a mumu-clad, chain-smoking woman of indeterminately mature years, who greeted me in a southern accent so thick that, if transmuted into liq-uid form, it would have held a knife upright. She told me she thought the script was terrific; she rattled off names of studio people she was sure would "adore" it enough to plunk down a few million dollars in production money. She then asked if I'd written anything else for films or TV and, when I answered in the negative, told me, "Honey, if I had your talent I'd get my tail on home and write." It was irresistible. After all, this was the only agent I'd even managed to get near. And, choosing to view the havoc in her office as a mere eccentricity, I signed a handwritten contract drawn up on her pale pink, xeroxed stationery.

Reeling with chutzpah from this heady encounter, I gave two weeks notice at Breakdown. Once free, I planned to settle down at my computer, write lots of movies and get, if not rich, at least richer than I was. My "agent" actually did get some studios and producers to read the script. Her tactics, however, could be disconcerting. At one point, for example, I was chagrined to discover the script had been delivered to a studio official along with an entire "secret recipe" key lime pie. Despite my wounded pride, such nonsense worked well enough to get me an appointment at Paramount with someone who'd liked the script and wanted to meet me. At the interview she said she thought I'd written a classy piece of work. But, of course, she added, Paramount didn't really make many classy pictures and she just wanted to wish me well. There were a couple of other nibbles, but it became clear after a while that nothing was actually going to happen.

I kept in touch with a few people at Breakdown, but Gary wasn't one of them. So, after I'd been gone for about a month, I was surprised when he called. He asked if I'd come back for a few weeks to fill in for someone who'd quit abruptly. My aspirations were still running high. And, though I didn't actually turn him down, I named a price a bit more than double the five dollars an hour he'd been paying me when I left, and he hung up. I felt badly about it later. I wanted to explain that I'd been motivated less by greed than by some kind of gamble I was making on myself. I thought about calling him and saying that, but I never did.

A Normal Evening with Audrey

I stayed at the Chateau Marmont, where Stravinsky once lived and John Belushi died of a drug overdose. It's set on a hillside above Sunset Boulevard; a white building with terraces shaded by red and blue awnings; inside, a solemn, dignified, faintly seedy air. From the garage entrance at night, you can see the women walk along Sunset Strip, sometimes alone, sometimes in groups of three or four. A few are extremely pretty. In the morning, I looked out the window of my room at a hillside of white stucco houses with Spanish roof tiles amid tall trees. The tropical sunlight made it appear no city is more visible than L.A., but I'd seen nothing to write about. I had to change my assignment or give it up. Instead of writing about a place, maybe I'd find a person who wants to be seen, perhaps wants to be a movie star. I phoned Ben, an old friend who lived in L.A. working as a free-lance writer.

He said, "Audrey. She's twenty years old."

"What does that mean?"

"What the automobile is to Detroit, the twenty-year-old woman is to L.A."

Ben picked me up at 8 P.M. in a Mercedes sports car, and we drove to the house in the Hollywood hills where Audrey lived with Dan, Ben's war buddy. Dan opened the door. What I saw was behind him, in the air, long naked legs and clacking slippers, descending a slanted ladder from a loft. I took in Dan's presence—tall, lean, square-shouldered—but down the ladder came the legs, the legs, the legs, then a bathrobe, then Audrey's face. She had bourbon-colored hair, almond-shaped hazel eyes, high round cheekbones, and a striking overbite.

She said nothing to me, not even hello, just nodded, then her legs clacked back up the ladder, disappeared in the loft, and came clacking down again in a very short pink cotton dress. The shoulder straps kept sliding down her arms. She kept pushing them up, as if that were how the dress is worn, in a ceaseless effort to stop it from falling off, exposing naked breasts. She came and went, pushing at the straps, giving play to her body, squandering energy.

Audrey finally sat down beside Dan.

"I should be a movie star. . . . I *am* a movie star," she said. "Sometimes I feel so frustrated. I mean here I am." She was gathering toward a fuller statement, but decided against it, abruptly stopped.

The smoke from Audrey's cigarette began gliding toward Dan's face. He said, "Watch your cigarette." She put it out immediately; self-correcting instincts quick as fear. Dan, about twice her age, had a New York definitive edge. He announced that he wasn't going with us to *Oolala*, a disco. Audrey wouldn't be herself if he were there. She pleaded with him to come along, saying to me, "Dan is a great dancer," but he was firm. He said the evening might lead to something for her, perhaps being "discovered." She had no job, nothing to do. Audrey kissed him goodnight, said she'd be home in an hour and a half.

With Ben at the wheel of the Mercedes and Audrey on a pillow between the seats, we entered Saturday night traffic along Sunset Boulevard. Audrey slipped a tape into the cassette recorder. The music of the movie *Flashdance* filled the car with stunning clarity. I asked Audrey if she'd seen the movie.

"Three times."

I asked about her family. She said her mother and younger sister lived in San Pedro, then sighed as if, really, she couldn't talk about all that. "Life is fun. Let's keep it that way." She said her real name isn't Audrey. "It's Lucinda May."

"You ought to be Lucinda May."

She said she'd think about it, then asked if she ought to have her teeth fixed. I said, "Don't change anything."

"Someone connected with the movies advised me not to take acting lessons. I might lose my unique qualities."

Streets went by streaming brilliance. The music was sensual, and, despite the grim, compulsive beat, seemed medieval, not modern, yearning for joy beyond this world. Audrey sang along, soothed by it and the voluptuous leather upholstery and the electrified balmy night.

About 11 P.M. we walked into *Oolala*. The disco beat hit like punches to the chest. The room was huge; very crowded. Audrey abandoned us, heading into the bowels of the crowd where men kept stopping her, touching her as if she were a vital charge, whispering to her. Her pink dress appeared and disappeared, a signal in the shifting sea of fabrics. Ben and I went to the bar. Audrey joined us. She gave Ben a batch of business cards and scraps of napkin scribbled with telephone numbers and names. I asked, "How will you remember which faces go with the names?"

"It doesn't matter. I love Dan."

"What do the men say?"

In a grim, mechanical voice, Audrey said, "Hello. My name is Umberto. Have you ever been to Italy? I said no. Would you like to come to my place in the valley and do something? I said no."

She went back into the crowd, then out onto the dance floor. Her partner was a man with black hair, wearing a brown leather jacket, a little taller than Audrey, very handsome. He danced in a way that set her off, doing one or two steps, smooth and contained. Audrey was looser; extravagant.

"I like Audrey's overbite and screwy teeth. She looks unfinished. Adolescent."

"Dan thinks she could make pimples the thing to have," said Ben.

A man joined us at the bar, a Latin with a broad, easy smile declaring his right to know you. Ben introduced him as Mario. He asked, so I told him what I was doing in L.A., following Audrey around. "I might be able to help you," he said, though I hadn't asked, "but L.A. is a complicated city. There are many different levels. Would you be interested in the true story of a murder?" As we talked, I noticed a girl in jeans and high heels, dancing alone. She was whirling as if there were no other dancers. Mario followed my stare and said, "Her name is Linda. She is seventeen."

"Lovely."

"Give me your business card, my friend. I'll send her to you."

When Mario left, I said to Ben, "He was doing business?"

"Believe him."

Believe, not understand, two plus two makes four.

"Linda has nice shoes," I said.

"Bad girls have the nicest shoes."

A woman started dancing with Linda, following her steps and whirling flights; magnetized. Linda was oblivious. Nobody or anybody could have her, whirling in a trance, as if to be lovely were lonely or insane.

Audrey returned. She said, "Hide me."

Ben and I shuffled between her and a gnomish man who'd come up behind her. He had the big head and mangled, sallow, studious face of an old world rabbi. He was reading the crowd. I wondered if he was another Mario. His expression was a mixture of curiosity and distaste. Muscles in his face moved, straining toward the dancers, exceedingly critical.

I asked Audrey if she knew Linda. She looked, figuring her out. "She wants to be rescued. My best friend was like that. Dan gave her his Rolex because she was going to have it fixed for him, but she committed suicide. So he can't get it back. The police confiscated everything in her apartment."

"I'm sorry."

"He's got another Rolex. Do you want to go to a party?"

Minutes later we were in the Hollywood hills following a road through heavy foliage. I saw a coyote in our headlights. They walked the hills. Whores walked Sunset Boulevard. We soared through the night in a Mercedes convertible. I remembered Audrey collecting papers; men from whom she walked away. Her glory. Being desired, walking away. We lost her at the party.

It was very late when Ben drove me back to the Chateau. I hadn't seen anything to write about. Ben was in good spirits, reciting verse along Mulholland Drive, booming lines:

> Ramon Fernandez, tell me, if you know,
> Why, when the singing ended and we turned
> Toward town . . .

Ben had been a specialist in jungle combat, spending most of the war behind enemy lines. I'd heard he could take a man's head off, in the middle of a sentence, so quickly the head went on speaking, unaware it was dead. As we drove, he talked about Bangkok, a green city with beautiful temples and women dragged in from the countryside for Europeans and Americans. They became whores who worked in the bars, he said, and lost their hearing because music was always very loud. They had to drink with customers, going off all night to make themselves vomit so they could drink more. He said they danced on the bar, exquisite women with numbers hanging around their necks. Others were handcuffed to beds for West German businessmen. Thirty handcuffed whores died one night when a house burned. Ben wondered about Thai men, why they put up with it.

"Oh! Blessed rage for order," he said, his hands lightly on the wheel, shaping the curves, coming down into the lights.

Jean Baudrillard

Los Angeles by Night

There is nothing to match flying over Los Angeles by night. A sort of luminous, geometric, incandescent immensity, stretching as far as the eye can see, bursting out from the cracks in the clouds. Only Hieronymus Bosch's hell can match this inferno effect. The muted fluorescence of all the diagonals: Wilshire, Lincoln, Sunset, Santa Monica. Already, flying over San Fernando Valley, you come upon the horizontal infinite in every direction. But, once you are beyond the mountain, a city ten times larger hits you. You will never have encountered anything that stretches as far as this before. Even the sea cannot match it, since it is not divided up geometrically. The irregular, scattered flickering of European cities does not produce the same parallel lines, the same vanishing points, the same aerial perspectives either. They are medieval cities. This one condenses by night the entire future geometry of the networks of human relations, gleaming in their abstraction, luminous in their extension, astral in their reproduction to infinity. Mulholland Drive by night is an extraterrestrial's vantage point on earth, or conversely, an earth dweller's vantage point on the galactic metropolis.

Dawn in Los Angeles, coming up over the Hollywood hills. You get the distinct feeling that the sun only touched Europe lightly on its way to rising properly here, above this plane geometry where its light is still that brand new light of the edge of the desert. Long-stemmed palm trees, swaying in front of the electronic billboard, the only vertical signs in this two-dimensional world.

At 6 A.M. a man is already telephoning from a public phonebox in Beverly Terrace. The neon signs of the night are going out as the daytime ones become visible. The light everywhere reveals and illuminates the absence of architecture. This is what gives the city its beauty, this city that is so intimate and warm, whatever anyone says of it: the fact is it is in love with its limitless horizontality, as New York may be with its verticality.

Kids

The handsomeness of the young Californians had made a great impression on him, accustomed, as he was, to European resorts and European bodies. "They are like Greeks," he said, "with their muscles and their bronzed skins." Then he executed an awkward dance, his eyes alight with humor. "We are Greeks without brains," he sang. "We are Greeks without brains. That's the song they sing." PETER VIERTEL

M.F.K. Fisher

The First Oyster

The intramural complexities of the faculty at Miss Huntingdon's School for Girls have become much clearer to me since I left there, but even at sixteen I knew that Mrs. Cheever's social position was both uncomfortable and lonely.

She had her own office, which was certainly more than any snobbish Latin teacher could boast. She was listed as part of the school's administration in the discreet buff and sepia catalog; I cannot remember now just what her title was, except that it implied with high-sounding ambiguity that she was the house-keeper without, of course, using that vulgar word itself.

She was a college graduate, even though it was from some domestic-science school instead of Smith or Mount Holyoke.

She was, above all, a lady.

She was almost a super-lady, mainly because it was so obvious that the rest of the faculty, administration as well as teachers, considered her a cook. When she stepped occasionally after dinner into the library, where I as an honor Sophomore was privileged to carry demitasses to the Seniors and the teachers on alternate Wednesday nights, I could see that she was snubbed almost as thoroughly as her well-fed colleagues snubbed the school nurse, one notch below the housekeeper on the social scale but also a colleague as far as the catalog went.

No malicious, inverted, discontented boarding-school teacher on God's earth, however, could snub the poor nurse as much as Mrs. Cheever could. Her coarsely genteel face under its Queen Mary coiffure expressed with shocking clarity the loathing she felt for that gentle ninny who dealt out pills and sticking plasters, and all the loneliness and bitter social insecurity of her own position showed in the way Mrs. Cheever stood proudly alone in the crowded library, smiling with delicacy and frightful pleasure at the nurse, whose hand trembled clumsily as she sipped at her little coffee cup and tried to look like a college graduate.

The two women studiously spoke to no one, mainly because no one spoke to them. Perhaps once or twice, long since, the nurse may have said a timid nothing to the housekeeper, but Mrs. Cheever would have bitten out her own tongue before loosening it in charity toward a sister outcast.

Once it almost looked as if she would have a friend on the faculty, when a new gym teacher came. So often athletic people were not exactly . . . that is, they seldom had M.A.'s, even if they seemed really quite lady-like at times. And Mrs. Cheever felt sure that the new colleague would be as scornful as she was herself of all the pretentious schoolma'ams, with their airs and graces.

But after the first week, during which the little gym teacher stood shyly by the housekeeper for coffee, or nibbled in her room on the pink grapes and small frosted cakes that Mrs. Cheever sent her, the other women discovered that not only was she from Barnard . . . *summa cum laude, parbleu!* . . . but that she had the most adorable little cracked voice, almost like a boy's. It was perfect with her hair, so short and boyish too, and by the end of the second week three of the teachers were writing passionate notes to her, and Mrs. Cheever once more stood magnificently alone on her occasional visits to the library after dinner.

Perhaps loneliness made her own food bitter to her, because Mrs. Cheever was an obvious dyspeptic. The rest of us, however: Miss Huntingdon herself, remote and saint-like; Miss Blake, her shadow, devoted, be-wigged, a skin-and-bone edition of Krafft-Ebing; all the white women of the school, fat, thin, frantic or calm, and all the Filipino servants, pretty little men-dolls as mercurial as monkeys, and as lewd; all the girls, who felt like victims but were really the raison d'être of this strange collection within the high walls . . . Mrs. Cheever fed us four times a day with probably the best institutional food in America.

She ran her kitchens with such skill that in spite of ordinary domestic troubles like flooded basements and soured cream, and even an occasional extraordinary thing like the double murder and hara-kiri committed by the head-boy one Good Friday, our meals were never late and never bad.

There were about seventy boarders and twenty-five women, and for morning-recess lunch a pack of day-girls, and most of us ate with the delicacy and appreciation of half-starved animals. It must have been sickening to Mrs. Cheever to see us literally wolfing her well-planned, well-cooked, well-served dishes. For in spite of doing things wholesale, which some gastronomers say is impossible with any finesse, the things we ate at Miss Huntingdon's were savory and interesting.

Mrs. Cheever, for instance, would get a consignment of strange honey from the Torrey pine trees, honey which only a few people in the world were supposed to have eaten. I remember it now with some excitement, as a grainy greenish stuff like some I once ate near Adelboden in the Bernese Alps, but then it was to most of us just something sweet and rather queer to put on hot biscuits. Tinned orange marmalade would have done as well.

At Thanksgiving she would let the Filipinos cover the breakfast tables with dozens of odd, beautiful little beasts they had made from vegetables and fruits and nuts, so that the dining room became for a while amazingly funny to us, and we were allowed to make almost as much noise as we wanted while we ate forbidden things like broiled sausage and played with the crazy toys. The boys would try not to laugh too, and even Mrs. Cheever would incline her queenly topknot less scornfully than usual when spoken to.

Saturday noons we could eat sandwiches and cocoa or pink punch on the hockey field, and have ice cream from the soda fountain in the village if we told Mrs. Cheever between eight and nine that morning. I sometimes went without it, or got another girl to order for me, simply because I could not bear to go into the little office and have the housekeeper look at me. She made me feel completely unattractive, which is even worse at sixteen than later.

She would sit stiffly at her desk, waiting for orders with an expression of such cold impersonal nausea on her face that I could hardly believe the gossip that she had made a fat sum weekly by charging us almost double what the drug store got for its cartons of ice cream and its incredibly sweet sauces.

She would make precise notations on a sheet of paper while we mumbled our orders, and sometimes even suggested in her flat clear voice that salted pecans might be better than strawberry syrup on chocolate-ice-cream-with-butterscotch-sauce. Her expression of remote anguish never changed, even when she reminded us, with her eyes resting coldly on a bulging behind or a spotty chin, that we were limited to one pint apiece.

It was for festivals like Easter and Old Girls' Day, though, that she really exercised her talents. Now I can see that she must have filled many hours of snubbed isolation in plans for our pleasure, but then I only knew that parties at Miss Huntingdon's School for Girls were really fun, mostly because the food was so good. Mrs. Cheever, callously ignored by the girls except for a few minutes each Saturday morning, and smiled at condescendingly by her unwilling colleagues with university degrees, turned our rare bats into what could truly be called small gastronomic triumphs . . . and the more so because they were what they were within high walls.

Old Girls' Day, for instance, meant to all but the Seniors, who had to be nice to the returning alumnae, that we spent a long gray warm June day on the sand and the rocks, and that we could wear our full pleated gym-bloomers and *no stockings*, and take pictures of each other with our Brownies, and, best of all, that at half past noon a procession of house-boys would come down the cliffs from the school with our lunch for us in big baskets.

There would be various things, of course, like pickles and napkins and knives and probably sandwiches and fruit, although how Mrs. Cheever managed it with the school full of hungry shrieking postgraduates is more than I can guess. Perhaps she even sent down devilled eggs to make it a real picnic.

I don't remember, because all that we thought about then, or could recall now if we ever dared to think at all of those days, were the hot crisp fried halves of young chickens, stiff and tempting. We could have all we wanted, even three or four, and we could eat with our fingers, and yell, and gobble. It was wonderful.

There must have been chaperones, but they seemed not to exist down there in the warmth and the silly freedom, and when a stately figure stood for an instant on the cliff top, wrapped fussily in an afternoon gown for the Old Girls, and looked down at us with her face set in a sour chill smile, we waved our greasy drumsticks hilariously up at her, and cried,

> *Miss-is Chee-ver*
> *Miss-is Chee-ver*
> *Miss-is Chee-ver*
> *Rah-ah-ah-ah,*

almost as if she were a whole basketball game between the Golds and the Purples. For one moment, at least, in the year, we were grateful to her for our deliciously full mouths.

She did her conscientious best to be sensible in her menus, and fed us better garden things and fresher cream and milk than most of us have eaten since, but there must have been a dreadful impatience in her for such pap, so that occasionally she would give us the Torrey pine-honey for breakfast, or have the Chinese cook put chives over the Friday fish instead of a cream sauce.

Once, for the Christmas Party, she served Eastern oysters, fresh oysters, oysters still in their shells.

Nothing could have been more exotic in the early twenties in Southern California. The climate was still considered tropical, so that shellfish imported alive from the East were part of an oil-magnate's dream, or perhaps something to be served once or twice a year at Victor Hugo's, in a private room with pink candleshades and a canary. And of course any local molluscs were automatically deemed inedible, at least by *nice* people.

The people, that Christmas Party night, were indeed nice. We wore our formals: skirts not less than eight nor more than fifteen inches from the floor, dresses of light but not bright colors and of materials semi-transparent or opaque, neck-lines not more than three inches below the collar bone and sleeves long or elbow-length. We all passed the requirements of the catalog, but with such delectable additions as long chiffon scarves twined about our necks in the best Nita-Naldi-bronchitic manner, or great artificial flowers pinned with holiday abandon on our left shoulders. Two or three of the Seniors had fox furs slung nonchalantly about them, with the puffy tails dangling down over their firmly flattened young breasts in a most fashionable way.

There may even have been a certain amount of timid make-up in honor of Kris Kringle and the approaching libertinage of Christmas vacation, real or devoutly to be hoped for, but fortunately the dining room was lighted that night by candles only.

Mrs. Cheever had outdone herself, although all we thought then was that the old barn had never looked so pretty. The oblong tables, usually in ranks like dominoes in their box, were pushed into a great horseshoe, with a little table for Miss Huntingdon and Miss Blake and the minister and the president of the trustees in the middle, and a sparkling Christmas tree, and . . . yes! . . . a space for dancing! And there were candles, and the smells of pine branches and hot wax, and place cards all along the outer edge of the horseshoe so that the Freshmen would not sit in one clot and the other groups in theirs.

We marched once around the beautiful room in the flickering odorous candlelight, singing, "God Rest You Merry, Gentlemen" or some such thing to the scrapings of the assistant violin instructor and two other musicians, who in spite of their trousers had been accurately judged unable to arouse unseemly longings in our cloistered hearts.

Then we stood by the chairs marked with our names, and waited for the music to stop and Miss Huntingdon and the minister to ask the blessings in their fluty voices. It was all very exciting.

When I saw that I was to sit between a Senior and a Junior, with not a Freshman in sight, I felt almost uplifted with Christmas joy. It must mean that I was Somebody, to be thus honored, that perhaps I would even be elected to the Altar Guild next semester. . . .

I knew enough not to speak first, but could not help looking sideways at the enormous proud nose of Olmsted, who sat at my left. She was president of the Seniors, and moved about the school in a loose-limbed dreamy way that seemed to me seraphic. Inez, the Junior, was less impressive, but still had her own string of horses in Santa Barbara and could curse with great concentration, so many words that I only recognized *damn* and one or two others. Usually she had no use for me, but tonight she smiled, and the candlelight made her beady eyes look almost friendly.

The grace done with, we pulled our chairs in under the unaccustomed silkiness of our party-dress bottoms with less noise than usual, and the orchestra flung itself into a march. The pantry doors opened, and the dapper little houseboys pranced in, their smooth faces pulled straight and their eyes snapping with excitement.

They put a plate in front of each of us. We all looked mazily at what we saw, and waited with mixed feelings until Miss Huntingdon had picked up her fork (where, I wonder now, did Mrs. Cheever even find one hundred oyster forks in a California boarding school?), before we even thought of eating. I heard Inez mutter under her breath, several more words I did not recognize except as such, and then Olmsted said casually, "How charming! Blue Points!"

There was a quiet buzz . . . we were being extremely well-bred, all of us, for the party . . . and I know now that I was not the only Westerner who was scared shaky at the immediate prospect of eating her first raw oyster, and was putting it off for as long as possible.

I remembered hearing Mother say that it was vulgar as well as extremely unpleasant to do anything with an oyster but swallow it as quickly as possible, without *thinking*, but that the after-taste was rather nice. Of course it was different with tinned oysters in turkey dressing: they could be chewed with impunity, both social and hygienic, for some reason or other. But raw, they must be swallowed whole, and rapidly.

And alive.

With the unreasoning and terrible persnicketiness of a sixteen-year-old I knew that I would be sick if I had to swallow anything in the world alive, but especially a live oyster.

Olmsted picked up one deftly on the prongs of her little fork, tucked it under her enormous nose, and gulped. "Delicious," she murmured.

"Jesus," Inez said softly. "Well, here goes. The honor of the old school. Oi!" And she swallowed noisily. A look of smug surprise crept into her face, and she said in my ear, "Try one, Baby-face. It ain't the heat, it's the humidity. Try one. Slip and go easy." She cackled suddenly, watching me with sly bright eyes.

"Yes, do," Olmsted said.

I laughed lightly, tinklingly, like Helen in *Helen and Warren*, said, "Oh, I *love* Blue Points!" and got one with surprising neatness into my mouth.

At that moment the orchestra began to play, with sexless abandon, a popular number called, I think, "Horses." It sounded funny in Miss Huntingdon's dining room. Olmsted laughed, and said to me, "Come on, Kennedy. Let's start the ball rolling, shall we?"

The fact that she, the most wonderful girl in the whole school, and the most intelligent, and the most revered, should ask me to dance when she knew very well that I was only a Sophomore, was so overwhelming that it made even the dream-like reality that she had called me Kennedy, instead of Mary Frances, seem unimportant.

The oyster was still in my mouth. I smiled with care, and stood up, reeling with the thought of dancing the first dance of the evening with the senior-class president.

The oyster seemed larger. I knew that I must down it, and was equally sure that I could not. Then, as Olmsted put her thin hand on my shoulder blades, I swallowed once, and felt light and attractive and daring, to know what I had done. We danced stiffly around the room, and as soon as a few other pairs of timid girls came into the cleared space by the tree, headed toward Miss Huntingdon's table.

Miss Huntingdon herself spoke to me by name, and Miss Blake laughed silently so that her black wig bobbled, and cracked her knuckles as she always did when she was having a good time, and the minister and Olmsted made a little joke about Silent Sophomores and Solemn Seniors, and I did not make a sound, and nobody seemed to think it strange. I was dumb with pleasure at my own importance . . . practically the Belle of the Ball I was! . . . and with a dawning gastronomic hunger. Oysters, my delicate taste buds were telling me, oysters are *simply marvelous!* More, more!

I floated on, figuratively at least, in Olmsted's arms. The dance ended with a squeaky but cheerful flourish, and the girls went back to their seats almost as flushed as if they were returning from the arms of the most passionate West Point cadets in white gloves and coats.

The plates had been changed. I felt flattened, dismayed, as only children can about such things.

Olmsted said, "You're a funny kid, Kennedy. Oh, green olives!" when I mumbled how wonderful it had been to dance with her, and Inez murmured in my ear, "Dance with me next, will you, Baby-face? There are a couple of things boys can do I can't, but I can dance with you a damn sight better than that bitch Olmsted."

I nodded gently, and smiled a tight smile at her, and thought that she was the most horrible creature I had ever known. Perhaps I might kill her some day. I was going to be sick.

I pushed back my chair.

"Hey, Baby-face!" The music started with a crash, and Inez put her arms surely about me, and led me with expert grace around and around the Christmas tree, while all the candles fluttered in time with my stomach.

"Why don't you talk?" she asked once. "You have the cutest little ears I ever saw, Baby-face . . . like a pony I had, when I was in Colorado. How do you like the way I dance with you?"

Her arm tightened against my back. She was getting a crush on me, I thought, and here it was only Christmas and I was only a Sophomore! What would it be by April, the big month for them? I felt somewhat flattered, because Inez was a Junior and had those horses in Santa Barbara, but I hated her. My stomach felt better.

Miss Huntingdon was watching me again, while she held her water glass in her white thin fingers as if it had wine in it, or the Holy Communion. She leaned over and said something to Miss Blake, who laughed silently like a gargoyle and cracked her knuckles with delight, not at what Miss Huntingdon was saying but that she was saying anything at all. Perhaps they were talking about me, saying that I was nice and dependable and would be a good Senior president in two more years, or that I had the cutest ears. . . .

"Relax, kid," Inez murmured. "Just pretend . . ."

The pantry door swung shut on a quick flash of gray chiffon and pearls, almost at my elbow, and before I knew it myself I was out of Inez' skillful arms and after it. I had to escape from her; and the delightful taste of oyster in my mouth, my new-born gourmandise, sent me toward an unknown rather than a known sensuality.

The thick door shut out almost all the sound from the flickering, noisy dining room. The coolness of the pantry was shocking, and Mrs. Cheever was even more so. She stood, queenly indeed in her beautiful gray evening dress and her pearls and her snowy hair done in the same lumpy rhythm as Mary of England's, and her face was all soft and formless with weeping.

Tears trickled like colorless blood from her eyes, which had always been so stony and now looked at me without seeing me at all. Her mouth, puckered from years of dyspepsia and disapproval, was loose and tender suddenly, and she sniffed with vulgar abandon.

She stood with one arm laid gently over the scarlet shoulders of the fat old nurse, who was dressed fantastically in the ancient costume of Saint Nicholas. It became her well, for her formless body was as generous as his, and her ninny-simple face, pink-cheeked and sweet, was kind like his and neither male nor female. The ratty white wig sat almost tidily on her head, which looked as if it hardly missed its neat black-ribboned nurse's cap, and beside her on the pantry serving table lay the beard, silky and monstrous, ready to be pulled snug against her chins when it was time to give us all our presents under the Christmas tree.

She looked through me without knowing that I stood staring at her like a paralyzed rabbit. I was terrified, of her the costumed nurse and of Mrs. Cheever so hideously weeping and of all old women.

Mrs. Cheever did not see me either. For the first time I did not feel unattractive in her presence, but rather completely unnecessary. She put out one hand, and for a fearful moment I thought perhaps she was going to kiss me: her face was so tender. Then I saw that she was putting oysters carefully on a big platter that sat before the nurse, and that as she watched the old biddy eat them, tears kept running bloodlessly down her soft ravaged cheeks, while she spoke not a word.

I backed toward the door, hot as fire with shock and the dread confusion of adolescence, and said breathlessly, "Oh, excuse me, Mrs. Cheever! But I . . . that is, *all* the Sophomores . . . on behalf of the Sophomore Class I want to thank you for this beautiful, this *simply marvelous* party! Oysters . . . and . . . and everything . . . It's all *so* nice!"

But Mrs. Cheever did not hear me. She stood with one hand still on the wide red shoulders of the nurse, and with the other she put the oysters left from the Christmas Party on a platter. Her eyes were smeared so that they no longer looked hard and hateful, and as she watched the old woman eat steadily, voluptuously, of the fat cold molluscs, she looked so tender that I turned anxiously toward the sureness and stability of such small passions as lay in the dining room.

The pantry door closed behind me. The orchestra was whipping through "Tales from the Vienna Woods," with the assistant violin instructor doubling on the artificial mocking bird. A flock of little Filipino boys skimmed like monkeys into the candlelight, with great trays of cranberry sauce and salted nuts and white curled celery held above their heads, and I could tell by their faces that whatever they had seen in the pantry was already tucked far back behind their eyes, perhaps forever.

If I could still taste my first oyster, if my tongue still felt fresh and excited, it was perhaps too bad. Although things are different now, I hoped then, suddenly and violently, that I would never see one again.

— Octavio Paz —

The Pachuco

When I went to live in the United States, I stayed for a while in Los Angeles, a city with around a million inhabitants of Mexican descent. At first sight the visitor is struck, apart from the purity of the sky and the ugliness of the scattered and ostentatious buildings, by the city's vaguely Mexican atmosphere, an atmosphere impossible to convey in words. This impression of Mexico—a taste for cheap ornaments, for carelessness, passion, and reserve—floats in the air. I say floats because it neither mixes with nor melts into that other world, that North American world built on precision and efficiency. It floats but does not oppose; it sways, at the whim of the wind, sometimes as shapeless as a cloud and sometimes as direct and erect as a rocket. It hugs the ground, falls into pleats, expands, contracts, sleeps, or dreams: beauty in tatters. It floats, never coming to the point of existing or disappearing.

Somewhat the same thing happens with the Mexicans one meets on the street. Though they have lived there many years, wear the same clothes, speak in the same way, and are ashamed of their origins, no one would take them for real North Americans. And not because physical features count for as much as is commonly thought. The thing that seems to me to distinguish them from the

Editors' note: The pachuco is a young Mexican-American with a taste for flashy clothes and special jargon and usually belonging to a neighborhood gang.

rest of the people is their furtive, restless air—of maskers, of creatures who fear the gaze of a stranger as if it could strip them bare. When you talk to them you notice that emotionally they are like a pendulum, a crazy pendulum which oscillates violently and unrhythmically.

This state of mind, or mindlessness, has produced what is called the *pachuco*—a strange word that has no precise meaning, or rather, like all popular creations, is charged with a multiplicity of meanings. Whether we like it or not, they are Mexicans and represent one of the extremes to which the Mexican character can go.

Incapable of adjusting to a civilization that spurns them anyhow, the pachucos have found no answer to a hostile environment except an exacerbated affirmation of their personality. Other minorities do not react in the same way. Negroes, for instance, hounded as they are by racial intolerance, try to "pass," to sneak into society. They want to be just like their fellow citizens. Mexicans, faced with a less violent form of rejection, far from attempting a problematic adaptation to local fashions, affirm their differences, underline them, do all they can to make them noticeable. By means of a grotesque dandyism and anarchic behavior, they call attention not so much to the injustice or incapacity of a society which has not been able to assimilate them as to their personal determination to go on being different.

There is no point in trying to understand the reasons for this conflict, and even less in trying to remedy it. Everywhere there are minorities who lack the opportunities afforded others. What is characteristic here is the obstinate desire to be different, the anguish with which the Mexican, orphaned from both value and validity, flaunts his difference before the world. The pachuco has lost his birthright—his language, religion, customs, beliefs. All that he has left is a body and soul bare to the elements, naked to stares. His mask protects him; it hides him at the same time that it makes him conspicuous.

His clothes, aggressively fancy and so obvious that they require no further analysis, show that he makes no claim to belonging to any sect or clique. *Pachuquismo* is an open society in a country abundant in religious and tribal customs destined to satisfy the American need to belong to something more vital and concrete than the abstract morality of the American Way of Life. The pachuco costume is neither a uniform nor the vestments of a rite. It is just a style. Like all styles, it depends on novelty (which Leopardi called the dam of death), and on imitation.

The novelty of the costume lies in its exaggeration. The pachuco takes fashion to its ultimate limits and transforms it into art. Nowadays one of the guiding principles of American fashion is comfort; in returning everyday clothes to the realm of aesthetics, the pachuco has come back to the "impractical," the nonfunctional. And so he denies the very principles of the model which inspired him. Hence his aggressiveness.

This rebellion is only a meaningless gesture, since it is simply an exaggeration of the modes against which he is trying to revolt and not a return to the dress of his ancestors—or a new sartorial invention. Usually it is by their clothing that eccentrics emphasize their determination to cut themselves off from society, either to found a new and tighter clique or to assert their singularity. With the pachucos there is an evident ambiguity: on the one hand their clothes isolate them and make them conspicuous; on the other, the way they dress represents an act of homage to a society they are trying to deny.

This duality is also expressed in another, perhaps more profound, way: the pachuco is a clown, an unabashed and sinister clown, who has no intention of inciting laughter but does mean to terrify. This sadistic attitude is linked with a longing for self-abasement, which it seems to me is the true key to his character. The pachuco knows that it is dangerous to stand out and that his conduct exasperates society; no matter, he seeks for and attracts persecution and scandal. It is the only way in which he can establish a more vital relationship with the society that he is irritating. As a victim he can take his place in a world which has hitherto taken no notice of him; as an outlaw, he may become one of its accursed heroes, _le maudit_.

The irritation behind the American attitude to him springs, I think, from a view of the pachuco as a mythical—and as such all the more potentially dangerous—being. His menace springs from his singularity. Americans have always found the hybrid both disturbing and fascinating. Around the pachuco a cluster of ambivalent notions arises; his uniqueness seems to feed on powers that are now malevolent, now beneficent. To some he suggests extraordinary erotic powers, to others he hints a perversity which may be aggressive. A symbol of love and happiness, or of horror and abomination, the pachuco seems to be the incarnation of freedom, disorder, the forbidden—in short, someone who deserves to be liquidated, but also someone with whom it is possible to achieve a dark, secret contact.

Passively, contemptuously, the pachuco suffers all these contradictory implications to accumulate around his head, until (not without a certain wounded self-satisfaction) he sees them erupt into a bar brawl or a police raid or a riot. And then, in persecution, he realizes his true, his authentic role, his supreme, his denuded essence, as the pariah, the man who belongs nowhere, the outsider.

Jane Vandenburgh

Failure to Zigzag

It was the look, the thought, of her own hair that always filled Charlotte with hopelessness. The braids went trundling down her back like her grandparents' twin sentinels. They made her feel like a refugee, as if she were another Annelli Verdonner. Annelli, like Williman, was another Charlotte felt she ought to be particularly kind to but could never quite bring herself to be. Like Charlotte's, Annelli's braids were obviously constructed by someone else—hers were white blonde, skinny, pinned up with ribbons in bun-shaped twists at the sides of her head above her translucent ears. They made her look years younger than anyone in their grade. The fact of braids, Charlotte had decided, had the effect of making a girl look old-fashioned, too well tended, too often handled. The country from which Annelli Verdonner had come had been taken over by the Russians at the end of the Second World War and had disappeared from the map of the world.

The more regular girls at Glendale High wore flips or pixies, bubbles or a single, bouncing ponytail. The point was not to be knock-down beautiful, which tended to stir things up, but rather to be cute. Moms of girls looked like Doris Day, their grandmothers like Mamie Eisenhower. A very stylish woman from the country club might try to look like a grayer, more Republican Jackie Kennedy, as long as she didn't look "Eastern." Looking "Eastern," sounding

"Eastern," or sending your children east to go to school all showed you thought you were better than everybody else. In Glendale, in 1962, it was better to be the same.

There were no Negroes living in Glendale then, by unwritten covenant. If anyone was Jewish in Charlotte's school, the fact was never mentioned. Even the hoods, like Bob Davidson, weren't real greasers since they weren't Mexican. Mexicans lived in their own neighborhoods and went to their own schools, and for the kids at Glendale High, were the stuff of lore. Mexican girls had deadly beehives, hairdos that were ratted up, hairsprayed, never taken down to be washed, used to hide razor blades for girl fights and for the breeding of black widow spiders. Spitcurls were stuck to the cheeks of Mexican girls with little X's of scotchtape, X's inexplicably left there after the curls were already good and stuck.

The cute, sweet, nice girls of Glendale High didn't swear. They didn't swear, scream, fight, or have pierced ears. They learned to dance at cotillion and learned their pleasant manners at charm school, where they also learned that manners, once learned, might also occasionally be ignored. They didn't get pregnant or have girl fights, which were fought by different rules than the fights of boys. The fingernails of Mexican girls illustrated this: they were long, sharp, and as red as if they'd already been dipped in blood. Charlotte knew all about girl fights, this being the way she fought the enemies in her dreams.

Boys' fights were different, were fought more simply, as men fought wars: to crush, to annihilate. In girl fights the impulse was less singular. Girls fought a fight to humiliate, to make the other ugly, to rip the blouse away, to tear off a bra and expose the other publicly. They fought with boys surrounding them and watching, fought so these boys would laugh and cheer.

"We could iron it," Patsy was saying. "Or we could use that stuff Negroes use, that junk like a perm that reverses the process?" They were trying to figure out how to make Charlotte's hair fall straight. Because it was braided wet it fell down her back in a curtain of waves when they let it down. When brushed out Charlotte's hair, like Katrinka's, turned wild, electric. Patsy's parents were out and they were babysitting Brian. He was in the den down the hall watching TV. They were in the bedroom with the door locked, drinking rum and coke.

"But it would stink up the house," Patsy went on. "It always stunk up the house when Mom used to give me a Tony. We're not supposed to stink up the house when my parents are out." She had cotton balls stuffed between her toes, a trick, like the use of orange sticks for cuticles, they'd gotten out of charm school. "Why don't we just cut it?" Patsy asked. "I mean, what could they really do to you if you came home with it trimmed?"

"Throw me out of the house."

Tom Wolfe

The Pump House Gang

Our boys never hair out. The black panther has black feet. Black feet on the crumbling black panther. Pan-thuh. Mee-dah. Pam Stacy, sixteen years old, a cute girl here in La Jolla, California, with a pair of orange bell-bottom hip-huggers on, sits on a step about four steps down the stairway to the beach and she can see a pair of revolting black feet without lifting her head. So she says it out loud, "The black panther."

Somebody farther down the stairs, one of the boys with the *major* hair and khaki shorts, says, "The black feet of the black panther."

"Mee-dah," says another kid. This happens to be the cry of a, well, *underground* society known as the Mac Meda Destruction Company.

"The pan-thuh."

"The poon-thuh."

All these kids, seventeen of them, members of the Pump House crowd, are lollygagging around the stairs down to Windansea Beach, La Jolla, California, about 11 A.M., and they all look at the black feet, which are a woman's pair of black street shoes, out of which stick a pair of old veiny white ankles, which lead up like a senile cone to a fudge of tallowy, edematous flesh, her thighs, squeezing out of her bathing suit, with old faded yellow bruises on them, which she probably got from running eight feet to catch a bus or something.

She is standing with her old work-a-hubby, who has on *sandals*: you know, a pair of navy-blue anklet socks and these sandals with big, wide, new-smelling tan straps going this way and that, *for keeps*. Man, they look like orthopedic sandals, if one can imagine that. Obviously, these people come from Tucson or Albuquerque or one of those hincty adobe towns. All these hincty, crumbling black feet come to La Jolla-by-the-sea from the adobe towns for the weekend. They even drive in cars all full of thermos bottles and mayonnaisey sandwiches and some kind of latticework wooden back support for the old crock who drives and Venetian blinds on the back window.

"The black panther."

"Pan-thuh."

"Poon-thuh."

"Mee-dah."

Nobody says it to the two old crocks directly. God, they must be practically fifty years old. Naturally, they're carrying every piece of garbage imaginable: the folding aluminum chairs, the newspapers, the lending-library book with the clear plastic wrapper on it, the sunglasses, the sun ointment, about a vat of goo—

It is a Mexican standoff. In a Mexican standoff, both parties narrow their eyes and glare but nobody throws a punch. Of course, nobody in the Pump House crowd would ever even jostle these people or say anything right to them; they are too cool for that.

Everybody in the Pump House crowd looks over, even Tom Coman, who is a cool person. Tom Coman, sixteen years old, got thrown out of his garage last night. He is sitting up on top of the railing, near the stairs, up over the beach, with his legs apart. Some nice long willowy girl in yellow slacks is standing on the sidewalk but leaning into him with her arms around his body, just resting. Neale Jones, sixteen, a boy with great lank perfect surfer's hair, is standing nearby with a band-aid on his upper lip, where the sun has burnt it raw. Little Vicki Ballard is up on the sidewalk. Her older sister, Liz, is down the stairs by the Pump House itself, a concrete block, fifteen feet high, full of machinery for the La Jolla water system. Liz is wearing her great "Liz" styles, a hulking rabbit-fur vest and black leather boots over her Levis, even though it is about eighty-five out here and the sun is plugged in up there like God's own dentist lamp and the Pacific is heaving in with some fair-to-middling surf. Kit Tilden is lollygagging around, and Tom Jones, Connie Carter, Roger Johnson, Sharon Sandquist, Mary Beth White, Rupert Fellows, Glenn Jackson, Dan Watson from San Diego, they are all out here, and everybody takes a look at the panthers.

The old guy, one means, you know, he must be practically fifty years old, he says to his wife, "Come on, let's go farther up," and he takes her by her fat upper arm as if to wheel her around and aim her away from here.

But she says, "No! We have just as much right to be here as they do."

"That's *not the point*—"

"Are you going to—"

"*Mrs. Roberts*," the work-a-hubby says, calling his own wife by her official married name, as if to say she took a vow once and his word is law, even if he is not testing it with the blond kids here—"farther up, *Mrs. Roberts.*"

They start to walk up the sidewalk, but one kid won't move his feet, and oh, god, her work-a-hubby breaks into a terrible shaking Jello smile as she steps over them, as if to say, Excuse me, sir, I don't mean to make trouble, please, and don't you and your colleagues rise up and jump me, screaming *Gotcha*—

Mee-dah!

But exactly! This beach *is* verboten for people practically fifty years old. This is a segregated beach. They can look down on Windansea Beach and see nothing but lean tan kids. It is posted "no swimming" (for safety reasons), meaning surfing only. In effect, it is segregated by age. From Los Angeles on down the California coast, this is an era of age segregation. People have always tended to segregate themselves by age, teenagers hanging around with teenagers, old people with old people, like the old men who sit on the benches up near the Bronx Zoo and smoke black cigars. But before, age segregation has gone on within a larger community. Sooner or later during the day everybody has melted back into the old community network that embraces practically everyone, all ages.

But in California today surfers, not to mention rock 'n' roll kids and the hot-rodders or Hair Boys, named for their fanciful pompadours—all sorts of sets of kids—they don't merely hang around together. They establish whole little societies for themselves. In some cases they live with one another for months at a time. The "Sunset Strip" on Sunset Boulevard used to be a kind of Times Square for Hollywood hot dogs of all ages, anyone who wanted to promenade in his version of the high life. Today "The Strip" is almost completely the preserve of kids from about sixteen to twenty-five. It is lined with go-go clubs. One of them, a place called It's Boss, is set up for people sixteen to twenty-five and won't let in anybody over twenty-five, and there are some terrible I'm-dying-a-thousand-deaths scenes when a girl comes up with her boyfriend and the guy at the door at It's Boss doesn't think she looks under twenty-five and tells her she will have to produce some identification proving she is young enough to come in here and live The Strip kind of life and—she's *had* it, because she can't get up the ID and nothing in the world is going to make a woman look stupider than to stand around trying to argue *I'm younger than I look, I'm younger than I look*. So she practically shrivels up like a Peruvian shrunken head in front of her boyfriend and he trundles her off, looking for some place you can get an old doll like this into. One of the few remaining clubs for "older people," curiously, is the Playboy Club. There are apartment houses for people twenty to thirty only, such as the Sheri Plaza in Hollywood and the E'Questre Inn in Burbank. There are whole suburban housing developments, mostly private developments, where only people over forty-five or fifty can buy a house. Whole towns, meantime, have become identified as "young": Venice, Newport Beach, Balboa—or "old": Pasadena, Riverside, Coronado Island.

Behind much of it—especially something like a whole nightclub district of a major city, "The Strip," going teenage—is, simply, money. World War II and the prosperity that followed pumped incredible amounts of money into the population, the white population at least, at every class level. All of a sudden here is an area with thousands of people from sixteen to twenty-five who can get their hands on enough money to support a whole nightclub belt and to have the cars to get there and to set up autonomous worlds of their own in a fairly posh resort community like La Jolla—

—Tom Coman's garage. Some old bastard took Tom Coman's garage away from him, and that means eight or nine surfers are out of a place to stay.

"I went by there this morning, you ought to see the guy," Tom Coman says. Yellow Stretch Pants doesn't move. She has him around the waist. "He was out there painting and he had this brush and about a thousand gallons of ammonia. He was really going to scrub me out of there."

"What did he do with the furniture?"

"I don't know. He threw it out."

"What are you going to do?"

"I don't know."

"Where are you going to stay?"

"I don't know. I'll stay on the beach. It wouldn't be the first time. I haven't had a place to stay for three years, so I'm not going to start worrying now."

Everybody thinks that over awhile. Yellow Stretch just hangs on and smiles. Tom Coman, sixteen years old, piping fate again. One of the girls says, "You can stay at my place, Tom."

"Um. Who's got a cigarette?"

Pam Stacy says, "You can have these."

Tom Coman lights a cigarette and says, "Let's have a destructo." A destructo is what can happen in a garage after eight or ten surfers are kicked out of it.

"Mee-dah!"

"Wouldn't that be bitchen?" says Tom Coman. Bitchen is a surfer's term that means "great," usually.

"Bitchen!"

"Mee-dah!"

It's incredible—that old guy out there trying to scour the whole surfing life out of that garage. He's a pathetic figure. His shoulders are hunched over and he's dousing and scrubbing away and the sun doesn't give him a tan, it gives him these . . . *mottles* on the back of his neck. But never mind! The hell with destructo. One only has a destructo spontaneously, a Dionysian . . . *bursting out*, like those holes through the wall during the Mac Meda Destruction Company Convention at Manhattan Beach—Mee-dah!

Something will pan out. It's a magic economy—yes!—all up and down the coast from Los Angeles to Baja California kids can go to one of these beach towns and live the complete surfing life. They take off from home and get to the beach, and if they need a place to stay, well, somebody rents a garage for twenty bucks a month and everybody moves in, girls and boys. Furniture—it's like, one means, you know, one *appropriates* furniture from here and there. It's like the Volkswagen buses a lot of kids now use as beach wagons instead of woodies. Woodies are old station wagons, usually Fords, with wooden bodies, from back before 1953. One of the great things about a Volkswagen bus is that one can . . . *exchange* motors in about three minutes. A good VW motor exchanger can go up to a parked Volkswagen, and a few ratchets of the old wrench here and it's up and out and he has a new motor. There must be a few nice old black panthers around wondering why their nice hubby-mommy VWs don't run so good anymore—but—then—they—are—probably—puzzled—about—a—lot of things. Yes.

Saint Aloysius

Twice a year the parish held fundraising bazaars. They were on weekends in October and May and were the backbone of the finances for the grammar school and church. They were held on the blacktop of the schoolyard. There were never any rides, but plenty of food and games of chance and amusement. It was the duty of the parents of the schoolchildren to contribute some of their time in the organizing and actual running of the bazaar.

My father ran the jingleboard. He carried metal rings on a metal rod with a magnet at one end and bellowed out the prices for the rings. They were bought, or rather rented, by the patrons of the board and thrown at a table filled with coins and bills. When one landed clearly on a coin or the face of a bill it became yours. He picked up the ricocheting rings from the ground and table with the magnet. He was the perfect barker for a carnival somewhere out of a 1950s movie, making up little rhymes and jingles as the day went on, more and more people enticed by his words as the evening went on. He was quite adept at the game himself, having been running the board for ten years by the time I entered that school.

There were other games too. The goldfish pond where a person threw ping pong balls, three for a quarter, at a table filled with bowls of the fish swimming in colored water, some of them with orange tails whispery thin against the background of blue, red, or green colored water. Mrs. Tabor, whose daughter was in my first grade class, was always the one to run this particular booth.

There was another fish pond at those bazaars. My mother, I remember, always worked at this one. It was a booth covered in front with cardboard. Portholes were cut in the cardboard and children for the cost of a dime were given bamboo poles with a string tied to one end and a fishhook at the end of that string. The poles were lowered into the portholes and my mother tied cheap toys onto the hook and tugged at the string. Thereupon the child would retrieve the pole, string, and hook from out of the hole and take his prize. It was the only sure winner in the entire operation.

When I first began school there at Saint Aloysius I had a sister in the eighth grade, a brother in the sixth, another sister in the fourth, and finally my brother Felix in the second. I remember being at the bazaar with my oldest sister that first year. At that time it was still felt I needed to be with someone older and being with my sister and her friends had its drawbacks. I had to use the girls' restroom, the boys' being far too dirty, rowdy, and violent for the six-year-old child I was. Even later when I was old enough(?), wise enough(?), dumb enough(?) to use that restroom it remained a place of fear and uncertainty. It was a place of flooded floors and overflowing toilets, sweating Mexican men and Seconal swallowing, zombie-eyed cholos passing the pills and cheap wine. It was the scene of the first sight of knives cutting flesh, bottles breaking skulls, and the strangeness of being fearful, but curious, of being scared enough to cry, but not wanting to miss a thing that tears might blind me from.

One Saturday afternoon in those first formative years I walked with my then buddy Jeffrey Leon. We bought raspadas from Mr. Salazar and his boy scout troop and crushed the confetti eggs we had spent all week preparing on the heads of our classmates. Not within the scrutiny of our parents we snuck peeks as best we could under the mini-skirts of the seventh and eighth grade girls and the teased-hair high-school cholas. We knew there was something up under those skirts and between those long legs which everyone talked about and desired and which would be ours to partake of someday, though we didn't know at the time what it was for sure.

Bingo games were held in the Old Hall throughout the weekends. It was the only parish hall, but always referred to as the Old Hall. In the cafeteria the food prepared by the parish mothers was sold: corn dogs and *buñuelos*, tamales, tostadas, tortas and tacos, burritos and menudo always for the morning after. When they were setting the booths up for the weekends it was probably some of the best times that were ever had during the school year. During recess and lunch breaks the children of the school stood within the booths acting out what each knew or thought the weekend would be like. The yard would be filled with strange cars and trucks and the men of the parish building the booths leaving little room for any football, basketball, or sockball.

On one such weekend while I was in the third grade I asked my father's permission to visit a friend who lived close by. It was the first time ever being allowed and I was getting older, more responsible perhaps. My friend Alfred and I went and looked at his older brother's *Playboy* magazines.

I used to love the mariachis who would play all decked out in their black suits and wide-brimmed sombreros, the guitaron thumping and the shrill trumpets getting louder. My father loved them too.

Sometime in the early seventies they stopped having these fundraisers, though I have heard they have started them up again. My nephew now goes to that school. They were ended because of the violence which always erupted. Cholos squaring off with each other in the crowd of people. I remember the fight that ended the show for years. The church and school lying somewhere on mutual ground, it was more than likely the bad boys from Florence against their counterparts from Watts. I stood and watched it all. It was the third night in a row. Sticks, knives, and beer bottles filled the air.

I can remember the panic and fear which engulfed me. I was alone for what was probably the first time on the streets. No brother, no sister, mother or father within reach, just lost in a crowd more than a thousand strong. I heard the commotion starting, growing and getting nearer. Glass broke and curses flew. People screamed and cried. Father José in his heavy Castilian accent stood in the middle of it, speaking in a combination of both English and Spanish and called upon the Lord to help settle the matter.

Some of my family was there though I didn't know where at the time. I heard firecrackers which I later learned was gunfire. I saw one dark, skinny vato walk by me with the bottom of a beer bottle firmly embedded in the side of his head. I felt sick. People ran scared. More people stuck around to see how it would turn out. The sheriffs then came to bust some heads themselves. Everyone left then, including myself, for fear of being arrested. I walked home alone at night for the first time, the sirens speeding toward where I had just left. School. Church. Someone died. The neighborhood. Perhaps it was the vato loco with the beer bottle bottom for a crown. I felt a fear I hoped I would never feel again.

— Randall Sullivan —

The Leader of the Pack

See, Dad, since you were a kid, they've invented a whole lot of ways for us to get into trouble. THE BEAVER TO WARD CLEAVER

On the morning after fifteen-year-old Mark Miller was shot to death in the parking lot of the Hot Trax teen nightclub on Van Nuys Boulevard, two photographs accompanied the front-page story in the *San Fernando Valley Daily News*. One was of the spectacularly handsome boy in the black tuxedo he wore on the night he was elected prom king at Montclair Prep, a distinguished private school in the Valley. The other was of the letters "FFF" scrawled in the blood that had spilled onto the pavement from Mark's head.

The detectives who stood under the hot August sun inside the yellow crime-scene ribbons that afternoon recognized the signature of Fight for Freedom, an association of Valley teenagers who had become the object of an uneasy, even belligerent, fascination for certain members of the Los Angeles Police Department. "A white, middle-class street gang" was how the police described FFF to the *Daily News*. Yet off the record the cops seemed to have problems with this description. The members of FFF did not appear to be bonded by either neighborhood loyalty or criminal enterprise, the glues traditionally holding L.A.'s black and Chicano gangs together, but rather by what the chief investigator on the scene would call "an attitude problem."

It came as something of a surprise to the police to discover that Mark Miller had not been a victim of FFF, but one of its members. During the previous school year, Mark had been voted the most valuable player on the football team at Montclair and was the star point guard on the basketball team. Still six months shy of his sixteenth birthday, he had already been the first love of more than a dozen young girls, most recently a thirteen-year-old Vidal Sassoon model; they had been celebrating their one-month anniversary on the night he was killed. "Mark was the most popular kid in the Valley," said his older brother, Larry, a star athlete and student-council member at North Hollywood High. Even cops found it curious that the most popular kid in the Valley would be a gang member.

Police in Los Angeles had been working to crush the adolescent insurrection that called itself Fight for Freedom since the early 1980s, back when FFF was still a punk-rock band headlining Friday-night shows at a dark, scabrous Hollywood cavern called Cathay de Grande. The band's lead singer was a stocky, scowling seventeen-year-old known as Ranger, a local legend among the habitués of a club scene that was siphoning hundreds of kids out of the suburbs every weekend. Along with bands like Black Flag and Suicidal Tendencies, FFF became a kind of punk cult, attracting a legion of mostly male fourteen- and fifteen-year-old devotees who followed the band from gig to gig.

Onstage, Ranger played it wild and free, exhorting his audience, taunting the cops who lurked in the darkened doorways, brandishing a broken beer bottle in one hand and fondling his crew-cut girlfriend with the other. An FFF concert was less a performance than an incitement to riot, building always to a mega-decibel climax at the playing of the band's anthem, "Where Were You in '42?"

Outsiders who stumbled in off Hollywood Boulevard saw a mob of thrashing skinheads wearing BELSEN WAS A GAS T-shirts and figured FFF for some neo-Nazi youth cabal. But for the hard-core punks who carpooled in from pastel tract houses in places like Canoga Park and Granada Hills, the message wasn't fascism but anarchy, boredom gone berserk and idealism inverted in a vast, amorphous mutiny against middle-class complacency. During "Where Were You in '42?" the crowd became a giant percussion section of overturned tables, broken chairs and shattered light bulbs. Kids did swan dives off the stage, gang-tackled the bouncers, pulled poseurs into the pit and slam-danced them into the emergency room at Cedars-Sinai.

By 1983, there wasn't a club left in Los Angeles that would allow FFF onstage, but when the band members walked out the front door, their audience followed them into the street. Fight for Freedom wasn't about music, Ranger said, it was about a way of life.

News that the members of FFF had outlived their careers as performing artists reached the public sector later that year, when security officers at North

Hollywood High reported that the former band members had ensconced themselves at the Yum Yum doughnut shop across the street from the campus, where an entourage of younger teenagers was growing around them. The cops came in to investigate the rumor that FFF was a drug ring but found a phenomenon they were unprepared for. The kids had modified their punk cuts into almost military-style flattops. Most were clean and neat white kids who used nicknames like Flaco, Waxer, Sapo, and Spooky, affecting an East L.A. cholo look of Dickies, chinos, flannel shirts, and either heavy black brogues or Creepers tennies. The kids flashed a lot of hand signals back and forth, seasoned their conversation with Spanish phrases and dealt with the authorities as if perpetrating some enormous inside joke.

The new FFF members weren't social outcasts but athletes and scholars, boys who had negotiated the blind curve of puberty and coasted into adolescence with an aplomb that made them the envy of their peers. "We were the best-looking guys, the most popular," said Damon Bain, recalling how he'd made the jump in the ninth grade from the surfer crowd. "FFF, we were the ones who always had the girls. So when we went punk, everyone freaked on us, like, 'What's goin' on?' We just said, 'Time for a change,' and everyone followed us who could, because we were the cool people."

Police officers who had merely been offended by FFF's appearance raised harsher objections when graffiti began to appear in affluent communities like Encino and Sherman Oaks. The two most common spray-ons were the FFF logo wrapped in the American flag or burning in the torch held aloft by the Statue of Liberty, occasionally supplemented by the four-part code Ranger had issued to his adherents: (1) be yourself; (2) live your own life; (3) fuck social values; (4) fight for freedom. Fifty complaints were reported within four months by neighborhood associations.

The cops sweated suspected FFF members but learned nothing. "These kids lie to you automatically," said Detective Paul Bishop. "It's a point of honor with them never to tell the police anything, even their real names. 'FFF?' they'll ask you. 'What's that?' "

"It was always being hassled by the cops, stopped on the street, taken in for bullshit, that really brought FFF together and made it last," said Damon Bain. "That made us think that maybe we really did stand for somethin', if they had to come down on us so hard."

In the Valley's high schools, it became part of the FFF mystique that no one who claimed to be a member really was. Everyone knew who really belonged. After the band broke up, Ranger would show up for one-dollar nights at the Cathay with fifty or sixty kids in tow and take the place over, inviting anyone who wanted to stand with him to step into the pit and slam.

"FFF basically took on Ranger's personality," explained Rick Ventre, a director of the Valley gang program Project Heavy. "He projected the image of a fighter, a tough guy whose skin was all black leather and metal studs."

Ranger had grown up out in the bleak, scorched foothills on the northern rim of Los Angeles County, in Sun Valley, where most of his neighbors spoke English as a second language. Early in his teens, when he was still Richard Yapelli, Jr., Ranger had been the first Anglo initiated into the Mexican gang Sol Trese, where he developed a repertoire of stories about stabbings with sharpened screwdrivers and shootings with pistol-grip shotguns that inflamed the imaginations of the white boys from the nicer neighborhoods to the south.

His myth grew when the other kids saw that Ranger walked like he talked, earning himself a reputation as a street fighter who not only never backed down but never lost. A student of military history, Ranger modeled FFF rumbles on World War II German army campaigns. He established a war council where he sat with three other senior members—a six-foot four-inch hulk called Oso, a sawed-off powder keg named Woody, and Shaun M.D., a scary skinhead with twenty-one-inch arms, amphetamine eyes and a scalp crosshatched by scars. The M.D. stood for Mr. Danger. "Definitely the baddest guy ever in FFF," said Damon Bain of Shaun M.D., who unnerved enemies when he girded for battle by massaging his forehead with broken glass. "If there was no punk gig, we'd show up at somebody's house with twenty or thirty guys," Damon said. "We scared 'em, took their girls, and there was nothin' anybody could do about it."

In an era of unisex, software, and techno-throb dance music, FFF came on with its crew cuts and overcoats like urban guerrillas from some underground outpost of macho. "The last real men," Project Heavy's Ventre called them, derisively. At North Hollywood High, FFF cut a swath of black and blue through the heavy-metal dopers who cruised in cars covered with Mötley Crüe and K-MET decals and feasted on the mophead mods who sat astride their mopeds in baggy pants. They sauntered through the hallways like slumming rock stars and loitered on the lawn outside, where the school's prettiest girls gathered around them at lunch like groupies on Grammy night.

When the weekend came, its numbers swelled, and FFF took on all comers, trashing the football teams from Notre Dame and Grant so totally that North Hollywood High's team backed down in public. An elite jock squad that recruited from private schools and named itself New Regime called FFF out one night at the Cathay and was beaten so badly it disbanded.

FFF's final test was the punk gang that had formed around the band Suicidal Tendencies, whose theme song went: "Sick of people—no one's real. Sick of trying—what's the point."

Based in a Venice neighborhood bordered by a black ghetto, a brown barrio, and the blue Pacific, Suicidal Tendencies' members wore bandannas and long-tailed white dress shirts. They had a reputation for carrying the theater of the strange into realms that even Ranger and Shaun M.D. would not enter. At punk gigs, if an FFF member did a dive off the stage, some kid from Suicidal Tendencies would climb a speaker stack fifty feet high and belly flop into the crowd. Two or three of them left by ambulance every night. "We were the badasses, but they were the crazies," said one FFFer. During the winter of 1983 and 1984, the two groups went to war at parking lots in Hollywood and Van Nuys. "They were from a tougher neighborhood, but every time they called us out, we wasted 'em," remembered Damon Bain. "After a while, people just accepted that we were unbeatable."

Mark Miller was the last and the youngest member formally initiated into FFF, recruited by Ranger personally. "Mark and I were like preppie jocks before that," his friend Tony Miller (no relation) recalled. "We were into Bermuda shorts, Polo sweaters, and Converse high-tops." The Miller Boys, as they billed themselves, had met as the stars of a Little League baseball team in Studio City. Both were blessed with dark good looks, and both were outstanding athletes. "We got a lot of women even back then," Tony said.

Tony joined FFF during the summer after seventh grade, sponsored by his older brother Rich, whose arms were already decorated with grotesque tattoos that he hid from their father under long-sleeved shirts. Tony had long considered Rich the family embarrassment but began to see the advantages of improved relations with his brother during the month he spent being chased around their condominium complex by a group of older kids who cruised on motocross bicycles like a troop of Hells Angels trainees. He absorbed about a beating a week, Tony recalled, until the August afternoon when Rich and two of his friends from FFF used billy clubs to dismount the boy bikers and worked them over until they bled from their ears.

"You start thinking that it's a good idea to have guys who will be there for you," Tony explained. "There's so much weirdness happening around." A week after Rich showed him what friends could do for you, Tony tossed the $700 New Romantic wardrobe his mother had bought him to start school in. He showed up that first week for classes wearing Creepers and an FFF flattop.

Twelve-year-old Mark introduced himself to FFF through his courtship of a fourteen-year-old girl named Jenny Lazarus. His friends teased Mark that Jenny's best feature was her friend Evie, who was dating Ranger at the time. In the younger boy, Ranger saw a burnished image of himself: good-looking, physically gifted, charismatic, a centerpiece in any setting. He began calling

Mark "little brother" and jumped him into FFF as a present for his thirteenth birthday.

For both Mark and Tony, their punk make-over was an enormous success at Reed Junior High. "After we joined FFF, it was incredible how the girls came after us," Tony recalled. "Everybody thought FFF was the baddest, the toughest, and girls love that shit, even the ones that say they don't. We were eighth graders, but we were hangin' out with older guys, people the other kids in our class were afraid to say hello to." The Miller Boys became the young princes of the punk scene, friendly rivals who made hard tackles on Friday afternoons, then celebrated in the pit at the Cathay until two the next morning, preening in the coed toilets and dating high-school girls. Ranger made Mark his protégé, and Tony was getting rich dealing marijuana and psychedelic mushrooms, using Rich as a bill collector. At the age of fourteen, Tony was renting suites at the new Le Mondrian Hotel on Sunset Strip, where he and Mark brought their girlfriends to order room service and dance on the balcony.

It was hard for parents to keep track of kids. Just about everyone's mother and father were divorced, and a street-smart suburban punk like Tony could create considerable confusion in the distance between his dad's condo in Studio City and his mom's house in Beverly Hills.

Mark's situation was a little different. His parents were divorced, too—had been when he was still in diapers—but they weren't really *apart*. Michael Miller had moved into a house just minutes away from the one his ex-wife rented on Riverside Drive in Studio City. Karen Miller won custody of their two sons, but Michael was at her front door constantly, a doting, obsessive, jealous father whose violent temper kept the household in a perpetual state of dread. Their parents' power struggle dominated the boys' upbringing, and Michael's denunciations of Karen's self-indulgent idealism and permissive parenting exploded into scenes that terrified Mark and his brother, Larry, who watched helplessly as their father performed such feats of strength as dragging their mother down a flight of stairs with a belt around her throat. Through the years, the parents continued to trade accusations and denials.

Larry, older by twenty-three months, "couldn't take sides," his mother said, "so he shut down emotionally, became very controlled." "I just decided not to let it affect me," Larry said. "Mark kept letting it affect him."

While Larry spread himself thin keeping contact with both parents, Mark drew closer to his mother, becoming her traveling companion, confidant, even, at times, her best friend. An attractive, gifted, troubled, idealistic, conflicted, self-dramatizing woman, Karen Miller was passionately attached to her younger son. "I saw a lot of myself in him," she admitted.

Karen had grown up in the expensive Valley community of Encino, raised in a lovely home on a lushly landscaped lot by a silent stepfather and a mother who committed suicide when her daughter was fourteen. On her own at age sixteen, Karen fled from her past into the youth movement of the 1960s, flowering on the south slopes of the Hollywood Hills, a cute and clever little blonde who alternated waiting on tables with writing whimsical articles for publications like the *L.A. Free Press*. Karen was all of nineteen in 1966 when she married Michael, a twenty-seven-year-old bail bondsman whose appreciation for the counterculture was limited to drugs, sex, and rock & roll. Like his young bride, Michael had grown up on his own, leaving his home in Michigan at age fifteen. Their relationship was one of those spontaneous combustions that become a general conflagration outside the bedroom, but from the beginning Karen was determined to have children. A DES baby, she had contracted cervical cancer at seventeen, undergone a series of operations to rebuild her female organs and tried "everything from fertilization pills to standing on my head to get pregnant." Both boys were born before she turned twenty-four.

The marriage was a heap of smoldering ashes by then. A story both parents told their children went back to the winter before Mark's birth. "Larry left his toy kettle on the burner one night, and the rubber melted and ruined the stove," Karen recalled. "The repairman came from the gas company and said, 'You need this and this and this.' I only had six dollars, and I said I couldn't afford it. Anyway, he came back an hour later with all the parts and said, 'Merry Christmas.' " A sweet little story, as Karen told it, except that after Mark was born, Michael didn't believe the baby was his. "He said it was the gasman's," Karen recalled.

With the two toddlers in tow, Karen moved out on her own, supporting herself with a mélange of occupations that included cocktail waitress and restaurant manager. She wrote a collection of children's stories about a crew of emotional monsters called the Gumballs who inhabited kitchen sinks and garbage pails.

When the boys were nine and eleven, their mother married her second husband, Bobby Lucero, who worked as banquet manager at the Valley's bastion of swank, the Sportsmen's Lodge. Bobby was a gentle character who liked to come home from work, put on a Grateful Dead T-shirt, and sail away on Jerry Garcia guitar solos. His peace was repeatedly shattered, though, by the battle that raged on, uninterrupted, between his new wife and her old husband: Michael was on the phone demanding to know if Karen had given Mark permission to wear an earring; Michael was in the driveway wondering where Karen had taken his kids; Michael was on the porch threatening legal action; Michael was in the living room promising to punch Bobby's lights out. "I was the one that got away," Karen said, "and he couldn't stand it." Neither could Bobby, who left after three years. "I don't want this kind of life," he told Karen.

She started to sink during the collapse of her second marriage, drinking heavily and agreeing to divide the kids, one week with their father, one week with her. Michael had become a successful private investigator, and he was generous to his sons with both time and money, taking them off for vacations in Maui, buying them surfboards and motor scooters, paying $7000 out of his own pocket for the tuition at Montclair Prep, the private school he had picked for Mark because it had "the best athletic programs of all those places."

Just before the split with Bobby, Karen caught herself in mid descent and joined Alcoholics Anonymous. She had started to work as a set decorator for television commercials; despite sporadic employment, she was able to bring home big checks when she had jobs.

At home, Karen maintained an open-door policy, and the house was full of boys who couldn't speak two words to their fathers, and girls who sounded her out on subjects ranging from birth control to careers in show business. Among Mark's friends, the place became known as Mama Miller's Mission.

"She bred a bad environment," Michael complained, "letting runaways stay at her house. She'd say they were kids with problems. So what? They're not our problems. Our problems are our kids."

"I respected kids," Karen said, "and I didn't scoff at what they were concerned about."

"Kids need discipline," Michael said, "but she couldn't even discipline herself. She wouldn't set standards."

"My kids always knew they were good enough for me," Karen said. "They didn't have to do or be anything but what they were."

The divisions between their parents were physically manifested in the boys: Larry inherited his mother's compact build and his father's long, angular face, while Mark wore Karen's high cheekbones and square chin atop his father's lanky, muscular body.

Larry was the son everyone called "the good kid"—a fine student, a class officer, banking money from a good job parking cars at a posh restaurant, never any trouble, forever being held up by their father as an example for Mark. Yet in many ways it was the older brother who envied the younger. "Mark had the looks and got all the girls," Karen explained. "They called by the dozens," Larry said.

Mark "couldn't understand why girls liked him so much," his mother recalled, "but I understood. He wasn't 'like a guy.' He showed his emotions, hugged and smooched and cried if he felt like it. There's two types of men that get most of the girls. One is the type like Michael that hates women and sees them as objects, and the other is the type like Mark that loves women and sees them as the most precious things on earth." Larry had ceased public displays of affection after his thirteenth birthday, Karen recalled, but Mark continued to sit his mother down on his knee and sing to her, even when friends were around. "Mark was very protective of me," Karen said. "I remember earlier in the year, we were driving home from a meeting, and these bad-looking guys stopped next to us at a light and started in with 'Hey baby this and hey baby that.' Mark jumped out of the car and told them, 'You don't talk to my mother that way.' I had to pull him back inside. I told him, 'You could have gotten us killed.' "

An indifferent student who received Cs and Ds even in the classes he liked, Mark struck some as a boy who had given up in advance on adulthood and thus was liberated to revel in the power of his youth. Sensitive and witty, a natural mimic, "he could charm anyone at any time," his mother said. "People were drawn to him."

While Larry found comfort in the mainstream, though, Mark was drawn to sharp edges and dark corners. When the older brother was decorating his bedroom with Springsteen posters, the younger was collecting the LPs of a band called the Germs, whose lead singer, Darby Crash, cut himself onstage with shards of glass and spawned a cult of kids who marked themselves on the left wrist with cigarette burns; he told an interviewer, "Blue circles and hard drugs are everything—one day you'll pray to me," a few months before his suicide by heroin overdose at age twenty-two.

Larry wanted to go to college on the beach in Santa Barbara and maybe be a plastic surgeon; he had heard it paid well. Mark had no idea what he wanted to do with his life and said money didn't matter. After Karen moved over the hill into Hollywood during the fall of 1984, Mark would come home from school and hike up the hill to the Cahuenga West Motel, a fading establishment filled with war vets and old men on welfare. "Mark liked to hear their stories," Karen recalled. "He'd spend his allowance on them, buy 'em cigarettes, invite 'em home for dinner."

Out on the street with his friends from FFF, though, Mark projected a ferocity that made him one of the most feared fifteen-year-olds in the Valley. Witnesses would identify him as the point man for a pack of FFFers who had pulled a group of mods off their mopeds and beaten them senseless on the sidewalk outside the Sherman Oaks Galleria one night in November of 1984 and as the leader of an assault team that had jumped a carload of heavy-metallers outside an ice-cream shop on Ventura Boulevard six months later. A seventeen-year-old longhair named Omar Davis testified that Mark had laid his scalp open to the bone with a steel chain while other FFFers stabbed him in the back with Buck knives.

"He was a chameleon. They're all chameleons," said Project Heavy's Ventre, who knew Mark by his FFF nickname, Stocko. "The kid was living two or three lives simultaneously."

The image Mark wanted his family to see slipped badly in February of 1985, when he was expelled from Montclair Prep for failing grades. His father punished him by taking away Mark's letterman's jacket and made an appointment with a psychiatrist—"a guy I know who was going to prepare a phony report about how Mark was getting treatment, had a lot of family problems, and should be let back in school," Michael explained. Mark said that he didn't want to return to Montclair and announced that from now on he wouldn't be spending any more time at his father's house, preferring instead to live full time with his mother. "She finally turned him against me," Michael complained bitterly.

Reluctantly, Michael agreed to send Mark to a therapist, handpicking family counselor Marshall Barnes because "he was a P.E. teacher with two boys of his own, not just book-learned."

Their boy's problem was his parents, Barnes told the Millers. It amazed him, the therapist said, that Mark could remember verbatim the harsh words that his mother and father had exchanged ten years earlier. Karen Miller seemed "more open to suggestion and change," Barnes thought, but Michael "was still very much involved in blame and anger, which made the process difficult." While in therapy, Mark upset his father by insisting that he wanted to stop playing sports. Mark didn't mean it, Michael said, but Barnes wasn't so sure: "You see that with these kids," he said. "They've been in organized sports for seven or eight years by the time they reach fifteen. They burn out."

In July, Mark disappeared for a week after a fight with his mother. It had to do with his first really serious girlfriend, a sixteen-year-old blond dancer named Honey Payton. "Michael had been trying to break up Mark and Honey for a long time," Karen said, "calling him pussy whipped and asking him why he spent all his time at her house. And [another girl] had been after Mark for a long time, and she got these guys who were friends of hers to call Mark and tell him what a slut Honey was, how she screwed three black guys on the steps at her school.

"I was furious at Mark for believing it, but he kept going on and on . . . so finally I threw a thong at him and said, 'Yeah, just like me fucking the gasman.' He immediately got quiet, never said another word. Then the next day he didn't come home."

They met a week later at Marshall Barnes's office. It was the first time in his life that his mother had sided with someone else against him, Mark said. He came home with Karen that afternoon but said he was going with a new girl, Natalie Molnar, now, and Honey was a thing of the past.

"You can't choose your son's friends," Karen said, "and you certainly can't choose his girlfriends."

Mark spent the summer adrift. He was scheduled to start classes as a sophomore at North Hollywood High, but he said he didn't know for sure what he would do. Karen took him to an AA meeting, where he became emotional during the first "sharing" of the evening and ran across the room to give the speaker a hug. Driving home one night, the two of them subsided into silence as the Mr. Mister song "Broken Wings" came on the radio.

> Baby I don't understand
> Why we can't just hold on
> To each other's hands

Karen began to cry. "That's us," Mark told her.

Michael saw Mark for the last time late in July. The two had spent very little time together since February. Michael rented a house at the beach shortly after Karen's move to Hollywood, and he attempted to persuade Mark to spend a month with him by putting a down payment on a surfboard. Mark, though, continued to avoid his father. Michael dropped by the campus where his son was attending summer school that afternoon in July, he recalled, to take Mark to the doctor to have a wart removed from his hand.

"He said he had to go to the house of a friend who was having some problems and needed him," Michael remembered. "I said, 'Mark, we have business to take care of. You know you have an appointment to have your wart removed.' He says, 'You get your wart removed,' slams the door and walks away. It was the last thing he ever said to me."

Nineteen eighty-five was the year youth on the loose made headlines in Los Angeles. All the big stories came out of the San Fernando Valley—three-quarters Caucasian, mostly middle class, an immense arid plain irrigated with water stolen from orange groves to the north, a place where a peculiar, essential, sun-kissed and smoggy, escapist and gridlocked version of the American dream had taken root.

> I'm gonna settle down and never more roam,
> And make the San Fernando Valley my home.

went the chorus of the song "San Fernando Valley," which rose to Number Two on the charts back in 1944, when Bing Crosby recorded it. Bing's partner Bob Hope made millions when he invested in land that would later become Ventura

Boulevard, the Valley's main street. On the adjoining acreage, houses were built by the hundreds after World War II—block after block of stucco bungalows, redwood ranch houses and sod lawns with sprinklers—subdivided into communities that sprawled into one another with boundaries that defined nothing more than the price of real estate.

The backyard barbecue, the single-family swimming pool, the supermarket were all born in the Valley, where carbon monoxide and summer heat collect under a sky stripped of ozone, and a population the size of Philadelphia's lives out a determined, if deluded, postindustrial fantasy of Middle America just minutes from the pervasive menace of Tinsel Town, constantly distracted by the glamour and decay that beckon from the other side of the hills.

Where else but the Valley would second graders be able to show first graders the homes of Michael Jackson and Pat Benatar during the bus ride to school? In the small and seedy city of Burbank, visitors tour the studios of NBC, Warner Brothers, and Disney—an entertainment industry larger than the economies of most *nations* on earth. Every other waitress is an actress-model, and ninety percent of our domestic pornography is produced here.

Even in a land that lives from trend to trend, however, the fundamental things still apply, and when "experts" from law enforcement and the social sciences were asked to comment on the Disturbing Developments among teenagers in the San Fernando Valley during the summer of 1985, virtually every one of them eventually arrived at the same bottom line: the Breakdown of the Nuclear Family. Divorce, single-parent households, absentee fathers, and working mothers—all categories in which Los Angeles ranks either first or second among major metropolitan areas—have increasingly left children to their own devices. What they have found, apparently, is one another.

Rat packing is the generic term authorities have applied to the phenomenon of teenagers banding together as an adolescent alternative to failed families, pointless public education, and No Future—a central punk concept. Rat packing means different things to different people. While the police trace the origins of rat packing to punk gangs like FFF, psychologists and social workers ascribe it to more domestic sources. The rat packs, they say, evolved from several separate small cores of kids who were skipping school together and found havens in homes where the adults were away at work during the day. Rotating from house to house, the rat packers learned to hide indoors until after school hours, then hit the streets before their parents came home from work. The police have reported runaway rat packers creating housing projects out of stolen Dempsey dumpsters or converting Goodwill depositories into one-bedroom apartments.

During the spring of 1985, several groups, including the West Valley members of FFF, discovered the vacated premises of the World of Women health spa on Ventura Boulevard and transformed the place into a Plato's Retreat for street kids, splattering the walls with raunchy graffiti and phallic imagery, filling the empty swimming pool with a detritus of wine and beer bottles, used condoms, discarded brassieres, and ragged skin magazines. GATES OF HELL was painted above the entrance to a stairway leading to a second-story office where those who dared rolled on the floor amid scraps of carpet, soiled panties, Vaseline jars, and vivid descriptions of acts that were widely regarded as unnatural back when Bob Hope owned the property.

"Kids who have been on the streets longer begin to take on a paraparental identity," explained Robert Bua, director of a Valley youth-counseling service called Bridge. "They keep their eye out for the dissatisfied thirteen-year-olds. . . . They are not followers; the rat packers are strong kids, leaders."

Larger rat packs, many modeling themselves on FFF, evolved into quasi gangs with names like Platte Rats, Burbank Punx Organization, Death Party, and Social Outcasts. Most outrageous was the conclave of upper-middle-class skinheads who called themselves the Mickey Mouse Club. Drawn from the relatively affluent West Valley community of Woodlands Hills, the Mickey Mousers lived out a *Clockwork Orange* orgy of crime and violence amid a landscape of hot tubs and franchise signs. Many Mickey Mousers had left home but continued to carry membership cards to the Mid Valley Racket Club, according to the police, where they kept lockers and used the showers. "What is your initiation process if someone should desire to be in your gang?" asked a reporter for the Taft High School *Tribune* of one Mickey Mouse Club member. "Be cool, hang out, and don't say shit" was his answer, but the police maintained that applicants gained admission by setting up their own parents' homes for burglaries, providing alarm codes, security schedules, and spare keys. "These are very sophisticated kids who like to use only the best equipment," said the LAPD's Bishop, a former school-patrol officer. "They don't break windows; they take a compressed-air gun and shoot the locks out."

While some police officers continued to use the designation *juvenile delinquent* to describe the rat packers, many public officials had discarded it in favor of the more discouraging word *incorrigible*. Perhaps it had to do with the national difficulty in separating social malaise from criminal behavior. Then again, it might have been a matter of sheer numbers. In March of 1985, *U.S. News & World Report* published a story datelined Canoga Park, California, in which the magazine estimated that in the Valley "as many as 30,000 troubled youths from middle- and upper-middle-class families" were "wasting their formative years" at some place other than home or school. "A shadow culture," Robert Bua called the rat packers. Los Angeles school officials reported that their Operation Stay in School Centers were processing 2000 truants a month.

More and more parents were adopting the attitude that extreme times called for extreme measures. By the spring of 1985, the single largest chapter of the national parents' organization Toughlove was meeting twice a week at Taft High School, calling themselves "Because I Love You": The Parent Support Group and adorning their automobiles with bumper stickers bearing the insignia of a heart held in a clenched fist.

Director Dennis Poncher apprised members of such tactics as removing a teenager's bedroom door to deny him or her any place of privacy, carrying telephones to and from work to prevent their unauthorized use by children, insisting upon a regular weekly urinalysis for problem kids, and refusing to allow runaways to return home without a signed contract. During an orientation speech for new enrollees, Poncher described with relish the evening he marched into his daughter Lesli's bedroom armed with a pair of scissors and shredded her wardrobe. "What you want is a household of cooperation, not togetherness," Poncher advised the adults sitting at school desks before him. "If you want to see *The Brady Bunch*, turn on the TV."

Toughlove's philosophy—"Your kid's problem is your kid's problem," as Poncher put it—found support among the leaders of such influential institutions as the San Fernando Valley Child Guidance Clinic. "These are simply kids who have a 'warped personality,' " asserted clinic director Stephan Fleisher. "Call it a conduct disorder or a character disorder. 'Bad kids' would be the more common parlance."

Rather than placing such children in the context of a cultural process, Fleisher suspected the root of the problem might be "genetics": "Research indicates that some kids are born with a lower level of anxiety than most of us. Whereas we play it straight because we fear the consequences, the conduct-disordered kid doesn't have that fear to inhibit his behavior."

At Dr. Fleisher's clinic, the staff's goal was "to create a conscience in a kid" by proceeding on a premise that would have horrified psychiatry's pioneers. "We increase shame and guilt," he explained.

Inevitably, the popularity of the new Get Tough attitude made it good government. In June of 1985, the police revived a long-dormant curfew law and used it to arrest minors for "loitering" after 10 P.M. in Westwood Village. A month later the city council passed a schedule of restrictions on L.A.'s three teen nightclubs, all located in the San Fernando Valley.

Toughlove members found their archvillain in the thirty-four-year-old manager of a Canoga Park club called Phases, Kevin Parr. A former fireman, scoutmaster, and Jaycee, he had spent seven years as a homosexual hustler on Santa Monica Boulevard and starred in a series of gay porno films. Blond and brown-eyed, an opportunistic idealist with a year-round tan and an earnest expression, Parr then transformed a windowless warehouse on Topanga Canyon Boulevard into a sanctuary for alienated youth, becoming a hero to the kids through such acts as his public firing of a security guard who laughed when a 250-pound girl with a Mohawk got up to dance on the club's center stage.

The teenagers who disturbed the Toughlove parents the most were the ones Phases's manager most admired. The Death Rockers, dressed all in black and notorious for partying in cemeteries, were "the most idealistic kids of all," Parr said. "They're all very concerned about the environment, nuclear war, human rights. They're like the hippies, only they feel more despair. Whereas the trendies, the ones who are into Duran Duran and Madonna—all they want is the latest designer labels. The Death Rockers wear thrift-store clothes, but they were the ones who sent in the largest donations to Live Aid. They're the kids who *care*. Yet they're the bad kids, and the trendies, the ones who are too cool to let anything matter, are the good kids. It's all twisted around."

The police raided Phases several times during the spring and threatened to suspend its license. The attention kids were suddenly receiving from the police, the politicians and the press produced the public impression of a situation that was out of control and hurtling toward a frightening climax. In March, the LAPD accused the FFF of shooting from cars at members of the Burbank Punx Organization. Later that month, at the Valley's Pickwick Drive-In, eighty BPO and FFF members rioted during a two-for-one screening. They "started coming in over the fences and through the exit gates . . . like little rats coming off a ship," the theater's manager told the *Daily News*.

In May, FBI agents arrested two sixteen-year-old boys who had met as classmates at a private school in Encino for a series of bank robberies that the pair committed while wearing police uniforms with clown masks and brandishing a .38 revolver. The police alleged the two were Mickey Mouse Club members.

On July 1st, the *Daily News* lead editorial was headlined RAT-PACKING REBELS: "These gangs should be viewed with the same alarm as their ghetto cohorts," the paper advised. "Members may drive BMWs, but they commit drive-by shootings all the same."

In a front-page story, the paper quoted an LAPD sergeant on the North Hollywood gang detail: "One day, some little rich kid will get killed, and the whole community will be up in arms."

Coast and Lowlands

The aspect of natural objects up and down the Pacific
Coast is as "aristocratic" as the comprehensive American
condition permits anything to be: it indeed appears to the
ingenious observer to represent an instinct on the part of
Nature, a sort of shuddering, bristling need, to brace herself in advance against the assault of a society so much less
marked with distinction than herself.   HENRY JAMES

Mary Austin

The Land

Pure desertness clings along the pits of the long valleys and the formless beds of vanished lakes. Every hill that lifts as high as the cloud line has some trees upon it, and deer and bighorn to feed on the tall, tufted, bunch grass between the boulders. In the year when Tonopah, turning upon itself like a swarm, trickled prospectors all over that country from Hot Creek to the Armagosa, Indians brought me word that the men had camped so close about the water holes that the bighorn died of thirst on the headlands, turned always in the last agony toward the man-infested springs.

That is as good a pointer as any if you go waterless in the country of Lost Borders: where you find cattle dropped, skeleton or skin dried, the heads almost invariably will be turned toward the places where water holes should be. But no such reminders will fend men from its trails. This is chiefly, I am persuaded, because there is something incomprehensible to the man-mind in the concurrence of death and beauty. Shall the tender opal mist betray you? the airy depth of mountain blueness, the blazonry of painted wind-scoured buttes, the far peaks molten with the alpenglow, cooled by the rising of the velvet violet twilight tide, and the leagues and leagues of stars? As easy for a man to believe that a beautiful woman can be cruel. Mind you, it is mostly men who go into the desert, who love it past all reasonableness, slack their ambitions, cast off old usages, neglect their families because of the pulse and beat of a life laid bare to its thews and sinews. Their women hate with implicitness the life like the land, stretching interminably whitey-brown, dim and shadowy blue hills that hem it, glimmering pale waters of mirage that creep and crawl about its edges. There was a woman once at Agua Hedionda—but you wouldn't believe that either.

If the desert were a woman, I know well what she would be like: deep-breasted, broad in the hips, tawny, with tawny hair, great masses of it lying smooth along her perfect curves, full lipped like a sphinx, but not heavy-lidded like one, eyes sane and steady as the polished jewel of her skies, such a countenance as should make men serve without desiring her, such a largeness to her mind as should make their sins of no account, passionate, but not necessitous, patient—and you could not move her, no, not if you had all the earth to give, so much as one tawny hair's-breadth beyond her own desires. If you cut very deeply into any soul that has the mark of the land upon it, you find such qualities as these.

California

All of a sudden the road took flight straight across the hills; it was wild and deserted, and there was a magnificent view of the sea. From time to time there were inns, all of them picturesque, built, in the western manner, like log cabins. Sometimes for signs they used old covered wagons with their green tarpaulin bonnets, but more often they had one or two wagon wheels leaning against the wall. Outside one of these places a live elephant sauntered around in a cage, and, close by, a lion, which drew the attention of the passing tourists. The inn at which we stopped would have promised an excellent meal had this been France; there were wooden benches, a huge chimney, small-paned windows, a beamed ceiling; but we were given drugstore food.

We left the highway and went down into a valley, descending by a narrow, twisting road. In a shady spot near a river, there was a camping site which had tables, benches, dutch ovens and even swings and trapezes; one had only to pitch a tent. People came in cars, of course, as it was too far away from everything to walk or bicycle. People voluntarily live in those trailers which I saw parked along all of the highways leading into Los Angeles. They are real caravans furnished with every comfort, but they may only park in areas reserved for them; the side roads, like the one we were following, are closed to them. The valley we were descending looked just like the country one might expect to find in California; it was enclosed by mountains on three sides, and on the fourth it spread out in a wide expanse and then dropped to the sea, which could be seen in the distance. The entire bowl-like area was planted with orange trees in rows as regular as the orchards one sees in old tapestries: what I had not expected, however, were the long rows of small brown stoves, or smudge pots, for the valley was fairly high, and there was danger of freezing on winter nights; these prevented the harvest from being entirely lost. Like Minutemen of the Revolutionary War, men are specially picked for the job of rushing to the scene, leaving their work as soon as the alarm is sounded, to light and tend the tiny, protective fires.

The little car went forward, jolting its way across bumpy fields; it plowed through the soil, it got stuck, climbed up hills covered with rock and scrub—hills where N. loves to ride. We took the road to Ojai once again. On its lovely site Ojai was as depressing as any village in the Middle West: it was a sad, white street lined with banks and shops and cut at right angles by more white streets.

We shopped for dinner. It was the first time I had entered a market. One might say it was an agricultural show: the smooth and shining fruit, the vegetables in full bloom, all had the false lustre and magnificence of hybrid produce: they were not marred by the hazards of sun and rain. . . .

We left at seven o'clock, for San Francisco was three hundred miles away. The road was built on the mountainside like a cornice, and it fell steeply to the sea, undulating dizzily above the abyss. There was not a house, not a car, not a plant nor domestic animal: man was far away. In our car which protected us and carried us, we felt that we were just as lost as if we had been on foot crossing the plateaus of Southern France or the heaths of Corsica; it was a kind of place dreamed up for a Humphrey Bogart who kills his wife seemingly by accident. We were amazed when, after two hours, we suddenly discovered a log cabin inn, with a porch full of flowers, standing at the edge of a cliff: people did occasionally pass by here. We ate bacon and eggs. The countryside was shimmering with sunlight, but we had to pay for the serene view. The breakfast cost the same price as a dinner. The innkeeper was surprised to see us traveling alone. One does not often see women unaccompanied by men driving along the California highways.

It was eleven o'clock when we finally came to Monterey. It was there that the battle was fought in which Mexico lost Southern California to America. Monterey is an old port and has faithfully preserved its Mexican past. A sign invited us to follow the markers along the highway which would lead us to the chief curiosities of the town. Notices placed before the old worm-eaten wooden houses gave their history. The houses of famous governors and notorious bandits were labeled with equal care. There was a theater about a hundred years old and a *posada* which had been used as an assayor's office where the miners had deposited their precious gold dust. There were many picturesque spots; the walls were orange and apricot under the elms, and there were little brightly colored inns, but they gave the impression of museum pieces, and one felt one-self still in the U.S.A.

Down at the harbor, on the far side of a cluster of typically American houses, we were delighted to find ourselves once more in foreign country. A long wooden pier stretched out over the water between fishing boats painted in tropical colors; pink and silver fish, smooth and scaly, and laid out on blocks of ice, were sold in sheds on either side. Spread out on the ground were huge ab-alone shells, still damp with seaweed and covered with iridescent mother of pearl: these were five cents each. The smell of the market was as fresh as that of the sea, and at the end of the dock there were restaurants built on piles: they were wooden structures, and all had terraces and balconies exposed to the sun. The one we chose was built in Mexican style. It had yellow walls, and the wooden furniture, painted in lively colors, was simply designed; everything was fresh and bright. At night they lit candles in polished candelabra. We lunched on a balcony overlooking the fishing boats. The sun was bright, but a breeze tempered the heat. The cuisine was Italian, and we ate fresh fish and pizza: we ordered a "little" one, not very big, or big, or even medium-sized; they brought us a pie of tomato and anchovies which covered two plates. We were dumbfounded. The giant pizza must have been the size of a cartwheel.

The countryside had somewhat softened. We went through Carmel, one of the most well-known places on this coast: full of gardens, trees and flowers, the town itself is pretty. We did not have time to visit the Spanish Mission, but we crossed the *parc*; the English equivalent of this word, incidentally, does not al-ways have the same meaning in America as in Europe; it often means a site which the government takes under its protection. Sometimes one pays an en-trance fee. However, the park is left in its natural state, and here it was nothing more than part of the coast. After we had paid a dollar, we were allowed to con-tinue driving beside the sea instead of taking the main highway. The rocks and the huge breakers reminded me of Quiberon; it was very beautiful, but we missed the solitude we had found that morning: hundreds of motorists were coming from San Francisco to spend Sunday here. As soon as we had passed Carmel, however, we found ourselves once more in open spaces. We drove through immense pine forests; and, from time to time, at the bottom of a valley, or in a clearing, or coming out of a canyon, we would see in the distance a de-serted tavern, or a ranch, or else a camp or lodge. One would have liked to stop for several days in these out-of-the-way places, where in former times the monks had built their retreats. Often when the map indicated a village, we would find only a handful of houses half hidden by trees and separated by great silent space. I was on the lookout for Big Sur, where Henry Miller lived, but saw nothing more than a log cabin inn beside a filling station. The whole of this splendid coast had scarcely been touched by the hand of man.

In the Beginning

In other, olden times there were only phantoms. In the beginning, that is. If there ever was a beginning.

It was always a wild, rocky coast, desolate and forbidding to the man of the pavements, eloquent and enchanting to the Taliessins. The homesteader never failed to unearth fresh sorrows.

There were always birds: the pirates and scavengers of the blue as well as the migratory variety. (At intervals the condor passed, huge as an ocean liner.) Gay in plumage, their beaks were hard and cruel. They strung out across the horizon like arrows tied to an invisible string. In close they seemed content to dart, dip, swoop, careen. Some followed the cliffs and breakers, others sought the canyons, the gold-crested hills, the marble-topped peaks.

There were also the creeping, crawling creatures, some sluggish as the sloth, others full of venom, but all absurdly handsome. Men feared them more than the invisible ones who chattered like monkeys at fall of night.

To advance, whether on foot or on horseback, was to tangle with spikes, thorns, creepers, with all that pricks, clings, stabs, and poisons.

Who lived here first? Troglodytes perhaps. The Indian came late. Very late.

Though young, geologically speaking, the land has a hoary look. From the ocean depths there issued strange formations, contours unique and seductive.

As if the Titans of the deep had labored for eons to shape and mold the earth. Even millennia ago the great land birds were startled by the abrupt aspect of these risen shapes.

There are no ruins or relics to speak of. No history worth recounting. What was not speaks more eloquently than what was.

Here the redwood made its last stand.

At dawn its majesty is almost painful to behold. That same prehistoric look.

Topographical

It was twelve years ago on a day in February that I arrived in Big Sur—in the midst of a violent downpour. Toward dusk that same day, after a rejuvenating bath outdoors at the hot sulphur springs (Slade's Springs), I had dinner with the Rosses in the quaint old cottage they then occupied at Livermore Edge. It was the beginning of something more than a friendship. It would be more just, perhaps, to call it an initiation into a new way of life.

It was a few weeks after this meeting that I read Lillian Bos Ross's book, *The Stranger*. Till then I had been only a visitor. The reading of this "little classic," as it is called, made me more than ever determined to take root here. "For the first time in my life," to quote Zande Allen's words, "I felt to home in the world I was borned in."

Years ago our great American poet Robinson Jeffers began singing of this region in his narrative poems. Jack London and his friend George Stirling made frequent visits to Big Sur in the old days; they came on horseback, all the way from the Valley of the Moon. The general public, however, knew almost nothing of this region until 1937 when the Carmel-San Simeon highway, which skirts the Pacific for a distance of sixty miles or more, was opened up. In fact, until then it was probably one of the least known regions in all America.

The first settlers, mountain men mostly, of hardy pioneer stock, came around 1870. They were, as Lillian Ross puts it, men who had followed the buffalo trails and knew how to live on meat without salt. They came afoot and on horseback; they touched ground which no white men had ever set foot on before, not even the intrepid Spaniards.

So far as is known, the only human beings who had been here before were the Esselen Indians, a tribe of low culture which had subsisted in nomadic fashion. They spoke a language having no connection with that of other tribes in California or elsewhere in America. When the *padres* came to Monterey, around 1770, these Indians spoke of an ancient city called Excelen which was theirs but of which no vestiges have ever been found.

But perhaps I should first explain where the Big Sur region is located. It begins not far north of the Little Sur River (Malpaso Creek) and extends southward as far as Lucia, which, like Big Sur, is just a pin point on the map. Eastward from the coast it stretches to the Salinas Valley. Roughly, the Big Sur country comprises an area two to three times the size of Andorra.

Now and then a visitor will remark that there is a resemblance between this coast, the South Coast, and certain sections of the Mediterranean littoral; others liken it to the coast of Scotland. But comparisons are vain. Big Sur has a climate of its own and a character all its own. It is a region where extremes meet, a region where one is always conscious of weather, of space, of grandeur, and of eloquent silence. Among other things, it is the meeting place of migratory birds coming from north and south. It is said, in fact, that there is a greater variety of birds to be found in this region than in any other part of the United States. It is also the home of the redwoods; one encounters them on entering from the north and one leaves them on passing southward. At night one can still hear the coyote howling, and if one ventures beyond the first ridge of mountains one can meet up with mountain lions and other beasts of the wild. The grizzly bear is no longer to be found here, but the rattlesnake is still to be reckoned with. On a clear, bright day, when the blue of the sea rivals the blue of the sky, one sees the hawk, the eagle, the buzzard soaring above the still, hushed canyons. In summer, when the fogs roll in, one can look down upon a sea of clouds floating listlessly above the ocean; they have the appearance, at times, of huge iridescent soap bubbles, over which, now and then, may be seen a double rainbow. In January and February the hills are greenest, almost as green as the Emerald Isle. From November to February are the best months, the air fresh and invigorating, the skies clear, the sun still warm enough to take a sun bath.

From our perch, which is about a thousand feet above the sea, one can look up and down the coast a distance of twenty miles in either direction. The highway zigzags like the Grande Corniche. Unlike the Riviera, however, here there are but few houses to be seen. The old-timers, those with huge landholdings, are not eager to see the country opened up. They are all for preserving its virginal aspect. How long will it hold out against the invader? That is the big question.

The stretch of scenic highway referred to earlier was cut through at enormous expense, literally blasted out of the mountainside. It now forms part of the great international highway which will one day extend from the northern part of Alaska to Tierra del Fuego. By the time it is finished the automobile, like the mastodon, may be extinct. But the Big Sur will be here forever, and perhaps in the year A.D. 2000 the population may still number only a few hundred souls. Perhaps, like Andorra and Monaco, it will become a Republic all its own. Perhaps the dread invaders will not come from other parts of this continent but from across the ocean, as the American aborigines are said to have come. And if they do, it will not be in boats or in airplanes.

And who can say when this region will once again be covered by the waters of the deep? Geologically speaking, it is not so long ago that it rose from the sea. Its mountain slopes are almost as treacherous as the icy sea in which, by the way, one scarcely ever sees a sail boat or a hardy swimmer, though one does occasionally spot a seal, an otter, or a sperm whale. The sea, which looks so near and so tempting, is often difficult to reach. We know that the conquistadores were unable to make their way along the coast, neither could they cut through the brush which covers the mountain slopes. An inviting land, but hard to conquer. It seeks to remain unspoiled, uninhabited by man.

Often, when following the trail which meanders over the hills, I pull myself up in an effort to encompass the glory and the grandeur which envelops the whole horizon. Often, when the clouds pile up in the north and the sea is churned with white caps, I say to myself: "This is the California that men dreamed of years ago, this is the Pacific that Balboa looked out on from the Peak of Darien, this is the face of the earth as the Creator intended it to look."

Jack Kerouac

Big Sur

And in the morning (after sleeping by the creek in the white sand) I do see what was so scary about my canyon road walk—The road's up there on the wall a thousand feet with a sheer drop sometimes, especially at the cattle crossing, way up highest, where a break in the bluff shows fog pouring through from another bend of the sea beyond, scary enough in itself anyway as tho one hole wasnt enough to open into the sea—And worst of all is the bridge! I go ambling seaward along the path by the creek and see this awful thin white line of bridge a thousand unbridgeable sighs of height above the little woods I'm walking in, you just cant believe it, and to make things heart-thumpingly horrible you come to a little bend in what is now just a trail and there's the booming surf coming at you whitecapped crashing down on sand as tho it was higher than where you stand, like a sudden tidal wave world enough to make you step back or run back to the hills—And not only that, the blue sea behind the crashing high waves is full of huge black rocks rising like old ogresome castles dripping wet slime, a billion years of woe right there, the moogrus big clunk of it right there with its slaverous lips of foam at the base—So that you emerge from pleasant little wood paths with a stem of grass in your teeth and drop it to see doom—And you look up at that unbelievably high bridge and feel death and for a good reason: because underneath the bridge, in the sand right beside the sea cliff, *hump*, your heart sinks to see it: the automobile that crashed thru the bridge rail a decade ago and fell 1000 feet straight down and landed upside-down, is still there now, an upsidedown chassis of rust in a strewn skitter of sea-eaten tires, old spokes, old car seats sprung with straw, one sad fuel pump and no more people—

Big elbows of Rock rising everywhere, sea caves within them, seas plollocking all around inside them crashing out foams, the boom and pound on the sand, the sand dipping quick (no Malibu Beach here)—Yet you turn and see the pleasant woods winding upcreek like a picture in Vermont—But you look up into the sky, bend way back, my God you're standing directly under that aerial bridge with its thin white line running from rock to rock and witless cars racing across it like dreams! From rock to rock! All the way down the raging coast! So that when later I heard people say "Oh Big Sur must be beautiful!" I gulp to wonder why it has the reputation of being beautiful above and beyond its *fearfulness*, its Blakean groaning roughrock Creation throes, those vistas when you drive the coast highway on a sunny day opening up the eye for miles of horrible washing sawing.

Robinson Jeffers

November Surf

Some lucky day each November great waves awake and are drawn
Like smoking mountains bright from the west
And come and cover the cliff with white violent cleanness: then suddenly
The old granite forgets half a year's filth:
The orange-peel, eggshells, papers, pieces of clothing, the clots
Of dung in corners of the rock, and used
Sheaths that make light love safe in the evenings: all the droppings of the
      summer
Idlers washed off in a winter ecstasy:
I think this cumbered continent envies its cliff then. . . . But all seasons
The earth, in her childlike prophetic sleep,
Keeps dreaming of the bath of a storm that prepares up the long coast
Of the future to scour more than her sea-lines:
The cities gone down, the people fewer and the hawks more numerous,
The rivers mouth to source pure; when the two-footed
Mammal, being someways one of the nobler animals, regains
The dignity of room, the value of rareness.

Ideal Cosy Nook

There is a science-fiction story in which a number of very rich people wake up one morning in their luxury villas in the mountains to find that they are encircled by a transparent and insuperable obstacle, a wall of glass that has appeared in the night. From the depths of their vitrified luxury, they can still just discern the outside world, the real universe from which they are cut off, which has suddenly become the ideal world. But it is too late. These rich people will die slowly in their aquarium like goldfish. Some of the university campuses here remind me of this.

Lost among the pine trees, the fields, and the rivers (it is an old ranch that was donated to the university), and made up of little blocks, each one out of sight of the others, like the people who live in them: this one is Santa Cruz. It's a bit like the Bermuda Triangle (or Santa Barbara). Everything vanishes. Everything gets sucked in. Total decentering, total community. After the ideal city of the future, the ideal cosy nook. Nothing converges on a single point, neither the traffic, nor the architecture, nor authority. But, by that very token, it also becomes impossible to hold a demonstration: where could you assemble? Demonstrations can only go round and round in the forest, where the participants alone can see them. Of all the Californian campuses, famous for their spaciousness and charm, this is the most idealized, the most naturalized. It is the epitome of all that is beautiful. Famous architects designed the buildings and the bays of Carmel and Monterey stretch out all around. If the conviviality of the future already exists somewhere, then this must be the place. And yet this freedom, protected both by the pleasantness of the vegetation and by academic openness, becomes its own prisoner once again, immured in a natural and social overprotectedness which ends up producing all the agonies of the carceral universe (precisely by virtue of its walls, the carceral system may in certain conditions evolve in the direction of utopia more rapidly than open social systems). Society has become emancipated here as nowhere else on earth. The psychiatric hospitals have been opened up, public transport is free, and yet paradoxically this ideal has become closed in on itself as if behind a wall of glass.

A paradisiac and inward-looking illusion. We might understand what Lyotard calls the "Pacific Wall" as the wall of crystal that imprisons California in its own beatitude. But whereas the demand for happiness used to be something oceanic and emancipatory, here it comes wrapped up in a fetal tranquillity. Are there still passions, murders, and acts of violence in this strange, padded, wooded, pacified, convivial republic? Yes, but the violence is autistic and reactional. There are no crimes of passion, but there are rapes, and a case where a dozen women were murdered in two years before the killer was discovered. This is fetal violence, as gratuitous as "automatic writing." It seems an expression not so much of real aggression as of nostalgia for the old prohibitions (why does the number of rapes increase with the degree of sexual liberation?).

How sentimental these mixed dormitories seem, opening out here on to the forest, as if nature itself could be convivial and maternal, could herself stand as guarantor for the blossoming of sexuality and the ecology of manners, as if nature could look sympathetically upon any human society, as if one could have some relationship with her, outside the cruel universe of magic, which was not *stoical*, not the Stoics' relation between a blind, pitiless necessity and the even greater defiance, the even greater freedom one has to counterpose to it. Here, every last vestige of a heroic sense of destiny has disappeared. The whole place exudes an air of sentimental reconciliation with nature, with sex, with madness, and even with history (by way of a carefully corrected, revised Marxism).

Like many other aspects of contemporary America, Santa Cruz is part of *the post-orgy world*, the world left behind after the great social and sexual convulsions. The refugees from the orgy—the orgy of sex, political violence, the Vietnam War, the Woodstock Crusade, and the ethnic and anticapitalist struggles too, together with the passion for money, the passion for success, hard technologies etc., in short, the whole orgy of modernity—are all there, jogging along in their tribalism, which is akin to the electronic tribalism of Silicon Valley. Reduced pace of work, decentralization, air conditioning, soft technologies. Paradise. But a very slight modification, a change of just a few degrees, would suffice to make it seem like hell.

Linda Niemann

Boomer

I had been hanging around for a few years with a very party-time crowd, and my life was on a downward slide. I had gotten a Ph.D. and a divorce simultaneously. The fancy academic job never materialized, and I hung around Santa Cruz, getting to know my neighbors. Soon I was playing flute in a street band, eating donated sandwiches, and spending every night in clubs dancing the night away. My living room was full of strippers, poets, musicians, and drug dealers. Gradually there was less music and more drugs, and in a few years I was living in the mountains in a shack, my dogs had heartworm, my Chevy was a wreck, and while I thought of myself as a musician, the money, such as it was, came from dealing, and none of my friends worked.

When I saw the ad in the Sunday paper—BRAKEMEN WANTED—I thought of it as a chance to clean up my act and to get away. In a strategy of extreme imitation, I felt that by doing work this dangerous, I would have to make a decision to live, to protect myself. I would have to choose to stay alive every day, to hang on to the sides of those freight cars for dear life. The railroad transformed the metaphor of my life. Nine thousand tons moving at sixty miles an hour into the fearful night. I now would ride that image, trying to stay alive within it. I know that later, when I sat behind the moving train in the darkness of the caboose, window open and the unknown fragrances of the land filling the space, the blackness of the night was my friend. It felt good to be powerless and carried along by the destiny of that motion. I felt happy and at peace. I was where I belonged.

The railroad didn't believe in lengthy formal training. They offered a two-week class which covered the book of rules, a three-hundred-page document with a dual purpose—to keep trains from running into one another and to prevent any situation in which the company might get sued. Rules of the road which you had to learn were mixed in with rules which you had to ignore in order to get the work done. But you had to know that you were ignoring a rule so that in the winter, when company officials had time to sneak around testing, you could work by the book.

The rulebook was also in a continuous state of revision. Revisions appeared in the timetable which you carried with you at all times. Further revisions appeared in regular timetable bulletins which were posted at work. Soon your rulebook resembled a scrapbook, with paragraphs crossed out, pages pasted in, and notes on changes which were then crossed out and changed weeks later. It drove you crazy. You always had to be on the lookout for a company official hiding in the bushes while you did your work. This individual would pop out and ask you questions about the latest rule revisions. A notation of failure would then appear in your personal file. These notations were referred to as "Brownies," named after the official who devised the railroad demerit system. As trainmen were fond of pointing out, however, there was no merit system to go with it.

Out of seventeen student brakemen three of us were women. This was a large percentage, comparatively. The first women had been hired two years before, and they were around to give us advice. The point was to get through the class, ignore the sexist remarks and the scare tactics, and get over the probationary period known as the "derail." Then you were in the union and a railroader for life. Getting over the derail took sixty days, and if either the crews you worked with or the company officers had a complaint, you were out. At the end of two weeks of classroom instruction, you bought a railroad watch, they gave you switch keys and a two-dollar lantern, and you marked up as extra board brakemen. It was going to be sink or swim in this business. We drew numbers to determine our seniority dates—the most important factor in our careers. One or two numbers could mean that you worked or didn't.

On the last day of class, they took us down to the freightyard to grapple with the equipment. We practiced getting on and off moving cars, climbing the ladders and cranking down the handbrakes, lacing up the airhoses and cutting in the air, changing the eighty-five-pound knuckles that joined the cars together, and hand and lantern signals. These signals were the way members of the crew talked to each other, and they were an art form. An old head could practically order an anchovy pizza from a half mile away. You would see lights, arcs and circles, stabs of light. It would repeat. You would stand there confused. Finally you would walk down the track and find the foreman in a deep state of disgust.

"I told you to hang three cars, let two go to the runaround, one to the main, go through the crossovers, and line behind. Now can't you read a signal, dummy?"

The day after our practice session, I got into my car and tried to roll the window down. My arms didn't work. This was my first moment of doubt about being able to do the job. It was hard to get the upper-body strength required to hang on and ride for long distances on the side of cars. Terror at falling beneath the wheels was a big motivator, however. Terror and ridicule. There was a lot of both during the probationary period and the student trips. On student trips we tagged along with a regular crew and tried to learn something. To me, what we were doing made no sense whatsoever. Just getting used to the equipment had me so disoriented that I had no idea where we had gone or how the crew did anything. One of the crew suggested to me that I go to a toy store and look at the model trains, to see how switches work. They say, though, that whatever you start out doing railroading, it gets imprinted, and that's what you are most comfortable doing from then on. I couldn't have picked a better place to break in than Watsonville Junction. It was old-time, local-freight, full-crew switching. Kicking cars and passing signs. The basic stuff that you have to learn at first or you never get no matter how long you're out here.

The small switching yard at Watsonville classified all the perishable freight from the Salinas Valley and Hollister-Gilroy—the "salad bowl" of America. A break in the coastal range at Salinas allowed the fog to pour into the valley, cooling it, and allowing cool weather crops like artichokes, brussels sprouts, and lettuce to grow. Strawberry fields and apple orchards skirted the low hillsides. There were cool fresh days in midsummer. The packing houses and canneries were running around the clock, with rows of mostly women working the graveyard assembly lines. Clusters of yellow school buses bordered the fields, and farmworkers moved slowly through the orderly rows, bundled up against the fog and pesticides.

East of Eden

The Salinas Valley is in Northern California. It is a long narrow swale between two ranges of mountains, and the Salinas River winds and twists up the center until it falls at last into Monterey Bay.

I remember my childhood names for grasses and secret flowers. I remember where a toad may live and what time the birds awaken in the summer—and what trees and seasons smelled like—how people looked and walked and smelled even. The memory of odors is very rich.

I remember that the Gabilan Mountains to the east of the valley were light gay mountains full of sun and loveliness and a kind of invitation, so that you wanted to climb into their warm foothills almost as you want to climb into the lap of a beloved mother. They were beckoning mountains with a brown grass love. The Santa Lucias stood up against the sky to the west and kept the valley from the open sea, and they were dark and brooding—unfriendly and dangerous. I always found in myself a dread of west and a love of east. Where I ever got such an idea I cannot say, unless it could be that the morning came over the peaks of the Gabilans and the night drifted back from the ridges of the Santa Lucias. It may be that the birth and death of the day had some part in my feeling about the two ranges of mountains.

From both sides of the valley little streams slipped out of the hill canyons and fell into the bed of the Salinas River. In the winter of wet years the streams ran full-freshet, and they swelled the river until sometimes it raged and boiled, bank full, and then it was a destroyer. The river tore the edges of the farm lands and washed whole acres down; it toppled barns and houses into itself, to go floating and bobbing away. It trapped cows and pigs and sheep and drowned them in its muddy brown water and carried them to the sea. Then when the late spring came, the river drew in from its edges and the sand banks appeared. And in the summer the river didn't run at all above ground. Some pools would be left in the deep swirl places under a high bank. The tules and grasses grew back, and willows straightened up with the flood debris in their upper branches. The Salinas was only a part-time river. The summer sun drove it underground. It was not a fine river at all, but it was the only one we had and so we boasted about it—how dangerous it was in a wet winter and how dry it was in a dry summer. You can boast about anything if it's all you have. Maybe the less you have, the more you are required to boast.

The floor of the Salinas Valley, between the ranges and below the foothills, is level because this valley used to be the bottom of a hundred-mile inlet from the sea. The river mouth at Moss Landing was centuries ago the entrance to this long inland water. Once, fifty miles down the valley, my father bored a well. The drill came up first with topsoil and then with gravel and then with white sea sand full of shells and even pieces of whalebone. There were twenty feet of sand and then black earth again, and even a piece of redwood, that imperishable wood that does not rot. Before the inland sea the valley must have been a forest. And those things had happened right under our feet. And it seemed to me sometimes at night that I could feel both the sea and the redwood forest before it.

On the wide level acres of the valley the topsoil lay deep and fertile. It required only a rich winter of rain to make it break forth in grass and flowers. The spring flowers in a wet year were unbelievable. The whole valley floor, and the foothills too, would be carpeted with lupins and poppies. Once a woman told me that colored flowers would seem more bright if you added a few white flowers to give the colors definition. Every petal of blue lupin is edged with white, so that a field of lupins is more blue than you can imagine. And mixed with these were splashes of California poppies. These too are of a burning color— not orange, not gold, but if pure gold were liquid and could raise a cream, that golden cream might be like the color of the poppies. When their season was over the yellow mustard came up and grew to a great height. When my grandfather came into the valley the mustard was so tall that a man on horseback showed only his head above the yellow flowers. On the uplands the grass would be strewn with buttercups, with hen-and-chickens, with black-centered yellow violets. And a little later in the season there would be red and yellow stands of Indian paintbrush. These were the flowers of the open places exposed to the sun.

Under the live oaks, shaded and dusky, the maidenhair flourished and gave a good smell, and under the mossy banks of the water courses whole clumps of five-fingered ferns and goldy-backs hung down. Then there were harebells, tiny lanterns, cream white and almost sinful looking, and these were so rare and magical that a child, finding one, felt singled out and special all day long.

When June came the grasses headed out and turned brown, and the hills turned a brown which was not brown but a gold and saffron and red—an indescribable color. And from then on until the next rains the earth dried and the streams stopped. Cracks appeared on the level ground. The Salinas River sank under its sand. The wind blew down the valley, picking up dust and straws, and grew stronger and harsher as it went south. It stopped in the evening. It was a rasping nervous wind, and the dust particles cut into a man's skin and burned his eyes. Men working in the fields wore goggles and tied handkerchiefs around their noses to keep the dirt out.

The valley land was deep and rich, but the foothills wore only a skin of topsoil no deeper than the grass roots; and the farther up the hills you went, the thinner grew the soil, with flints sticking through, until at the brush line it was a kind of dry flinty gravel that reflected the hot sun blindingly.

I had spoken of the rich years when the rainfall was plentiful. But there were dry years too, and they put a terror on the valley. The water came in a thirty-year cycle. There would be five or six wet and wonderful years when there might be nineteen to twenty-five inches of rain, and the land would shout with grass. Then would come six or seven pretty good years of twelve to sixteen inches of rain. And then the dry years would come, and sometimes there would be only seven or eight inches of rain. The land dried up and the grasses headed out miserably a few inches high and great bare scabby places appeared in the valley. The live oaks got a crusty look and the sagebrush was gray. The land cracked and the springs dried up and the cattle listlessly nibbled dry twigs. Then the farmers and the ranchers would be filled with disgust for the Salinas Valley. The cows would grow thin and sometimes starve to death. People would have to haul water in barrels to their farms just for drinking. Some families would sell out for nearly nothing and move away. And it never failed that during the dry years the people forgot about the rich years, and during the wet years they lost all memory of the dry years. It was always that way.

Gertrude Stein

Everybody's Autobiography

We went first into the San Joaquin Valley, naturally this was interesting because Alice Toklas's pioneer grandfather had owned all his land there and Fresno and all about was exciting, after all if that is where you were and the names of it are that it is exciting. We tacked back and forward across the valley and we did like all we saw we liked smelling the oranges and the kind of nuts and fruits that had not been there I had never been there before but she had been there and the way they cut the tops of the trees to make a straight line as if they had been cut with a razor and the fig trees fig trees smell best of all and we went forward and back until we got a little higher and saw the California poppies growing which we had not seen growing wild since we had been in California, they were like they were and it gave me a shock to see them there, it began to be funny and to make me uneasy. Then we went up a little higher and then although it was still wintry we thought that we would go into the Yosemite, we had neither of us ever been there, that I had not been there was not astonishing, we had tended to go north not south from Oakland when we were children but that Alice Toklas had not been there was more surprising, her cousins who lived then in the San Joaquin Valley used to drive every year into the valley as they called the Yosemite the others were rivers but not valleys, and so we decided to go into the valley, I wanted to see the big trees I had never seen them and anyway we decided we would go into the valley, it was spring but it was a very cold one, there was rain and there was lots of snow yet and again.

We tried one road that led to big trees but it was raining and snowing and the road looked none too good and precipitous besides perhaps not but I felt that and so we went back again and finally got to Merced, there the sun was shining it was muddy but the sun was shining and the town of Merced looked like the kind of California I knew just a little country town and we ate something there and decided to go on. I am always afraid of precipices and I could not believe that in going into the Yosemite there would not be lots of them, they had told us not but naturally I did not believe them they said the road was not dangerous, of course the road is not dangerous roads rarely are but it is what you see when you don't see anything except the sky that gives you that funny feeling and makes what I call precipitous. No matter how wide the road and how large the curve it can be precipitous to me. So at Merced we wanted to go on but I thought I would feel better if somebody else was along and driving, so we asked was there any one, in France of course there would not have been any one but in Merced of course there was there was a boy at school who sooner or later would have to go home and his home was in the valley so he said he did not mind missing school that afternoon if we gave him a dollar and of course we did not mind and although he was very young he could drive anybody any where in America can. A good many can here in France but not so young as in America, in France they can all ride a bicycle any one can do that and go up any hill and never get off everybody has his specialty.

So we were driven into the valley and there was no precipice, how they made the road as it is and going always higher and never at any time in any place to feel as if you were jumping off and never necessary to change your speed it was a wonder. Later they told us perhaps it is so that you could go all the way from California to New York and at no time is there a grade which makes changing speeds necessary, the road is made in such a way and of course there are some precipitous spots but they all said certainly not and after the Yosemite Valley road I was almost ready to believe them.

The roads in America were lovely, they move along alone the big ones the way the railroad tracks used to move with really no connection with the country. Of course in a way that is natural enough as I always like to tell a Frenchman and he listens but he does not believe the railroad did not follow the towns made by the road but it made a road followed by the towns and the country, there were no towns and no roads therefore no country until the railroad came along, and the new big roads in America still make you feel that way, air lines they call some of them and they are they have nothing really to do with the towns and the country. The only thing that worried me not so much in California but still even there is the soft shoulder of the road as they called it, that the cement road had no finish to it as it has in France which keeps it from being a danger, I suppose the roads are too long to make that possible but still it is a pity, the smaller roads are too narrow as they have a soft shoulder, some day they will make them a little wider and finish the edge of them with a little edge to it, then they will be pleasanter for driving certainly in rain and anyway. However we did like driving on the American roads and the boy brought us safely into Yosemite.

It was high there and cold and we arrived a little late but the director of the valley offered to take us to see the big trees and we went. I liked that. The thing that was most exciting about them was that they had no roots did anybody want anything to be more interesting than that that the oldest and the solidest and the biggest tree that could be grown had no foundation, there it was sitting and the wind did not blow it over it sat so well. It was very exciting. Very beautiful and very exciting.

Mount Whitney

This is the true Mount Whitney, the one we named in 1864, and upon which the name of our chief is forever to rest. It stands, not like white Shasta, in a grandeur of solitude, but about it gather companies of crag and spire, piercing the blue or wrapped in monkish raiment of snowstorm and mist. Far below, laid out in ashen death, slumbers the desert.

Silence reigns on these icy heights, save when scream of Sierra eagle or loud crescendo of avalanche interrupts the frozen stillness, or when in symphonic fullness a storm rolls through vacant canyons with its stern minor. It is hard not to invest these great, dominating peaks with consciousness, difficult to realize that, sitting thus for ages in presence of all nature can work of light-magic and color-beauty, no inner spirit has kindled, nor throb of granite heart once responded, no Buddhistic nirvana-life, even, has brooded in eternal calm within these sphinxlike breasts of stone.

A week after my climb I lay on the desert sand at the foot of the Inyo Range and looked up at Mount Whitney, realizing all its grand individuality, and saw the drifting clouds interrupt a sun-brightened serenity by frown after frown of moving shadow; and I entered for a moment deeply and intimately into that strange realm where admiration blends with superstition, that condition in which the savage feels within him the greatness of a natural object, and forever after endows it with consciousness and power. For a moment I was back in the Aryan myth days, when they saw afar a snowy peak, and called it Dhavalagiri (white elephant), and invested it with mystic power.

These peculiar moments, rare enough in the life of a scientific man, when one trembles on the edge of mythmaking, are of interest, as unfolding the origin and manner of savage beliefs, and as awakening the unperishing germ of primitive manhood which is buried within us all under so much culture and science.

How generally the mythmaker has been extinguished in modern students of mountains may be realized by examining the tone of Alpine literature, which, once lifted above the fatiguing repetition of gymnastics, is almost invariably scientific.

Ruskin alone among prose writers on the Alps re-echoes the dim past, in ever-recurring mythmaking, over cloud and peak and glacier; his is the *Rig-Veda*'s idea of nature. The varying hues which mood and emotion forever pass before his own mental vision mask with their illusive mystery the simple realities of nature, until mountains and their bold, natural facts are lost behind the cloudy poetry of the writer.

Ruskin helps us to know himself, not the Alps; his mountain chapters, although essentially four thousand years old, are, however, no more an anachronism than the dim primeval spark which smoulders in all of us; their brilliancy is that spark fanned into flame.

To follow a chapter of Ruskin by one of Tyndall is to bridge forty centuries and realize the full contrast of archaic and modern thought.

This was the drift of my revery as I lay basking on the hot sands of Inyo, realizing fully the geological history and hard, materialistic reality of Mount Whitney, its mineral nature, its chemistry; yet archaic impulse even then held me, and the gaunt, gray old Indian who came slowly toward me must have subtly felt my condition, for he crouched beside me and silently fixed his hawk eye upon the peak.

At last he drew an arrow, sighted along its straight shaft, bringing the obsidian head to bear on Mount Whitney, and in strange fragments of language told me that the peak was an old, old man, who watched this valley and cared for the Indians, but who shook the country with earthquakes to punish the whites for injustice toward his tribe.

I looked at his whitened hair and keen, black eye. I watched the spare, bronze face, upon which was written the burden of a hundred dark and gloomy superstitions; and as he trudged away across the sands I could but feel the liberating power of modern culture, which unfetters us from the more than iron bands of self-made myths. My mood vanished with the savage, and I saw the great peak only as it really is—a splendid mass of granite 14,887 feet high, ice-chiselled and storm-tinted; a great monolith left standing amid the ruins of a bygone geological empire.

— Joan Didion —

Notes from a Native Daughter

It is very easy to sit at the bar in, say, La Scala in Beverly Hills, or Ernie's in San Francisco, and to share in the pervasive delusion that California is only five hours from New York by air. The truth is that La Scala and Ernie's are only five hours from New York by air. California is somewhere else.

Many people in the East (or "back East," as they say in California, although not in La Scala or Ernie's) do not believe this. They have been to Los Angeles or to San Francisco, have driven through a giant redwood and have seen the Pacific glazed by the afternoon sun off Big Sur, and they naturally tend to believe that they have in fact been to California. They have not been, and they probably never will be, for it is a longer and in many ways a more difficult trip than they might want to undertake, one of those trips on which the destination flickers chimerically on the horizon, ever receding, ever diminishing. I happen to know about that trip because I come from California, come from a family, or a congeries of families, that has always been in the Sacramento Valley.

You might protest that no family has been in the Sacramento Valley for anything approaching "always." But it is characteristic of Californians to speak grandly of the past as if it had simultaneously begun, *tabula rasa*, and reached a happy ending on the day the wagons started west. *Eureka*—"I Have Found It"—as the state motto has it. Such a view of history casts a certain melancholia over those who participate in it; my own childhood was suffused with the conviction that we had long outlived our finest hour. In fact that is what I want to tell you about: what it is like to come from a place like Sacramento. If I could make you understand that, I could make you understand California and perhaps something else besides, for Sacramento *is* California, and California is a place in which a boom mentality and a sense of Chekhovian loss meet in uneasy suspension; in which the mind is troubled by some buried but ineradicable suspicion that things had better work here, because here, beneath that immense bleached sky, is where we run out of continent.

In 1847 Sacramento was no more than an adobe enclosure, Sutter's Fort, standing alone on the prairie; cut off from San Francisco and the sea by the Coast Range and from the rest of the continent by the Sierra Nevada, the Sacramento Valley was then a true sea of grass, grass so high a man riding into it could tie it across his saddle. A year later gold was discovered in the Sierra foothills, and abruptly Sacramento was a town, a town any moviegoer could map tonight in his dreams—a dusty collage of assay offices and wagonmakers and saloons. Call that Phase Two. Then the settlers came—the farmers, the people who for two hundred years had been moving west on the frontier, the peculiar flawed strain who had cleared Virginia, Kentucky, Missouri; they made Sacramento a farm town. Because the land was rich, Sacramento became eventually a rich farm town, which meant houses in town, Cadillac dealers, a country club. In that gentle sleep Sacramento dreamed until perhaps 1950, when something happened. What happened was that Sacramento woke to the fact that the outside world was moving in, fast and hard. At the moment of its waking Sacramento lost, for better or for worse, its character, and that is part of what I want to tell you about.

But the change is not what I remember first. First I remember running a boxer dog of my brother's over the same flat fields that our great-great-grandfather had found virgin and had planted; I remember swimming (albeit nervously, for I was a nervous child, afraid of sinkholes and afraid of snakes, and perhaps that was the beginning of my error) the same rivers we had swum for a century: the Sacramento, so rich with silt that we could barely see our hands a few inches beneath the surface; the American, running clean and fast with melted Sierra snow until July, when it would slow down, and rattlesnakes would sun themselves on its newly exposed rocks. The Sacramento, the American, sometimes the Cosumnes, occasionally the Feather. Incautious children died every day in those rivers; we read about it in the paper, how they had miscalculated a current or stepped into a hole down where the American runs into the Sacramento, how the Berry Brothers had been called in from Yolo County to drag the river but how the bodies remained unrecovered. "They were from away," my grandmother would extrapolate from the newspaper stories. "Their parents had no *business* letting them in the river. They were visitors from Omaha." It was not a bad lesson, although a less than reliable one; children we knew died in the rivers too.

When summer ended—when the State Fair closed and the heat broke, when the last green hop vines had been torn down along the H Street road and the tule fog began rising off the low ground at night—we would go back to memorizing the Products of Our Latin American Neighbors and to visiting the great-aunts on Sunday, dozens of great-aunts, year after year of Sundays. When I think now of those winters I think of yellow elm leaves wadded in the gutters outside the Trinity Episcopal Pro-Cathedral on M Street. There are actually people in Sacramento now who call M Street Capitol Avenue, and Trinity has one of those featureless new buildings, but perhaps children still learn the same things there on Sunday mornings:

> Q. *In what way does the Holy Land resemble the Sacramento Valley?*
> A. *In the type and diversity of its agricultural products.*

And I think of the rivers rising, of listening to the radio to hear at what height they would crest and wondering if and when and where the levees would go. We did not have as many dams in those years. The bypasses would be full, and men would sandbag all night. Sometimes a levee would go in the night, somewhere upriver; in the morning the rumor would spread that the Army engineers had dynamited it to relieve the pressure on the city.

After the rains came spring, for ten days or so; the drenched fields would dissolve into a brilliant ephemeral green (it would be yellow and dry as fire in two or three weeks) and the real-estate business would pick up. It was the time of year when people's grandmothers went to Carmel; it was the time of year when girls who could not even get into Stephens or Arizona or Oregon, let alone Stanford or Berkeley, would be sent to Honolulu, on the *Lurline.* I have no recollection of anyone going to New York, with the exception of a cousin who visited there (I cannot imagine why) and reported that the shoe salesmen at Lord & Taylor were "intolerably rude." What happened in New York and Washington and abroad seemed to impinge not at all upon the Sacramento mind. I remember being taken to call upon a very old woman, a rancher's widow, who was reminiscing (the favored conversational mode in Sacramento) about the son of some contemporaries of hers. "That Johnston boy never did amount to much," she said. Desultorily, my mother protested: Alva Johnston, she said, had won the Pulitzer Prize, when he was working for the *New York Times*. Our hostess looked at us impassively. "He never amounted to anything in Sacramento," she said.

Hers was the true Sacramento voice, and, although I did not realize it then, one not long to be heard, for the war was over and the boom was on and the voice of the aerospace engineer would be heard in the land. VETS NO DOWN! EXECUTIVE LIVING ON LOW FHA!

Later, when I was living in New York, I would make the trip back to Sacramento four and five times a year (the more comfortable the flight, the more obscurely miserable I would be, for it weighs heavily upon my kind that we could perhaps not make it by wagon), trying to prove that I had not meant to leave at all, because in at least one respect California—the California we are talking about—resembles Eden: it is assumed that those who absent themselves from its blessings have been banished, exiled by some perversity of heart. Did not the Donner-Reed Party, after all, eat its own dead to reach Sacramento?

I have said that the trip back is difficult, and it is—difficult in a way that magnifies the ordinary ambiguities of sentimental journeys. Going back to California is not like going back to Vermont, or Chicago; Vermont and Chicago are relative constants, against which one measures one's own change. All that is constant about the California of my childhood is the rate at which it disappears. An instance: on Saint Patrick's Day of 1948 I was taken to see the legislature "in action," a dismal experience; a handful of florid assemblymen, wearing green hats, were reading Pat-and-Mike jokes into the record. I still think of the legislators that way—wearing green hats, or sitting around on the veranda of the Senator Hotel fanning themselves and being entertained by Artie Samish's emissaries. (Samish was the lobbyist who said, "Earl Warren may be the governor of the state, but I'm the governor of the legislature.") In fact there is no longer a veranda at the Senator Hotel—it was turned into an airline ticket office, if you want to embroider the point—and in any case the legislature has largely deserted the Senator for the flashy motels north of town, where the tiki torches flame and the steam rises off the heated swimming pools in the cold Valley night.

It is hard to *find* California now, unsettling to wonder how much of it was merely imagined or improvised; melancholy to realize how much of anyone's memory is no true memory at all but only the traces of someone else's memory, stories handed down on the family network. I have an indelibly vivid "memory," for example, of how Prohibition affected the hop growers around Sacramento: the sister of a grower my family knew brought home a mink coat from San Francisco, and was told to take it back, and sat on the floor of the parlor cradling that coat and crying. Although I was not born until a year after Repeal, that scene is more "real" to me than many I have played myself.

I remember one trip home, when I sat alone on a night jet from New York and read over and over some lines from a W. S. Merwin poem I had come across in a magazine, a poem about a man who had been a long time in another country and knew that he must go home:

> . . . But it should be
> Soon. Already I defend hotly
> Certain of our indefensible faults,
> Resent being reminded; already in my mind
> Our language becomes freighted with a richness
> No common tongue could offer, while the mountains
> Are like nowhere on earth, and the wide rivers.

You see the point. I want to tell you the truth, and already I have told you about the wide rivers.

It should be clear by now that the truth about the place is elusive, and must be tracked with caution. You might go to Sacramento tomorrow and someone (although no one I know) might take you out to Aerojet-General, which has, in the Sacramento phrase, "something to do with rockets." Fifteen thousand people work for Aerojet, almost all of them imported; a Sacramento lawyer's wife told me, as evidence of how Sacramento was opening up, that she believed she had met one of them, at an open house two Decembers ago. ("Couldn't have been nicer, actually," she added enthusiastically. "I think he and his wife bought the house next *door* to Mary and Al, something like that, which of course was how *they* met him.") So you might go to Aerojet and stand in the big vendors' lobby where a couple of thousand components salesmen try every week to sell their wares and you might look up at the electrical wallboard that lists Aerojet personnel, their projects and their location at any given time, and you might wonder if I have been in Sacramento lately. MINUTEMAN, PO-LARIS, TITAN, the lights flash, and all the coffee tables are littered with airline schedules, very now, very much in touch.

But I could take you a few miles from there into towns where the banks still bear names like The Bank of Alex Brown, into towns where the one hotel still has an octagonal-tile floor in the dining room and dusty potted palms and big ceiling fans; into towns where everything—the seed business, the Harvester franchise, the hotel, the department store, and the main street—carries a single name, the name of the man who built the town. A few Sundays ago I was in a town like that, a town smaller than that, really, no hotel, no Harvester franchise, the bank burned out, a river town. It was the golden anniversary of some of my relatives and it was 110 degrees and the guests of honor sat on straight-backed chairs in front of a sheaf of gladioluses in the Rebekah Hall. I mentioned visiting Aerojet-General to a cousin I saw there, who listened to me with interested disbelief. Which is the true California? That is what we all wonder.

Let us try out a few irrefutable statements, on subjects not open to interpretation. Although Sacramento is in many ways the least typical of the Valley towns, it *is* a Valley town, and must be viewed in that context. When you say "the Valley" in Los Angeles, most people assume that you mean the San Fernando Valley (some people in fact assume that you mean Warner Brothers), but make no mistake: we are talking not about the valley of the sound stages and the ranchettes but about the real Valley, the Central Valley, the fifty thousand square miles drained by the Sacramento and the San Joaquin Rivers and further irrigated by a complex network of sloughs, cutoffs, ditches, and the Delta-Mendota and Friant-Kern canals.

A hundred miles north of Los Angeles, at the moment when you drop from the Tehachapi Mountains into the outskirts of Bakersfield, you leave Southern California and enter the Valley. "You look up the highway and it is straight for miles, coming at you, with the black line down the center coming at you and at you . . . and the heat dazzles up from the white slab so that only the black line is clear, coming at you with the whine of the tires, and if you don't quit staring at that line and don't take a few deep breaths and slap yourself hard on the back of the neck you'll hypnotize yourself."

Robert Penn Warren wrote that about another road, but he might have been writing about the Valley road, U.S. 99, three hundred miles from Bakersfield to Sacramento, a highway so straight that when one flies on the most direct pattern from Los Angeles to Sacramento one never loses sight of U.S. 99. The landscape it runs through never, to the untrained eye, varies. The Valley eye can discern the point where miles of cotton seedlings fade into miles of tomato seedlings, or where the great corporation ranches—Kern County Land, what is left of DiGiorgio—give way to private operations (somewhere on the horizon, if the place is private, one sees a house and a stand of scrub oaks), but such distinctions are in the long view irrelevant. All day long, all that moves is the sun, and the big Rainbird sprinklers.

Every so often along 99 between Bakersfield and Sacramento there is a town: Delano, Tulare, Fresno, Madera, Merced, Modesto, Stockton. Some of these towns are pretty big now, but they are all the same at heart, one- and two- and three-story buildings artlessly arranged, so that what appears to be the good dress shop stands beside a W. T. Grant store, so that the big Bank of America faces a Mexican movie house. *Dos Peliculas, Bingo Bingo Bingo.* Beyond the downtown (pronounced *down*town, with the Okie accent that now pervades Valley speech patterns) lie blocks of old frame houses—paint peeling, sidewalks cracking, their occasional leaded amber windows overlooking a Foster's Freeze or a five-minute car wash or a State Farm insurance office; beyond those spread the shopping centers and the miles of tract houses, pastel with redwood siding, the unmistakable signs of cheap building already blossoming on those houses which have survived the first rain. To a stranger driving 99 in an air-conditioned car (he would be on business, I suppose, any stranger driving 99, for 99 would never get a tourist to Big Sur or San Simeon, never get him to the California he came to see), these towns must seem so flat, so impoverished, as to drain the imagination. They hint at evenings spent hanging around gas stations, and suicide pacts sealed in drive-ins.

But remember:

Q. In what way does the Holy Land resemble the Sacramento Valley?
A. In the type and diversity of its agricultural products.

U.S. 99 in fact passes through the richest and most intensely cultivated agricultural region in the world, a giant outdoor hothouse with a billion-dollar crop. It is when you remember the Valley's wealth that the monochromatic flatness of its towns takes on a curious meaning, suggests a habit of mind some would consider perverse. There is something in the Valley mind that reflects a real indifference to the stranger in his air-conditioned car, a failure to perceive even his presence, let alone his thoughts or wants. An implacable insularity is the seal of these towns. I once met a woman in Dallas, a most charming and attractive woman accustomed to the hospitality and social hypersensitivity of Texas, who told me that during the four war years her husband had been stationed in Modesto, she had never once been invited inside anyone's house. No one in Sacramento would find this story remarkable ("She probably had no *relatives* there," said someone to whom I told it), for the Valley towns understand one another, share a peculiar spirit. They think alike and they look alike. *I* can tell Modesto from Merced, but I have visited there, gone to dances there; besides, there is over the main street of Modesto an arched sign which reads:

WATER—WEALTH
CONTENTMENT—HEALTH

There is no such sign in Merced.

Richard Rodriguez

Credo

On Halloween night, all over Sacramento, children dressed up as ghosts or Frankensteins or dime-store skeletons with phosphorescent bones. But only Catholic school kids went to mass the next morning to honor the white-robed saints on the Feast of All Hallows. It was one of the "holy days of obligation"— a day on which I was obliged to go to morning mass, but for the rest of the day I was free—no school. I could ride my bicycle around Sacramento, watch public school kids walking to school. And people downtown were passing just another day. (They seemed not to know.)

In the secular calendar there was no day like Ash Wednesday. All day I would see on the heedless foreheads of classmates the Hindu-like smudge of dark ash, the reminder of death. (. . . Unto dust thou shalt return.) One year a girl at school was killed in a car crash shortly after Ash Wednesday. I took the lesson.

On these few occasions when secular Sacramento took up the sacred calendar they got it all wrong. Christmas downtown began in early November. Merchants would string tiny white lights up over K Street, where they shone through the night as pretty as heaven. But their Christmas ended in late afternoon on Christmas Eve—I saw department store clerks working against time to replace a holiday window display with deathly white piles of towels and sheets. In church, in early November there was Advent, the time for penance. On a table in front of the altar was a wreath with four candles stuck in, one of which was lit each week to mark the coming—the slow, slow coming—of Christ. In church, Christmas began at midnight mass, Christmas Eve. And the holy season continued until the Feast of Epiphany, the sixth of January, when carols were sung for the very last time and fir trees on the altar no longer cast their dark scent of damp earth.

The secular calendar whirled like a carnival wheel and offered carnival prizes—a fat Santa instead of the infant God; colored eggs and chocolate bunnies instead of the death and resurrection of Christ. During Holy Week all pictures and statues in church were shrouded by purple silk drapes. On Holy Thursday to commemorate the Last Supper of Christ there was a "white" mass at sunset (when stained-glass windows burned briefly before the light failed). After that mass, the sacrament was removed to a side altar and the red sanctuary lamp was extinguished, so that the next day, Good Friday, when women in scarves and men in work clothes came to church for "the three hours" they found an altar stripped bare and the tabernacle gaping.

In our house on Good Friday we behaved as if a member of our family had died. There was no radio or television. But I noticed that the Standard gas station right across from church stayed open for business as usual and I saw people at the laundromat watching their clothes tumble behind a round window—as if nothing in the world had happened. In Sacramento, the blue Easter morning seemed always to rhyme with the gospel account of the three Marys wending their way through a garden to discover an empty tomb. At church, at the altar, there were vestments of gold and the climbing voices of a Mozart mass, tossing rings sempiternal.

The wheels turned. Two wheels of time. The secular calendar made plain note of the hot first day of summer. Fall. Then winter. Ordinary time: Labor Day. The first day of school. Arithmetic class. An hour for spelling (a test every Friday). Recess. Church time: Benediction with classmates. Candles on St. Blaise's day. Ash. Palms in April. The red-eyed white dove descending, descending on Pentecost Sunday. Mary crowned with dying sweet flowers on the first day of May. The wheels turned. Second grade. Third grade. Fifth grade. Christmas. Epiphany. The secular calendar announced the vernal equinox. The low valley fog of late winter would slowly yield to the coming of Easter.

I went to the nine o'clock mass every Sunday with my family. At that time in my life, when I was so struck by diminished family closeness and the necessity of public life, church was a place unlike any other. It mediated between my public and private lives. I would kneel beside my brother and sisters. On one side of us would be my mother. (I could hear her whispered Spanish Hail Mary.) On the other side, my father. In the pew directly in front of us were the Van Hoyts. And in front of them were the druggist and his family. Over to the side was a lady who wore fancy dresses, a widow who prayed a crystal rosary. She was alone, as was the old man in front who cupped his face in his hands while he prayed. It was this same gesture of privacy the nuns would teach me to use, especially after Communion when I thanked God for coming into my soul.

The mass mystified me for being a public and a private event. We prayed here, each of us, much as we prayed on our pillows—most privately—all alone before God. And yet the great public prayer of the mass would go on. No one ever forgot where they were. People stood up together or they knelt at the right time in response to the progression of the liturgy. Every Sunday in summer someone fainted from heat, had to be carried out, but the mass went on.

I remember being puzzled very early by how different things were for the Protestants. Evangelical Christians would ring the doorbell to ask bluntly whether or not I was "saved." They proceeded to tell me about their own conversions to Christ. From classmates I would hear about Holy Rollers who jumped up and down and even fell to the floor at their services. It was funny. Hard to believe. My religion—the true religion—was so different. On Sunday afternoons, for a guilty few minutes, I'd watch an Oral Roberts prayer meeting on television. Members of the congregation made public confessions of sin, while people off camera shouted, "Hallelujah, sister! Hallelujah, brother, preach it!"

Sister and Brother were terms I used in speaking to my teachers for twelve years. Father was the name for the priest at church. I never confused my teachers or the priests with actual family members; in fact they were most awesome for being without families. Yet I came to use these terms with ease. They implied that a deep bond existed between my teachers and me as fellow Catholics. At the same time, however, Sister and Father were highly formal terms of address—they were titles, marks of formality like a salute or a curtsey. (One would never have spoken to a nun without first calling her Sister.) It was possible consequently to use these terms and to feel at once a close bond, and the distance of formality. In a way, that is how I felt with all fellow Catholics in my world. We were close—somehow related—while also distanced by careful reserve.

City

It seemed like a matter of minutes when we began rolling in the foothills before Oakland and suddenly reached a height and saw stretched out ahead of us the fabulous white city of San Francisco on her eleven mystic hills with the blue Pacific and its advancing wall of potato-patch fog beyond, and smoke and goldenness in the late afternoon of time. JACK KEROUAC

San Francisco

I have seen many cities which are built high above the water. Different as Marseilles, Algiers, Lisbon, and Naples are from each other, they all have one trait in common: their hills have been utilized in their elementary architecture; the streets curve around them, creep up in spirals so well placed that one has a glimpse of the sea from almost any point; the complicated plan one sees on the map appears simple and natural in reality. It is quite the opposite here: San Francisco is shocking in its obstinate abstraction—deliriously geometric. The blueprint seems to have been put on paper without the architect ever having seen the site. It is a drawing board with straight lines, like New York or Buffalo. The hills have simply been ignored; streets rise and fall without concern for their rigid design. As a result, one almost never sees the ocean; enclosed between the successive barriers which cut across the horizon, the streets have an insular calm: they are paved with red brick, reminding one of the tile floors of Dutch kitchens, and the white houses along them are three or four stories high. San Francisco does not have the lively teeming color of Barcelona or Marseilles; the memory of the prospectors, their camps, their brawling seems very remote. One can walk for a long time in a quiet bourgeois section without having the slightest notion that it is the heart of a mass composed of eight hundred thousand living parts.

Suddenly, at the top of an avenue like the others, we found ourselves on a cliff from which we saw the ocean; descending to the level area below was a road so steep that it seemed madness to risk going down in a car. This was another result of this abstract urbanism: the slopes are so abrupt that some are forbidden to cars; they discourage streetcars; they are only suitable for small cable cars, heirs of the old variety which were operated with horses: when the car arrived at the top, the horse simply made a semicircular turn, and, the balance thus shifted, the car was sent down again; now the conductor just moves to the other end of the car. Accidents sometimes occur, and a poll was recently made to find out if these cars should be retired from service. Public opinion was divided. Sentimental creatures, especially women, wished to keep them for the sheer love of tradition. One line will probably be kept in operation as a curiosity.

We did not get a very good look at San Francisco, because we only stayed there four days and knew no one, but we had a good time. We walked around, we window-shopped in Chinatown, admiring the silks, the jade, the dried ducks which hang naked and waxlike in their shop windows.

Telegraph Hill is a miniature Montmartre where artists' studios are ranged one above the other: there are also small cafes and little houses. We climbed it and contemplated the blue and gold of the bay from its summit. At the left, the Golden Gate shimmered in the sunlight; it was also through a public opinion poll that the molten copper color of this great metal bridge was chosen; all the flamboyance of the Riviera shone in its girders.

To the right is Bay Bridge, composed of two sections which rest on Treasure Island—the famous *Treasure Island* of Stevenson has no magic connotation here, for this island links San Francisco with the industrial cities on the far side of the bay: Oakland, Berkeley, Richmond. San Francisco no longer seems like an insular little town but like the heart of a huge city, with a population of three million people. There is the same animation in the business section as in New York or Chicago: Market Street is another Broadway, and when you go to the outskirts, you find the boundless desolation of great cities: unfinished avenues like those of Queens or Los Angeles: stations, depots, garages, deserted crossroads. But hemmed around by factories, industrial suburbs, toil and poverty, the bay is still a luxuriant paradise. A small island, floating on the water, looks like a quiet Eden: it is, in fact, a prison.

We went down to the fishermen's wharf. Small boats bobbed up and down in narrow basins between wooden docks; the little square was surrounded by restaurants with bay windows, where people ate fish and lobsters, while in the doorways they sold fritters, shellfish, shrimp, and prawns frozen in blocks of ice. The odor of burning fat mingled with the smell of seaweed. But compared to the old port of Marseilles with its sea chanteys and sea urchins, the place was very tame. . . .

Southeast of San Francisco, along the flat marshy coast, stretches a vast industrial suburb. Trucks run along the highroad, which smells of gasoline; I know few less attractive spots. But here, too, you only have to take a side road, and after a few miles you have shaken off the twentieth century. The peninsula is covered by an ancient sequoia forest, less imposing than those I had seen in technicolor films but with more unusual tints; the ruddy trunks had the quiet beauty of old Persian rugs, faded silks and tarnished gold. From the coast road you have a view of both sides of the sea; the forest stretches out in dark green masses just as it has grown for many millions of years, on the left towards the open sea, on the right towards the bay. . . .

We went to dine in a little Chinese place, like the one we had enjoyed the day before. When it was time to leave, we did not feel like going to bed; we went down a street that opened onto the quay and across which a streamer pompously announced, "International Concession." We had been told that this was a street of evil haunts, but the street was dead. A few half-drunken sailors did not suffice to create the liveliness of a port. The bars with Hawaiian or Mexican decorations were empty; a pianist or a guitarist strummed away in the gloom. There was no one at the box offices of the "Variety Shows," though the pinup photos were attractive. People thronged to one place only—a dance hall, calling itself "The Gay Nineties," which tried to recreate a cabaret at the turn of the century. Here they drank whiskey or beer, sitting around little tables on pink plush chairs, while comics in checkered suits, moustachios and straw hats, and dancers in black stockings paraded across the stage: the show was amusing, for it was just like the sort always revived in Westerns. For a moment, the stage was empty, and all eyes were turned toward a screen on which sentimental old songs were projected; the band accompanied them, and everyone sang the chorus. For a moment, past and present really became one; fifty years ago people sang this way, and many of the lyrics were charming. Today the public is not just reviving an old-fashioned tradition: it joins in the game, roused by an altogether fresh enthusiasm. On the screen, the printed couplets had the poetry of images projected by magic lanterns at a time when movies and phonographs had not yet been invented.

Rudyard Kipling

From Sea to Sea

"You want to go to the Palace Hotel?" said an affable youth on a dray. "What in hell are you doing here, then? This is about the lowest place in the city. Go six blocks north to corner of Geary and Market; then walk around till you strike corner of Gutter and Sixteenth, and that brings you there."

I do not vouch for the literal accuracy of these directions, quoting but from a disordered memory.

"Amen," I said. "But who am I that I should strike the corners of such as you name? Peradventure they be gentlemen of repute, and might hit back. Bring it down to dots, my son."

I thought he would have smitten me, but he didn't. He explained that no one ever used the word "street," and that every one was supposed to know how the streets run; for sometimes the names were upon the lamps and sometimes they weren't. Fortified with these directions I proceeded till I found a mighty street full of sumptuous buildings four or five stories high, but paved with rude cobblestones in the fashion of the Year One. A cable car without any visible means of support slid stealthily behind me and nearly struck me in the back. A hundred yards further there was a slight commotion in the street—a gathering together of three or four—and something that glittered as it moved very swiftly. A ponderous Irish gentleman with priest's cords in his hat and a small nickel-plated badge on his fat bosom emerged from the knot, supporting a Chinaman who had been stabbed in the eye and was bleeding like a pig. The bystanders went their ways, and the Chinaman, assisted by the policeman, his own. Of course this was none of my business, but I rather wanted to know what had happened to the gentleman who had dealt the stab. It said a great deal for the excellence of the municipal arrangements of the town that a surging crowd did not at once block the street to see what was going forward. I was the sixth man and the last who assisted at the performance, and my curiosity was six times the greatest. Indeed, I felt ashamed of showing it.

There were no more incidents till I reached the Palace Hotel, a seven-storied warren of humanity with a thousand rooms in it. All the travel books will tell you about hotel arrangements in this country. They should be seen to be appreciated. Understand clearly—and this letter is written after a thousand miles of experiences—that money will not buy you service in the West.

When the hotel clerk—the man who awards your room to you and who is supposed to give you information—when that resplendent individual stoops to attend to your wants, he does so whistling or humming, or picking his teeth, or pauses to converse with some one he knows. These performances, I gather, are to impress upon you that he is a free man and your equal. From his general appearance and the size of his diamonds he ought to be your superior. There is no necessity for this swaggering self-consciousness of freedom. Business is business, and the man who is paid to attend to a man might reasonably devote his whole attention to the job.

In a vast marble-paved hall under the glare of an electric light sat forty or fifty men; and for their use and amusement were provided spittoons of infinite capacity and generous gape. Most of the men wore frock coats and top hats—the things that we in India put on at a wedding breakfast if we possessed them— but they all spat. They spat on principle. The spittoons were on the staircases, in each bedroom—yea, and in chambers even more sacred than these. They chased one into retirement, but they blossomed in chiefest splendour round the Bar, and they were all used, every reeking one of 'em. Just before I began to feel deathly sick, another reporter grappled me. What he wanted to know was the precise area of India in square miles. I referred him to Whittaker. He had never heard of Whittaker. He wanted it from my own mouth, and I would not tell him. Then he swerved off, like the other man, to details of journalism in our own country. I ventured to suggest that the interior economy of a paper most concerned the people who worked it. "That's the very thing that interests us," he said. "Have you got reporters anything like our reporters on Indian newspapers?" "We have not," I said, and suppressed the "thank God" rising to my lips. "*Why* haven't you?" said he. "Because they would die," I said. It was exactly like talking to a child—a very rude little child. He would begin almost every sentence with: "Now tell me something about India," and would turn aimlessly from one question to another without the least continuity. I was not angry, but keenly interested. The man was a revelation to me. To his questions I returned answers mendacious and evasive. After all, it really did not matter what I said. He could not understand. I can only hope and pray that none of the readers of the *Pioneer* will ever see that portentous interview. The man made me out to be an idiot several sizes more drivelling than my destiny intended, and the rankness of his ignorance managed to distort the few poor facts with which I supplied him into large and elaborate lies. Then thought I: "The matter of American journalism shall be looked into later on. At present I will enjoy myself."

No man rose to tell me what were the lions of the place. No one volunteered any sort of conveyance. I was absolutely alone in this big city of white folk. By instinct I sought refreshment and came upon a barroom full of bad Salon pictures, in which men with hats on the backs of their heads were wolfing food from a counter. It was the institution of the "Free Lunch" that I had struck. You paid for a drink and got as much as you wanted to eat. For something less than a rupee a day a man can feed himself sumptuously in San Francisco, even though he be bankrupt. Remember this if ever you are stranded in these parts.

Later, I began a vast but unsystematic exploration of the streets. I asked for no names. It was enough that the pavements were full of white men and women, the streets clanging with traffic, and that the restful roar of a great city rang in my ears. The cable cars glided to all points of the compass. I took them one by one till I could go no farther. San Francisco has been pitched down on the sand bunkers of the Bikaneer desert. About one-fourth of it is ground reclaimed from the sea—any old-timer will tell you all about that. The remainder is ragged, unthrifty sand hills, pegged down by houses.

From an English point of view there has not been the least attempt at grading those hills, and indeed you might as well try to grade the hillocks of Sind. The cable cars have for all practical purposes made San Francisco a dead level. They take no count of rise or fall, but slide equally on their appointed courses from one end to the other of a six-mile street. They turn corners almost at right angles; cross other lines, and, for aught I know, may run up the sides of houses. There is no visible agency of their flight; but once in a while you shall pass a five-storied building, humming with machinery that winds up an everlasting wire cable, and the initiated will tell you that here is the mechanism. I gave up asking questions. If it pleases Providence to make a car run up and down a slit in the ground for many miles, and if for twopence-halfpenny I can ride in that car, why shall I seek the reasons of the miracle? Rather let me look out of the windows till the shops give place to thousands and thousands of little houses made of wood—each house just big enough for a man and his family. Let me watch the people in the cars, and try to find out in what manner they differ from us, their ancestors. They delude themselves into the belief that they talk English—*the* English—and I have already been pitied for speaking with "an English accent." The man who pitied me spoke, so far as I was concerned, the language of thieves. And they all do.

Night fell over the Pacific, and the white sea-fog whipped through the streets, dimming the splendors of the electric lights. It is the use of this city, her men and women, to parade between the hours of eight and ten a certain street, called Kearney Street, where the finest shops are situated. Here the click of heels on the pavement is loudest, here the lights are brightest, and here the thunder of the traffic is most overwhelming. I watched Young California and saw that it was at least expensively dressed, cheerful in manner, and self-asserting in conversation. Also the women are very fair. The maidens were of generous build, large, well groomed, and attired in raiment that even to my inexperienced eyes must have cost much. Kearney Street, at nine o'clock, levels all distinctions of rank as impartially as the grave. Again and again I loitered at the heels of a couple of resplendent beings, only to overhear, when I expected the level voice of culture, the staccato "Sez he," "Sez I," that is the mark of the white servant girl all the world over.

This was depressing because, in spite of all that goes to the contrary, fine feathers ought to make fine birds. There was wealth—unlimited wealth—in the streets, but not an accent that would not have been dear at fifty cents. Wherefore, revolving in my mind that these folk were barbarians, I was presently enlightened and made aware that they also were the heirs of all the ages, and civilised after all.

McTeague

On weekdays the street was very lively. It woke to its work about seven o'clock, at the time when the newsboys made their appearance together with the day laborers. The laborers went trudging past in a straggling file—plumbers' apprentices, their pockets stuffed with sections of lead pipe, tweezers, and pliers; carpenters, carrying nothing but their little pasteboard lunch baskets painted to imitate leather; gangs of street workers, their overalls soiled with yellow clay, their picks and long-handled shovels over their shoulders; plasterers, spotted with lime from head to foot. This little army of workers, tramping steadily in one direction, met and mingled with other toilers of a different description—conductors and swing men of the cable company going on duty; heavy-eyed night clerks from the drugstores on their way home to sleep; roundsmen returning to the precinct police station to make their night report; and Chinese market gardeners teetering past under their heavy baskets. The cable cars began to fill up; all along the street could be seen the shopkeepers taking down their shutters.

Between seven and eight the street breakfasted. Now and then a waiter from one of the cheap restaurants crossed from one sidewalk to the other, balancing on one palm a tray covered with a napkin. Everywhere was the smell of coffee and of frying steaks. A little later, following in the path of the day laborers, came the clerks and shopgirls, dressed with a certain cheap smartness, always in a hurry, glancing apprehensively at the powerhouse clock. Their employers followed an hour or so later—on the cable cars for the most part—whiskered gentlemen with huge stomachs, reading the morning papers with great gravity; bank cashiers and insurance clerks with flowers in their buttonholes.

At the same time the school children invaded the street, filling the air with a clamor of shrill voices, stopping at the stationers' shops or idling a moment in the doorways of the candy stores. For over half an hour they held possession of the sidewalks, then suddenly disappeared, leaving behind one or two stragglers who hurried along with great strides of their little thin legs, very anxious and preoccupied.

Toward eleven o'clock the ladies from the great avenue a block above Polk Street made their appearance, promenading the sidewalks leisurely, deliberately. They were at their morning's marketing. They were handsome women, beautifully dressed. They knew by name their butchers and grocers and vegetable men. From his window McTeague saw them in front of the stalls, gloved and veiled and daintily shod, the subservient provision men at their elbows, scribbling hastily in the order books. They all seemed to know one another, these grand ladies from the fashionable avenue. Meetings took place here and there; a conversation was begun; others arrived; groups were formed; little impromptu receptions were held before the chopping blocks of butchers' stalls or on the sidewalk around boxes of berries and fruit.

From noon to evening the population of the street was of a mixed character. The street was busiest at that time; a vast and prolonged murmur arose—the mingled shuffling of feet, the rattle of wheels, the heavy trundling of cable cars. At four o'clock the school children once more swarmed the sidewalks, again disappearing with surprising suddenness. At six the great homeward march commenced; the cars were crowded, the laborers thronged the sidewalks, the newsboys chanted the evening papers. Then all at once the street fell quiet; hardly a soul was in sight; the sidewalks were deserted. It was supper hour. Evening began; and one by one a multitude of lights, from the demoniac glare of the druggists' windows to the dazzling blue-whiteness of the electric globes, grew thick from street corner to street corner. Once more the street was crowded. Now there was no thought but for amusement. The cable cars were loaded with theatergoers—men in high hats and young girls in furred opera cloaks. On the sidewalks were groups and couples—the plumbers' apprentices, the girls of the ribbon counters, the little families that lived on the second stories over their shops, the dressmakers, the small doctors, the harness makers—all the various inhabitants of the street were abroad, strolling idly from shop window to shop window, taking the air after the day's work. Groups of girls collected on the corners, talking and laughing very loud, making remarks upon the young men that passed them. The tamale men appeared. A band of Salvationists began to sing before a saloon.

Then, little by little, Polk Street dropped back to solitude. Eleven o'clock struck from the powerhouse clock. Lights were extinguished. At one o'clock the cable stopped, leaving an abrupt silence in the air. All at once it seemed very still. The only noises were the occasional footfalls of a policeman and the persistent calling of ducks and geese in the closed market. The street was asleep.

Day after day, McTeague saw the same panorama unroll itself. The bay window of his Dental Parlors was for him a point of vantage from which he watched the world go past.

Jack Kerouac

The Railroad Earth

There was a little alley in San Francisco back of the Southern Pacific station at Third and Townsend in redbrick of drowsy lazy afternoons with everybody at work in offices in the air you feel the impending rush of their commuter frenzy as soon they'll be charging en masse from Market and Sansome buildings on foot and in buses and all well-dressed thru workingman Frisco of Walkup?? truck drivers and even the poor grime-bemarked Third Street of lost bums even Negroes so hopeless and long left East and meanings of responsibility and *try* that now all they do is stand there spitting in the broken glass sometimes fifty in one afternoon against one wall at Third and Howard and here's all these Millbrae and San Carlos neat-necktied producers and commuters of America and Steel civilization rushing by with San Francisco *Chronicles* and green *Call-Bulletins* not even enough time to be disdainful, they've got to catch 130, 132, 134, 136 all the way up to 146 till the time of evening supper in homes of the railroad earth when high in the sky the magic stars ride above the following hotshot freight trains.—It's all in California, it's all a sea, I swim out of it in afternoons of sun hot meditation in my jeans with head on handkerchief on brakeman's lantern or (if not working) on books, I look up at blue sky of perfect lostpurity and feel the warp of wood of old America beneath me and have insane conversations with Negroes in several-story windows above and everything is pouring in, the switching moves of boxcars in that little alley which is so much like the alleys of Lowell and I hear far off in the sense of coming night that engine calling our mountains.

But it was that beautiful cut of clouds I could always see above the little S.P. alley, puffs floating by from Oakland or the Gate of Marin to the north or San Jose south, the clarity of Cal to break your heart. It was the fantastic drowse and drum hum of lum mum afternoon nathin' to do, ole Frisco with end of land sadness—the people—the alley full of trucks and cars of businesses nearabouts and nobody knew or far from cared who I was all my life three thousand five hundred miles from birth-O opened up and at last belonged to me in Great America.

Now it's night in Third Street the keen little neons and also yellow bulb-lights of impossible-to-believe flops with dark ruined shadows moving back of torn yellow shades like a degenerate China with no money—the cats in Annie's Alley, the flop comes on, moans, rolls, the street is loaded with darkness. Blue sky above with stars hanging high over old hotel roofs and blowers of hotels moaning out dusts of interior, the grime inside the word in mouths falling out tooth by tooth, the reading rooms tick tock bigclock with creak chair and slant boards and old faces looking up over rimless spectacles bought in some West Virginia or Florida or Liverpool England pawnshop long before I was born and across rains they've come to the end of the land sadness end of the world gladness all you San Franciscos will have to fall eventually and burn again. But I'm walking and one night a bum fell into the hole of the construction job where theyre tearing a sewer by day the husky Pacific & Electric youths in torn jeans who work there often I think of going up to some of em like say blond ones with wild hair and torn shirts and say "You oughta apply for the railroad its much easier work you dont stand around the street all day and you get much more pay" but this bum fell in the hole you saw his foot stick out, a British MG also driven by some eccentric once backed into the hole and as I came home from a long Saturday afternoon local to Hollister out of San Jose miles away across verdurous fields of prune and juice joy here's this British MG backed and legs up wheels up into a pit and bums and cops standing around right outside the coffee shop—it was the way they fenced it but he never had the nerve to do it due to the fact that he had no money and nowhere to go and O his father was dead and O his mother was dead and O his sister was dead and O his whereabout was dead was dead.—But and then at that time also I lay in my room on long Saturday afternoons listening to Jumpin' George with my fifth of tokay no tea and just under the sheets laughed to hear the crazy music "Mama, he treats your daughter mean," Mama, Papa, and dont you come in here I'll kill you etc.

getting high by myself in room glooms and all wondrous knowing about the Negro the essential American out there always finding his solace his meaning in the fellaheen street and not in abstract morality and even when he has a church you see the pastor out front bowing to the ladies on the make you hear his great vibrant voice on the sunny Sunday afternoon sidewalk full of sexual vibratos saying "Why yes Mam but de gospel do say that man was born of woman's womb—" and no and so by that time I come crawling out of my warmsack and hit the street when I see the railroad ain't gonna call me till 5 AM Sunday morn probably for a local out of Bayshore in fact always for a local out of Bayshore and I go to the wailbar of all the wildbars in the world the one and only Third-and-Howard and there I go in and drink with the madmen and if I get drunk I git.

The whore who come up to me in there the night I was there with Al Buckle and said to me "You wanta play with me tonight Jim, and?" and I didnt think I had enough money and later told this to Charley Low and he laughed and said "How do you know she wanted money always take the chance that she might be out just for love or just out for love you know what I mean man dont be a sucker." She was a goodlooking doll and said "How would you like to oolyakoo with me mon?" and I stood there like a jerk and in fact bought drink got drink drunk that night and in the 299 Club I was hit by the proprietor the band breaking up the fight before I had a chance to decide to hit him back which I didnt do and out on the street I tried to rush back in but they had locked the door and were looking at me thru the forbidden glass in the door with faces like undersea—I should have played with her shurrouruuruuruuruuruuruurkdiei.

Maxine Hong Kingston

Twisters and Shouters

In the Tenderloin, depressed and unemployed, the jobless Wittman Ah Sing felt a kind of bad freedom. Agoraphobic on Market Street, ha ha. There was nowhere he had to be, and nobody waiting to hear what happened to him today. Fired. Aware of Emptiness now. Ha ha. A storm will blow from the ocean or down from the mountains, and knock the set of the City down. If you dart quick enough behind the stores, you'll see that they are stage flats propped up. On the other side of them is ocean forever, and the great Valley between the Coast Range and the Sierras. Is that snow on Mount Shasta?

And what for had they set up Market Street? To light up the dark jut of land into the dark sea. To bisect the City diagonally with a swath of lights. We are visible. See us? We're here. Here we are.

What else this street is for is to give suggestions as to what to do with oneself. What to do. What to buy. How to make a living. What to eat. Unappetizing. The street was full of schemes: FIRE SALE. LOANS. OLD GOLD. GUNS NEW AND USED. BOUGHT AND SOLD. GOING OUT OF BUSINESS. OUR PAIN YOUR GAIN. Food. Fast food joints. Buy raw, sell cooked. If he got ahold of food, he'd just eat it, not sell it. But we're supposed to sell that food in order to buy, cook, and eat different foods. Eat indirect. If you're the more imaginative type, go to the mud flats, collect driftwood, build yourself a cart or a stand, sell umbrellas on rainy and foggy days, sell flowers, sell fast portable hot dogs, tacos, caramel corn, ice-cream sandwiches, hamburgers. Daedalate the lineup from cow to mouth, and fill up your life. If a human being did not have to eat every day, three times a day, ninety per cent of life would be solved.

Clothes are no problem; there are now and then neckties hanging on bushes, and, quite often, a coat on a fence, a watch and shoes at the beach.

Musicians have a hard time of it. Sax players and guitarists and a bass player have left their instruments in pawn shops; they're away perhaps forever, trying to make money, and to eat. A lot of hocked jewelry sits in the windows overnight; the real diamonds, they keep in the twirlinglock safe. These cellos and jewels belonged to people who for a while appreciated more than food. The nature of human beings is also that they buy TVs, coffee tables, nightstands, sofas, daddy armchairs for dressing the set of their life dramas.

Market Street is not an avenue or a boulevard that sweeps through arches of triumph. Tangles of cables on the ground and in the air, open manholes, construction for years. Buses and cars trying to get around one another, not falling into trenches, and not catching tires in or sliding on tracks, lanes taken up by double and triple parking. Pedestrians stranded on traffic islands. How am I to be a *boulevardier* on Market Street? I am not a *boulevardier*; I am a bum-how, I am a fleaman.

Now what? Where does a fleaman go for the rest of the evening, the rest of his adult life? The sets haven't started at the Black Hawk, but no more spending extravagant money on music. Music should be overflowing everywhere. It's time to find out how much free music there is. And no hanging out at the Albatross anymore, taken over by scary spades. To feel the green earth underfoot, he could walk on the green Marina, look at the moon over the sea, and perhaps a second moon in the sea. Keep track of moon phases; are you going through changes in sync with werewolves? But something about that nightlight on the grass that looked sick, like the Green Eye Hospital. *I saw: Hospitals*. No walk in the Palace of the Legion of Honor either, not to be by himself in that huge dark; better to have a companion, and impress her at high noon, Wittman Ah Sing as Hercules chained to the columns and pulling them down, while shouting Shakespeare. If he went to Playland-at-the-Beach, he would get freaked out by the Laughing Lady. Haaw. Haaaw. Haaaaw. He had yet to walk across the Golden Gate at night, but did not just then feel like being suspended in the open cold above the Bay; the breath of the cars would not be warm enough. Continue, then, along Market.

No *boulevardiers* here. Who's here? Who are my familiars? Here I am among my familiars, yeah, like we're Kerouac's people, tripping along the street.

> Soldiers, sailors,
> the panhandlers and drifters,
> (no) zoot suiters, the hoodlums,
> the young men who washed dishes in cafeterias
> > from coast to coast,
> the hitchhikers, the hustlers, the drunks,
> the battered lonely young Negroes,
> the twinkling little Chinese,
> the dark Puerto Ricans (and braceros and pachucos)
> and the varieties of dungareed Young Americans
> > in leather jackets
> > who were seamen and mechanics and garagemen
> > > everywhere . . . .
> The same girls who walked in rhythmic pairs,
> the occasional whore in purple pumps and red raincoat
> > whose passage down these sidewalks was always
> > so sensational,
> the sudden garish sight of some incredible homosexual
> > flouncing by with an effeminate shriek of
> > > general greeting to everyone, anyone:
> > > "I'm just *so* knocked out and you *all* know it,
> > > you *mad* things!"
> > > —and vanishing in a flaunt of hips. . . .

Well, no such red and purple whore or resplendent homosexual. Might as well expect a taxi door to open and out step a geisha in autumn kimono, her face painted white with tippy red lips and smudge-moth eyebrows, white *tabi* feet winking her out of sight on an assignation in the floating demimonde.

Shit. The "twinkling little Chinese" must be none other than himself. "Twinkling"?! "Little"?! Shit. Bumkicked again. If King Kerouac, King of the Beats, were walking here tonight, he'd see Wittman and think, "Twinkling little Chinese." Refute "little." Gainsay "twinkling." A man does not twinkle. A man with balls is not little. As a matter of fact, Kerouac didn't get "Chinese" right either. Big football player white all-American jock Kerouac. Jock Kerouac. I call into question your naming of me. I trust your sight no more. You tell people by their jobs. And by their nation. And the wrong nation at that. If Ah Sing were to run into Kerouac—grab him by the lapels of his lumberjack shirt.

Pull him up on his toes. Listen here, you twinkling little Canuck. What do you know, Kerouac? What do you know? You don't know shit. I'm the American here. I'm the American walking here. Fuck Kerouac and his American road anyway. *Et tu*, Kerouac. Aiya, even you. Just for that, I showed you, I grew to six feet. May still be growing.

Bay Blues

Every night, at the end of America
We taste our wine, looking at the Pacific.
How sad it is, the end of America!

LOUIS SIMPSON, Lines Written
Near San Francisco

Baghdad-by-the-Bay

By the dawn's early light Coit Tower standing starkly silhouetted against the first faint flush in the east . . . A sun-and-windswept corner on Montgomery Street, where you can look west and see a wall of thick, dirty fog rising geniilike from the Pacific, while a finger of whiter, puffier stuff feels its way into the Bay, twisting this way and that till it conforms to every contour, snugly and coldly . . . And the poor man's perfume of Skid Road—a melancholy mixture of frying grease, stale beer, and harsh deodorants that clings to your clothes and your thoughts for hours.

The smug majesty of the City Hall's famed dome, higher (and dirtier) than Washington's, and so far above the conniving that goes on beneath it . . . The few surviving little wooden houses of Telegraph Hill, clinging together for mutual protection against concrete newcomers slowly pushing them out on a limbo . . . And Fisherman's Wharf at 7 A.M., with its tiny fleet of tiny ships lined up in neat display, and proud sea gulls strutting past to review them.

The hangers-on outside the Public Library in Civic Center, singing an *a cappella* chorus of futility against the roaring backdrop of a metropolis in motion—Market Street . . . That occasional white ferryboat drifting over from the Oakland mole and dipping respectfully beneath the aloof bridge that doomed so many of its side-wheeling sisters . . . And block after block of flatiron buildings along Columbus Avenue—sharp edges of a city that grew in too many directions at once.

The incongruity of a lonely foghorn calling somewhere in the Bay as you stroll hatless down a sun-swept street—and the grotesque sight of this jumbled city from Twin Peaks, a sardonic, hysterical travesty on the dreams of those who stood there after the Great Fire and planned the Perfect City . . . Long-forgotten cable-car slots wandering disconsolately and alone up steep hills that are now flattened, with a contemptuous snort, by high-powered, twin-engined buses . . . And the Saturday-night symphony audiences arriving breathlessly at the Opera House from streetcars, on foot, in shabby automobiles—a far and enjoyable cry from the Friday-afternoon trade slinking slowly up in limousines that actually look bored.

University of California's Medical Center (where they discovered vitamin E) rearing up like a spectacular movie set against the darkness of Mount Sutro and Parnassus Heights, while in the pre-dawn hush of Golden Gate Park, far below, squirrels sit unafraid in the middle of the silent roads, and ducks waddle importantly along the bridle paths . . . The full magnificence of the Pacific bursting into your consciousness as you swing past the Cliff House . . . And the monumental mechanical madness of the Kearny, Geary, Third, and Market intersection, where traffic, honking the horns of its dilemma, squeezes painfully through a bottleneck with a "Stop" sign for a cork.

The too-bright mask of Chinatown's restaurants and bars, sometimes standing half empty, while upstairs, in the tenementlike apartments, live six Chinese in one room . . . The glittering Golden Horseshoe during opera season, a constant reminder that there are Upper Classes even in a public building paid for by the masses . . . And the eye-bulging sight, from atop the Fifteenth Avenue hill, of the little white new houses marching through the Sunset District toward the Pacific like stucco lemmings that decided, just in time, not to hurl themselves into the sea.

St. Francis Wood, Pacific Heights, and Sea Cliff, where the homes have room to puff out their chests in the satisfaction of success; and the ornate frame buildings just west of Van Ness—before 1906 the mansions of the mighty, today living out their long lives as boardinghouses for those who are also merely existing . . . Those two distinguished neighbors, the Mark Hopkins and the Fairmont, staring blankly at each other across California Street in the silence of 5 A.M. when even the cable slots cease their friendly gibberish . . . And the corner of Jackson and Kearny, a one-worldly blend of China, Italy, and Mexico, where, all within a few steps, you can eat chow mein, top it off with chianti, and then step into a Spanish movie.

The inner excitement of Stockton Tunnel, as the jampacked buses wiggle noisily through, autos somehow squeeze past, and school kids run excitedly along the inside walk; and North Beach, with its 1001 neon-spattered joints alive with the Italian air of garlic and the juke-boxed wail of American folk songs . . . The dismal reaches of lower Market after midnight; the city within a city that is the deep Mission District, and the bittersweet juxtaposition of brusquely modern Aquatic Park against the fortresslike jumble of red brick where Ghirardelli makes his chocolate.

The crowded garages and the empty old buildings above them, the half-filled night clubs and the overfilled apartment houses, the saloons in the skies and the families huddled in basements, the Third Street panhandlers begging for handouts in front of pawnshops filled with treasured trinkets, the great bridges and the rattletrap streetcars, the traffic that keeps moving although it has no place to go, the thousands of newcomers glorying in the sights and sounds of a city they've suddenly decided to love, instead of leave.

The warm magic of a spring day in "the city that knows no seasons" and all seasons—the children frolicking like sea lions on the Beach, the white-faced office workers turning their eager faces to the sun from the flatness of apartment house roofs, the cops shedding their coats and their dignity at every street corner, the whole city shrinking pleasantly together in the rare wonder of it all . . . The new buses on Market Street, snorting along in the ghostly shadows of streetcars that are no longer there—except in the memories of those who remember the madness of the street with the four-track mind, it's quieter now along the Nightmare Alley that used to frighten timid old ladies—but somehow it's no longer Market Street . . . And the white-stucco false fronts of the Western Addition houses which were mere children in the days of the fire-quake—old relics with their faces lifted, feeling young and popular again in this overcrowded era when there's a sweetheart for every hearth.

The old, bent Italians who have spent the best years of their lives shining shoes at North Beach bootblack stands—still able to smile although the Promised Land has given them not gold in the streets, but boots in their faces . . . The silent sun worshipers who crowd the benches on the tiny plateau of Union Square, comfortably parked for an hour—while in the streets all around them anxious automobiles poke their noses into the garage entrances, then draw back angrily at the implacably pleasant signs: "Sorry—Parking Space Full" . . . And wonderful, parklike Dolores Street, which bobs up and down in its own divided way from Market Street—straight into a past that had time and space for grassy parks in the middle of streets, lawns in front of houses, and sidewalks big enough for games of hopscotch under shade trees.

The picturesque firehouse on California Street, occupied by Engine Fifteen and topped off by the most magnificent weather vane in town—so definitely a part of the past that you expect a horse-drawn engine to come pounding out any moment . . . The oppressive atmosphere of Playland-at-the-Beach on a cold, wet day—the barkers standing still and silent in their overcoats, the Fun House an empty cavern of gloom, the merry-go-round playing a tinny prayer for sunshine . . . The lush green lawns of Julius Kahn Playground in the Pacific Heights sector, where the proletariat may romp in the shadow of mansions which stand coldly with their backs turned . . . And the Russ Building at five o'clock—suddenly becoming a Tower of Babble as the secretaries and stenos, so tired just an hour earlier, clatter out on their high heels like children freed from school.

The mad jumble of architecture that distinguishes Russian Hill—huge apartments and tiny back houses, formal gardens and unkempt patches of lawn, empty lots and mysteriously unfinished apartment houses . . . The garlic-flavored signs on the stores and offices along Columbus Avenue, singing their own Italian Street Song for your eyes and reminding you dreamily of faraway places you've never seen . . . Tenth and Mission, a notable Baghdadian intersection, where there is a service station on each of the four corners—plenty of free air, plenty of free water, plenty of free enterprise . . . And the Nob Hill gentlemen who walk their dogs in Huntington Park on many a midnight—their pajama bottoms peeking out from beneath their overcoats, their manner still as majestic as a floorwalker's.

The "Little Ghetto" of the Fillmore-McAllister area, rubbing narrow shoulders with "Little Osaka" and "Little Harlem"—a few thought-provoking blocks majoring in minorities . . . The massed neon signs along lower O'Farrell Street, their raucous red heightened by the driving rain, their reflections casting a weird upward glow on every strange passing face . . . The little bookshop in Old St. Mary's, always with a half-dozen volumes ranged in its small windows quite conservatively—so that you could never accuse it of advertising . . . And McDonald's fantastic secondhand bookstore on Mission, a cavernous treasure trove for the bargaining literati, stacked from floor to ceiling with everything from *True Detective Tales* to *Das Kapital*—with Mr. McDonald himself, a character straight from Dickens, presiding urbanely over his cut-rate classics.

The lovely homes ranged along the bluffs of Sea Cliff, where the residents may gaze at the Golden Gate Bridge from the ocean side: an exclusive view for the exclusive few . . . The unbathed Skid Rowgues who line up for a sunbath in front of the Salvation Army on Howard Street—men with darkness in their hearts trying to get color in their cheeks . . . The never-changing downstairs lounge at the Mark, where the Same Old Faces sit in the Same Old Places and talk the talk of people with nothing to talk about except each other; the Social Register—ringing up a "No Sale". . . And the shiny black limousines lined up for rent on Geary Street near Powell—the trappings of millionaires, available for a few dollars to those who need a King-for-a-Day Dream.

The scores of tiny coffeeshops in the theatrical hotel sector, serving breakfast in the afternoon to pancaked girls who go to work with the sunset and to bed with the sunrise—leading upside-down lives in a world which is hardly right-side up . . . The tiny restaurant that nestles on California Street between the great buildings of the financial district—and is known as "Mom's Home Cooking". . . That fantastic old theatre 'way out on Mission, which was built solely to put a competitor out of business; when that was accomplished, it closed . . . And the clusters of spotlights which bathe the Shell Building in gold, creating a forever amber landmark on the skyline.

The psychopathic ladies of the night who patrol streets like Larkin and Mission in the endless hours before dawn—speaking to passing men in a dead voice that invites no answer . . . The deadpanned old men sitting silently by the hour in the pool halls of Market Street and North Beach, watching others enjoy themselves from behind Life's eightball . . . the row after row of tiny, all-alike hotels along Turk, Eddy, and Ellis streets—as monotonous, as hard to identify as the men who inhabit them . . . And lower Mason Street at three in the morning—a hurly-burlycue of boisterous soldiers and sailors, double-parked cabs, dames who've had that one too many, all-night drugstores and hamburgers; just about all that's left of the town they called "Frisco!"

Grant Avenue and Post Street, the crossroads of Baghdad-by-the-Bay, where (if you stand there long enough) you can see everybody in San Francisco . . . The always freshly painted buildings of Alcatraz, glowing so brightly in the afternoon sun that for a second you forget it's inhabited by men who are deserted together on an island . . . That institution called the Bay City Grill, where the old-time waiters still follow the ancient habit, at times, of totaling your check for you right on the tablecloth . . . And the shabby gospel singers, shouting out their hearts and the glory of God at Third and Howard—while their audience lounges around on fireplugs and against telephone poles, shutting their ears and listening only with their half-closed eyes.

The frank, open window of Telegraph Hill's miniature castles, whose occupants gape at the gapers every bit as blandly as the gapers gape at them . . . The "Portals of the Past" service station on the crest of Nob Hill, a stone's throw from the Pacific-Union Club—whose front door is also a portal of the past . . .

The death of a dream in cluttered-up-run-down Sutro Heights—once the pride of a millionaire, now a sore sight for eyes that remember its beauties and turn away from its decay of today . . . And the huge neon star that revolves slowly and majestically atop the Sir Francis Drake to advertise a saloon in the sky—easily outshining the small electric cross that marks a church in the dark valley below.

Tourists standing smellbound at Fisherman's Wharf, staring in disbelief at the huge pots of boiling water and asking the question they always ask: "You mean you *actually* throw them in *alive*?"—as the attendant, too bored to answer, nods curtly and reaches for the sacrificial crab . . . The wonderful contrast of that neat little chicken ranch under the massive approach to the Golden Gate Bridge at Fort Point—the chickens cluck-clucking around as though well satisfied that while they might not be able to build such a miracle as the span overhead, neither can a man lay an egg . . . And out-of-townies staring through open mouths at the ring of lobsters on display in the windows of Bernstein's Fish Grotto on Powell Street—tourist-trapped by San Francisco's oldest shell game.

Chinatown's fine ladies and merchants, heading up Grant Avenue around eleven o'clock each morning for the little places that serve a tiffin of tea and steamed buns—an old Spanish custom among the Chinese . . . The shadowy waiting station of the long-dead Powell Street Railroad Company at Fulton Street and Seventh Avenue—a sentimemento of the days when the cable cars ran out to the Park instead of into the red . . . The long-ago-and-faraway atmosphere at Robert's-at-the-Beach on a Sunday night, filled with oldsters who become slightly nostalcoholic and youngsters who aren't yet aware that they're filling up with memories for future use . . . And Kearny Street in the Hall of Justice Region, one part of the rundown-down-town sector that preserves some of the rough, tough color of an earlier San Francisco—as unpretty as it's unphony.

The treat of treating your eyes to true magic—at sundown, on the terrace behind the Cliff House, with the endless Beach sprawled out on your left, the Gold Gate yawning with dignity at your right, and Seal Rocks in front of you, thrill-houetted sharply against a sun sinking with amazing swiftness into the great ocean . . . Baghdad-by-the-Bay!

Kenneth Rexroth

San Francisco Letter

There has been so much publicity recently about the San Francisco Renaissance and the New Generation of Revolt and Our Underground Literature and Cultural Disaffiliation that I for one am getting a little sick of writing about it, and the writers who are the objects of all the uproar run the serious danger of falling over, "dizzy with success," in the immortal words of Comrade Koba. Certainly there is nothing underground about it anymore. For ten years after the Second World War there was a convergence of interest—the Business Community, military imperialism, political reaction, the hysterical, tear and mud drenched guilt of the ex-Stalinist, ex-Trotskyite American intellectuals, the highly organized academic and literary employment agency of the Neo-antireconstructionists—what might be called the meliorists of the White Citizens' League, who were out to augment the notorious budgetary deficiency of the barbarously miseducated Southron male schoolmarm by opening up jobs "up North." This ministry of all the talents formed a dense crust of custom over American cultural life—more of an ice pack. Ultimately the living water underneath just got so damn hot the ice pack has begun to melt, rot, break up, and drift away into Arctic oblivion. This is all there is to it. For ten years or more, seen from above, all that could be discerned was a kind of scum. By very definition, scum, ice packs, crusts, are surface phenomena. It is what is underneath that counts. The living substance has always been there—it has just been hard to see—from above.

It is easy to understand why all this has centered in San Francisco. It is a long way from Astor Place or Kenyon College. It is one of the easiest cities in the world to live in. It is the easiest in America. Its culture is genuinely (not fake like New Orleans—white New Orleans, an ugly Southern city with a bit of the Latin past subsidized by the rubberneck buses) Mediterranean—laissez faire and *dolce far niente*. I for one can say flatly that if I couldn't live here I would leave the United States for someplace like Aix en Provence—so fast! I always feel like I ought to get a passport every time I cross the Bay to Oakland or Berkeley. I get nervous walking down the streets of Seattle with all those ghosts of dead Wobblies weeping in the shadows and all those awful squares peering down my neck. In New York, after one week of living on cocktails in taxicabs, I have to go to a doctor. The doctor always says—get out of New York before it kills you. Hence the Renaissance. I wrote a sociological job about it last winter in the *Nation*, you can read all about it there or in my forthcoming collected essays. But—like all squares—if you don't know already you won't know any more than you did before.

Most of the stuff written about San Francisco literary life has been pretty general, individuals have figured only as items in long and hasty lists. I want to talk at a little more length about a few specific writers and try to show how this disaffiliation applies to them, functions in their work.

In the first place. No literature of the past two hundred years is of the slightest importance unless it *is* "disaffiliated." Only our modern industrial and commercial civilization has produced an elite which has consistently rejected all the reigning values of the society. There were no Baudelaires in Babylon. It is not that we have lost sight of them in time. The nearest thing in Rome was Catullus, and it is apparent, reading him, that there stood behind him no anonymous and forgotten body of bohemians. He was a consort of the rich, of generals and senators, Caesar and Mamurra, and the girl he writes about as though she was, in our terms, an art-struck tart from the Black Cat, was, in fact, a notorious multimillionairess, "the most depraved daughter of the Clodian line." Tu Fu censured the Emperor, but he wanted to be recognized for it—he wanted to be a Censor. So the Taoism and Buddhism of Far Eastern culture function as a keel and ballast to the ship of State. The special ideology of the only artists and writers since the French Revolution who deserve to be taken seriously is a destructive, revolutionary force. They would blow up "their" ship of State—destroy it utterly. This has nothing to do with political revolutionarism, which in our era has been the mortal enemy of all art whatever. When the Bolsheviks, for a brief period, managed to persuade the culture bearers, demoralized by the world economic crisis and rising tide of political terrorism, that the political revolutionary and the artist, the poet, the moral *vates* were allies, Western European culture came within an ace of being destroyed altogether and finally, Capitalism cannot produce from within itself, from any of its "classes," bourgeois, petit bourgeois, or proletariat, any system of values which is not in essence of itself. The converse is a Marxist delusion. This is why "Marxist aestheticians" have gone to such lengths to "prove" that the artist, the writer, the technical and professional intelligentsia, are *not* declassés in modern society, but members of the petite bourgeoisie, and must "come over," in the words of Engels's old chestnut, "to the proletariat," that is, become the prostitutes of their brand of State Capitalism. Nothing could be more false. Artist, poet, physicist, astronomer, dancer, musician, mathematician are captives stolen from an older time, a different kind of society, in which, ultimately, *they* were the creators of all primary values. They are exactly like the astronomers and philosophers the Mongols took off from Samarkand to Karakorum. They belong to the *ancien régime*—all *anciens régimes* as against the nineteenth and twentieth centuries. And so they could only vomit in the faces of the despots who offered them places in the ministries of all the talents, or at least they were nauseated in proportion to their integrity. The same principles apply today as did in the days of Lamartine. Caught in the gears of their own evil machinery, the bosses may scream for an Einstein, a Bohr, even an Oppenheimer; when Normalcy comes back, they kick them out and put tellers in their place. The more fools the Einsteins for having allowed themselves to be used—as they always discover, alas, too late.

You may not think all this has anything to do with the subject, but it is the whole point. Poets come to San Francisco for the same reason so many Hungarians have been going to Austria recently. They write the sort of thing they do for the same reason that Hölderlin or Blake or Baudelaire or Rimbaud or Mallarmé wrote it. The world of poet-professors, Southern Colonels and ex-Left Social fascists from which they have escaped has no more to do with literature than do the leading authors of the court of Napoleon III whose names can be found in the endless pages of the *Causeries du lundi*. The *Vaticide Review* is simply the *Saturday Evening Post* of the excessively miseducated, and its kept poets are the Zane Greys, Clarence Budington Kellands and J. P. Marquands of Brooks Brothers Boys who got an overdose of T. S. Eliot at some Ivy League fog factory. It is just that simple.

Ralph J. Gleason

San Francisco Jazz Scene

San Francisco has always been a good-time town. For periods it has been a wide-open town. And no matter how tight they close the lid and no matter the 2 A.M. closing mandatory in California, it is still a pretty wide-open town.

A high-priced call girl, flush from the Republican convention and an automobile dealers conclave and happily looking forward to the influx of 20,000 doctors, 8,000 furniture dealers and divers other convention delegates, put it simply. "San Francisco is the town where everyone comes to ball, baby," she said.

This spirit of abandon goes hand in hand with a liking for jazz, because jazz is, no matter how serious you get about it, romantic music by and for romantics. What could be a better place for it to flourish than a town where everybody comes to ball, baby?

Because San Francisco is a small town with the charming lines of a big city, concentrated on the tip of a peninsula in a naturally air-conditioned dreamworld (it never gets *too* hot, nor *too* cold), there is a perpetual springtime air about searching for jazz. The fog is friendly; the clubs—dirty, dingy, crowded, smoky, and badly run like jazz clubs everywhere—somehow seem warmer. The audiences—Nob Hill slummers, bearded bohemians, crew-cut University of California sophomores and the casual tourist, gaping at the "big-name" jazz stars—are friendly. They want to tell you why they like the city, why they like its music and what Stan Getz said to them last time they heard him and do you remember the time Duke played the Fillmore Street ballroom and Al Hibbler sang "Trees"?

The San Francisco native is not suspicious. Here his jazz excursions seem safer, though still a glimpse of a different world, possibly because he can get back to his flat in the avenues, his Berkeley home, his Palo Alto patio, or his Sausalito barge, in half an hour and let the baby sitter go home.

It's an easy audience. The color line, though strictly drawn in prewar San Francisco (pre-World War II, that is) and still occasionally drawn today, is quite relaxed for a city so close to Mason & Dixon's line—it runs just south of here. The large Negro population has mixed for years with no tightening of lips or stiffness of necks at the jazz clubs.

These are some of the reasons why San Francisco has been for years and still is one of the best jazz towns in the country. Back before World War II, San Francisco radio boasted jazz programs where Ma Rainey records were played and Anson Weeks's band at the Palace Hotel had Ivie Anderson as vocalist. Paul Whiteman got his real start here, and the first explorers from New Orleans, Jelly Roll Morton, King Oliver, Bunk Johnson, Kid Ory and Mutt Carey, impregnated the area with a feeling for real jazz that was never this strong in any city outside New Orleans and Chicago.

One of the first jazz clubs (an organization, not a nightclub) began in San Francisco in the late thirties and begat the Lu Watters band whose splinter groups, led by Bob Scobey and Turk Murphy, today are the kings of revivalist jazz. One of the first modern jazz radio programs—Jimmy Lyons's KNBC show at the end of the forties and lasting into the fifties (back on the air now, incidentally, at the same spot)—paved the way for the cool-sounding Stan Getz and the swinging Gerry Mulligan style. Lyons's show started Dave Brubeck on his rise and was the genesis of a score of other jazz programs throughout the area. The *San Francisco Chronicle*, as far back as the thirties, did frequent interviews with jazz performers and since 1950 has offered thrice weekly coverage of recorded and in-person jazz on the same editorial basis as its coverage of classical music. For a decade Bay Area universities and colleges have offered jazz courses, sponsored jazz workshops and graduated a generation of jazz fans. It is no coincidence that Anson Weeks is still a bandleader here nor that his son, Jack, is a modern bassist with his own group. Succeeding generations of Northern Californians have supported them both. Families whose sixty-year-old senior citizens went dancing to Anson at the St. Francis or the Mark, and whose forty-year-old second generation drank beer to Lu Watters's Yerba Buena Jazz Band at the Dawn Club, have twenty-year-olds today who attend Sunday afternoon sessions at the Black Hawk or drop in to hear Jack Weeks at Fack's II.

Digging jazz today in San Francisco can be a capsule history of the music if you want it that way; or it can be all in one style. Down on the waterfront there are two jazz clubs catering to traditional fans and exploiting all the atmosphere of a dockside saloon it is possible to concentrate in one spot, including sawdust floor and old three-sheets. The Tin Angel, with a circular fireplace and a stage built by Turk Murphy, is home to George Lewis, Murphy, Kid Ory, and now and then Bob Scobey with the diehard traditional jazz fan rubbing shoulders with the sack-suited Nob Hiller down for a night on the town and bitterly resenting him. Across the street (actually the Embarcadero with a railroad switch line and the silhouettes of Matson liners as a backdrop) is Pier 23, a sailors' bar, where Burt Bales, a fine traditional pianist and one of the few dedicated jazzmen of that style left, plays as he pleases. The Sail 'N is a few blocks away and a host of other beer-and-wine or beer-only store fronts, such as the Hug-a-Mug, the Honey Bucket, and Burp Hollow, offer varying brands of Dixieland ranging from faithful imitations of Lu Watters (and if there is a San Francisco style in traditional jazz it is Watters's style with touches of Turk Murphy) to fraternity house Dixieland sans striped coats and straw hats. (San Francisco jazzmen, traditionalist style, are more apt to be in shirt sleeves or Brooks Brothers suits than uniforms.) In the middle of the downtown area (the business district and the hotel district is "downtown") the Hangover has been a West Coast Nick's for a decade with a good deal of the ad-agency "it's deductible" atmosphere. In recent years, the music has been the product of various versions of a house band selected by the owner and led, for almost two years now, by Earl Hines with such traditional "names" as Pops Foster, Muggsy Spanier, Joe Sullivan, and Meade Lux Lewis involved from time to time.

Modern jazz in San Francisco centers in and around the Black Hawk, a one-story, drab-looking club (once called the Stork Club, it lost a suit to you know who and changed its name, though the original is still etched in cement under the door mat) in the middle of the Tenderloin. The Hawk deals in modern jazz exclusively with names like Mulligan, Miles Davis, and Shorty Rogers. For several months each year, Dave Brubeck, who got his real start there and still lives in the Bay Area, returns to the Hawk for an extended series of appearances, playing for consecutive weekends, sometimes for three months at a time. Sunday afternoon sessions at the Black Hawk offer blowing time to young modernists. It is always a shock to come in out of the bright sunlight of a California Sunday afternoon to the dustiness of the Black Hawk, which, with the franker light of daytime, shows a frowsiness hidden by night—the mark of a true Tenderloin resident.

The other stronghold of modern jazz is The Cellar, a sort of homemade nightclub in a converted Chinese restaurant. (Several San Francisco clubs have had a history of conversion from Chinese restaurants or clubs.) It is located deep in the North Beach section—the Greenwich Village of San Francisco, close by Telegraph Hill. The Cellar has recently experimented with a series of jazz-and-poetry evenings in which San Francisco poets Kenneth Rexroth and Lawrence Ferlinghetti read their own poems while the jazz groups improvised in the background. The result of this, while far from aesthetically satisfactory to the performers involved, has been astounding in terms of attendance. Turn away crowds were at the first two sessions and brought considerable heat from the local representative of law and order, a squaresville type who hates jazz, hates musicians, poets and bohemians, and seems only to love his own authority.

Oddly enough, the only successful emergence of a big band in the Bay Area in recent years has taken place in Oakland, not San Francisco. Rudy Salvini, a young trumpeter and quondam high school teacher, has had a rehearsal band for some time which, under the wing of Pat Henry, Oakland disc jockey, has made a series of appearances at an Oakland ballroom to a curious young-old crowd. The band has been a workshop for local jazz arrangers and has recorded for San Francisco Jazz Records, one of the two local firms offering recording opportunities to young jazzmen. (The other is the exceptionally successful Fantasy Records, home label of Cal Tjader and Paul Desmond, and original recorder of Dave Brubeck.)

One of the curious aspects of San Francisco jazz is that, although the traditional jazz groups of Lu Watters and Turk Murphy have inspired considerable imitation, the modern jazz group of Dave Brubeck, despite its completely San Francisco personnel and its international reputation, has inspired no imitation at all. In the little hideaways where traditional jazz—second and third line— is played, there is always an overtone of Watters or Murphy and sometimes an outright copy. Obviously these men have made a tremendous impression on the musicians interested in that style.

On the other hand, at the Sunday afternoon sessions, at junior college and college amateur jazz concerts, at sessions near the University of California campus—the spots where the budding modern jazzmen sharpen their axes— no one steps up to the piano in a Brubeckian mood. There are, however, numerous saxophonists in whose playing there is a definite stamp of Paul Desmond, Brubeck's star boarder. But on an even greater number there is the stamp of Sonny Rollins, Charlie Parker, Stan Getz, the Modern Jazz Quartet and other Eastern jazz groups. The pervading influence in San Francisco modern jazz is Eastern, with the exception, if you can count it as such, of Gerry Mulligan.

A lot of jazz experimentation in the Bay Area never is heard in public at all.

Instead, the young musicians gather in apartments, garages (Lu Watters used to play in the Oakland hills), and hotel rooms for rehearsals. The recreation hall in the Musicians Union building is a favorite spot for blowing and there are several YMCA halls where jazz is encouraged. What is sadly needed, though, is some official union encouragement of the sort that is given the musicians in Seattle where the local AFM unit has sponsored a jazz workshop. In the Bay Area the jazz musician is on his own. This may produce a hardy crop of survivors, but it has also resulted in many potentially good jazzmen abandoning music or seeking the shelter of what few steady musical jobs there are. Another disappointing aspect of modern jazz in San Francisco is that it has brought forth no young singer of any stature. While traditional jazz has Turk Murphy and Clancy Hayes to sing its songs, there is a horrible shortage of modern singers.

Despite this, the Bay Area is alive with jazz talent. There is a constant struggle for new ideas and new concepts and a continuing experimentation that suggests more interesting developments in the future. Jazz concerts have always been successful here—the big traveling shows rack up huge grosses. Perhaps in future years more attention will be paid to local artists. In any case, the jazz fan, local or visiting, can find whatever type of jazz makes his pulse beat faster, intrigues his brain or merely causes his feet to tap. It's all here.

Allen Ginsberg

A Supermarket in California

What thoughts I have of you tonight, Walt Whitman, for I walked down the sidestreets under the trees with a headache self-conscious looking at the full moon.

In my hungry fatigue, and shopping for images, I went into the neon fruit supermarket, dreaming of your enumerations!

What peaches and what penumbras! Whole families shopping at night! Aisles full of husbands! Wives in the avocados, babies in the tomatoes!—and you, García Lorca, what were you doing down by the watermelons?

I saw you, Walt Whitman, childless, lonely old grubber, poking among the meats in the refrigerator and eyeing the grocery boys.

I heard you asking questions of each: Who killed the pork chops? What price bananas? Are you my Angel?

I wandered in and out of the brilliant stacks of cans following you, and followed in my imagination by the store detective.

We strode down the open corridors together in our solitary fancy tasting artichokes, possessing every frozen delicacy, and never passing the cashier.

Where are we going, Walt Whitman? The doors close in an hour. Which way does your beard point tonight?

(I touch your book and dream of our odyssey in the supermarket and feel absurd.)

Will we walk all night through solitary streets? The trees add shade to shade, lights out in the houses, we'll both be lonely.

Will we stroll dreaming of the lost America of love past blue automobiles in driveways, home to our silent cottage?

Ah, dear father, graybeard, lonely old courage-teacher, what America did you have when Charon quit poling his ferry and you got out on a smoking bank and stood watching the boat disappear on the black waters of Lethe?

Simone de Beauvoir

Berkeley

Today I had to speak at the University of California in Berkeley. A young writer, who ran a bookshop there, called for me in his car. He edited an avant-garde review influenced by Surrealism and Henry Miller. There is an intellectual regionalism in America; Henry Miller has little importance in New York, but on the West Coast, where he lives, he is taken for a genius. Many of his books are banned, but copies are passed around from hand to hand; passages have even been recorded. The bookshop to which V. took me reminded me a bit of Adrienne Yonnier's; it was quite small, with a tiny picture gallery. Many of the names I read on the shelves were unknown to me; I wanted to inform myself about the new generation of writers, and I asked his opinion; the replies I received were not at all identical with those I got in New York. No one seemed to agree about the older writers either, with the exception of Faulkner and Melville. It is true that in France we also have our coteries, our prejudices, our likes and dislikes, but here indecision symbolizes a certain disorder; writers, with no inkling of their future, turned their backs on their past. Yet nearly everyone agrees that there is a great revival of poetry.

While we were talking, V., himself a poet, gave me books and reviews and a record, a fragment of *Tropic of Cancer*. Books and records also figured in the conversation at the Faculty Club—an austere dining room all in black, with a big family table in the center and, around it, serious old gentlemen. As in France, but even more so, most of the universities are cut off from literary and artistic avant-garde movements. They seem to be as sharply cut off from life. We may certainly not look to the universities for the spark which will stimulate doubt and a sense of responsibility in the young people in their charge. The universities only confirm these young people in their apathy and conformity. I looked at the athletic-looking young people, the smiling young girls in my audience, and I thought that certainly, like the students in Los Angeles, there were no more than one or two who were concerned about the news of the day. They sometimes say that America is the land of youth. I am not so sure. Real youth is that which exerts itself in forging ahead to an adult future, not that which lives confined with accommodating resignation in the limits assigned to it.

Leonard Michaels

In the Fifties

I had a friend who was dragged down a courthouse stairway, in San Francisco, by her hair. She'd wanted to attend the House Un-American hearings. The next morning I crossed the Bay Bridge to join my first protest demonstration. I felt frightened and embarrassed. I was bitter about what had happened to her and the others she'd been with. I expected to see thirty or forty people like me, carrying hysterical placards around the courthouse until the cops bludgeoned us into the pavement. About two thousand people were there. I marched beside a little kid who had a bag of marbles to throw under the hoofs of the horse cops. His mother kept saying, "Not yet, not yet." We marched all day. That was the end of the fifties.

Sixties

Now, the city was beautiful, it was still the most beautiful city in the United States, but like all American cities it was a casualty of the undeclared war. There had been an undisclosed full-scale struggle going on in America for twenty years—it was whether the country would go mad or not.
NORMAN MAILER

———— *Mario Savio* ————

Why It Happened in Berkeley

There are many things that happened at Berkeley which will not be of interest to people elsewhere, and need not be; it is to be hoped that others will have their own problems to contend with, and will have interesting things of their own to do. Others should not have to get their experience second hand. But there are certain things that happened at Berkeley which it would be useful for people in other places to know about, as an aid in understanding themselves, as help to them in preparing revolts of their own.

There were some things which made the Berkeley revolt peculiarly Berkeley's, but other things made it a revolt among white middle-class youth that could happen at any state university. And it is the second set of factors which will probably be of most importance to people outside Berkeley.

Why did it happen in Berkeley? The important question to ask, rather, is: why did it happen in Berkeley *first?*—because there are several universities in the East and Midwest where, since last semester, little home-grown revolts have flared up.

Asking why it happened in Berkeley first is like asking why Negroes, and not Americans generally, are involved in securing access for all, to the good which America could provide for her people. This may seem strange to those who imagine America to be a virtual paradise except for certain groups, notably Negroes, who have been excluded. But this is a distortion. What oppresses the American Negro community is merely an exaggerated, grotesque version of what oppresses the rest of the country—and this is eminently true of the middle class, despite its affluence. In important ways the situation of students at Berkeley is an exaggerated representation of what is wrong with American higher education.

The forces influencing students at Berkeley—not merely those resulting from participation in the university itself, but also those deriving from student involvement in politics—these forces are likewise exaggerations of the forces to which society subjects other university students in other parts of the country. So probably the reason it could happen here first is this: while the same influences are present elsewhere, there is no university (none that I know of, at all events) where these influences are present in as extreme a form as here in Berkeley.

The influences upon students are of three main kinds: those deriving from personal history; "internal" problems resulting directly from being a student; and "external" problems deriving from after-class political activities. The external influences on students result primarily from involvement in the civil-rights movement, both in the Bay Area and in the South. The internal derive primarily from the style of the factorylike mass miseducation of which Clark Kerr is the leading ideologist. There are many impersonal universities in America; there is probably none more impersonal in its treatment of students than the University of California. There are students at many Northern universities deeply involved in the civil-rights movement; but there probably is no university outside the South where the effect of such involvement has been as great as it has been at Berkeley.

One factor which helps explain the importance of civil rights here is the political character of the Bay Area. This is one of the few places left in the United States where a personal history of involvement in radical politics is not a form of social leprosy. And, of course, there are geographical considerations. The Berkeley campus is very close to the urban problems of Oakland and San Francisco, but not right in either city. On campus it is virtually impossible for the thoughtful to banish social problems from active consideration. Many students here find it impossible not to be in some sense _engagé_. The shame of urban America (just south of campus or across the bay) forces itself upon the conscience of the community. At the same time it is possible to think about political questions by retreating from their immediate, physical, constant presence. Thus, at Columbia or CCNY it is difficult to tell where the city ends and the university begins, whereas at Berkeley there is a clearly demarcated university community, with places where students and faculty members can enjoy a certain sense of retreat and apartness. At Berkeley we are both close enough to gross injustice not to forget; and far enough away, and set well enough apart, so as neither to despair nor simply to merge into the common blight. Furthermore, ours is not a commuter school; the students live here at least part of the year. This makes possible a continuing community such as would be impossible at UCLA, for example. This community, with a great deal of internal communication, has been essential to the development of political consciousness. And there is a good deal for the students to communicate to one another. Over ten percent of the student body has taken part *directly* in civil-rights activity, in the South or in the Bay Area. These three thousand, all of whom have at least walked picket lines, are a leaven for the campus. And many more can be said to have participated vicariously: there is great and widespread interest in what those who "go South" have done and experienced. Of course, there is a natural receptivity for politics at Berkeley simply because this is a state-supported university: a good percentage of the student body comes from lower-middle-class or working-class homes; many who can afford to pay more for an education go, for example, to Stanford.

Now for those problems which have their origin within the university: the tale which follows is strictly true only for undergraduates in their first two years; there are some improvements during the second two years; but only graduate students can expect to be treated tolerably well.

It is surprising at first, after taking a semester of undergraduate courses here—except in the natural sciences or mathematics—to realize how little you have learned. It is alarming at the same time to recognize how much busy-work you have done: so many papers hastily thrown together, superficially read by some graduate-student teaching assistant. Even if you want to work carefully, it is difficult to do so in each of five courses, which often have unrealistically long reading lists—courses with little or no logical relationship to one another. Perhaps in the same semester, the student will "take" a superficial survey of all the major (and many minor) principles of biology, *and* a language course a good part of which is spent in a language "laboratory" very poorly integrated into the grammar and reading part of the course, a laboratory which requires its full hour of outside preparation but which benefits the student very little in terms of speaking ability in the foreign language. Perhaps, ironically, the semester's fare will include a sociology course in which you are sure to learn, in inscrutably "scientific" language, just what is so good and only marginally improvable in today's pluralistic, democratic America.

If you are an undergraduate still taking non-major courses, at least one of your subjects will be a "big" lecture in which, with field glasses and some good luck, you should be able, a few times a week, to glimpse that famous profile giving those four- or five-year-old lectures, which have been very conveniently written up for sale by the Fybate Company anyway. The lectures in the flesh will not contain much more than is already in the Fybate notes, and generally no more than will be necessary to do well on the examinations. Naturally, it will be these examinations which determine whether or not you pass the course. Such an education is conceived as something readily quantifiable: 120 units constitute a bachelor's degree. It is rather like the outside world—the "real" world—where values are quantified in terms of the dollar: at the university we use play money, course units. The teacher whom you will have to strain to see while he lectures will be very seldom available for discussion with his students; there is usually an hour set aside, in the course of each week, during which all of the students who want to speak with him will have to arrange to do so. In the face of physical impossibility, there are generally few such brave souls. If more came, it would make little difference; this system is rarely responsive to individual needs. There are too few teachers, and too little time. Indeed, if the professor is one of those really famous scholars of whom the university is understandably proud, then the primary reason there is not enough time for the problems of individual undergraduates is that the bulk of the professor's time (other than the six or eight hours spent in the classroom each week) is devoted to "research" or spent with graduate students. The moral of the piece is: if you want to get an education, you will have to get it yourself. This is true in any case, but it is not usually intended to be true in the sense that getting it yourself means *in spite* of the work at school. There are just too many nonsense hours spent by American students, hours to "do" much as one "does" time in prison.

In the course of one semester, doubtless there will be several opportunities for each unlucky student to come into contact with the administration of the university. This may be to request an exception from some university requirement. However formal the requirement may be, invariably at least once a semester, the student finds he cannot be excepted, not because the requirement is important but simply because it happens to be a *requirement*. Well, that is a problem common to bureaucracies of various kinds, but one wonders if this is the sort of thing that should be regularly encountered at a university. Yet this ordeal is what a large part of American college-age youth have to endure. We should ask not whether such intellectual cacophony and bureaucratic harassment are appropriate at universities—for certainly they are not—but rather, whether these local "plants" in what Clark Kerr calls the "knowledge industry" deserve the name university at all.

This is a somewhat overdrawn picture of life at Berkeley. The students are aware of meaningful activity going on outside the university. For there is some meaningful activity going on in America today—in the civil-rights movement, certainly. At the same time, but much more dimly, each student is aware of how barren of essential meaning and direction is the activity in which he is primarily involved, as a card-carrying student. I write "each student is aware" but I realize that this is to express more hope than fact. In less than a tenth of the students is this "awareness" a "consciousness." This consciousness of the poverty of one's immediate environment is a difficult thing to come by. In most it must remain a dim awareness. It is far easier to become aware of (and angry at) the victimization of others than to perceive one's own victimization. It is far easier to become angry when others are hurt. This is so for a number of reasons. Fighting for others' rights cannot engender nearly so great a guilt as striking rebelliously at one's own immediate environment. Also, it is simply easier to see the injustice done others—it's "out there." Many of us came to college with what we later acknowledge were rather romantic expectations, perhaps mostly unexpressed at first, about what a delight and adventure learning would be. We really did have unanswered questions searching for words, though to say so sounds almost corny. But once at college we quickly lose much of the romantic vision; although, fortunately, some never give in to the disappointment. Discovering that college is really high school grown up and not significantly more challenging, many console themselves with the realization that it is not much more difficult either.

The revolt began in the fall semester of 1964 as an extension of either vicarious or actual involvement in the struggle for civil rights. It was easy to draw upon this reservoir of outrage at the wrongs done to other people; but such action usually masks the venting, by a more acceptable channel, of outrage at the wrongs done to oneself. I am far from propounding a psychoanalytic theory of politics, yet most people whom I have met who are committed to radical political innovation are people who have experienced a good deal of personal pain, who have felt strong frustration in their own lives. This mechanism made possible the *beginning* of one pint-sized revolution on the Berkeley campus. The university set about denying students access to those facilities and rights on campus which had made possible student involvement in the civil-rights movement in the previous few years. Yet very rapidly the concern of the movement shifted from Mississippi to much closer to home; we soon began doing an awful lot of talking and thinking about the limitations of the university, the "Multiversity," the "knowledge industry"—these metaphors became ever more a part of the rhetoric of the movement. Civil rights was central in our fight because of business-community pressure on the university to crack down on campus-launched campaigns into the surrounding community—which had proven all too effective. University spokesmen have acknowledged that the need to respond to such pressures was the only "justification" for the ban on political activity. Nevertheless, the focus of our attention shifted from our deep concern with the victimization of others to outrage at the injustices done to ourselves. These injustices we came to perceive more and more clearly with each new attack upon us by the university bureaucracy as we sought to secure our own rights to political advocacy. The political consciousness of the Berkeley community has been quickened by this fight. The Berkeley students now demand what hopefully the rest of an oppressed white middle class will some day demand: freedom for all Americans, not just for Negroes!

—— *Tom Wolfe* ——

The Cops and Robbers Game

A very carnival! and it wasn't politics, what he said, just a prank, because the political thing, the whole New Left, is all of a sudden like *over* on the hip circuit around San Francisco, even at Berkeley, the very citadel of the Student Revolution and all. Some kid who could always be counted on to demonstrate for the grape workers or even do dangerous things like work for CORE in Mississippi turns up one day—and immediately everybody knows he has become a head. His hair has the long jesuschrist look. He is wearing the costume clothes. But most of all, he now has a very tolerant and therefore withering attitude toward all those who are still struggling in the old activist political ways for civil rights, against Vietnam, against poverty, for the free peoples. He sees them as still trapped in the old "political games," unwittingly supporting the oppressors by playing their kind of game and using their kind of tactics, while he, with the help of psychedelic chemicals, is exploring the infinite regions of human consciousness . . . Paul Hawken here in The Embassy—in 1965 he was an outstanding activist, sweat shirts and blue jeans and toggle coats, went on the March from Selma, worked as a photographer for CORE in Mississippi, risked his life to take pictures of Negro working conditions, and so on. Now he's got on a great Hussar's coat with gold frogging. His hair is all over his forehead and coming around his neck in terrific black Mykonos curls.

Warren Hinckle

A Social History of the Hippies

An elderly school bus, painted like a fluorescent Easter egg in orange, chartreuse, cerise, white, green, blue, and, yes, black, was parked outside the solitary mountain cabin, which made it an easy guess that Ken Kesey, the novelist turned psychedelic Hotspur, was inside. So, of course, was Neal Cassady, the Tristram Shandy of the Beat Generation, prototype hero of Jack Kerouac's *On the Road*, who had sworn off allegiance to Kerouac when the Beat scene became menopausal and had signed up as the driver of Kesey's fun and games bus, which is rumored to run on LSD. Except for these notorious luminaries, the Summit Meeting of the leaders of the new hippie subculture, convened in the lowlands of California's High Sierras during an early spring weekend last month, seemed a little like an Appalachian Mafia gathering without Joe Bananas.

Where was Allen Ginsberg, father goddam to two generations of the underground? In New York, reading his poetry to freshmen. And where was Timothy Leary, self-styled guru to tens or is it hundreds of thousands of turned-on people? Off to some nowhere place like Stockton, to preach the gospel of Lysergic Acid Diethylamide to nice ladies in drip dry dresses.

The absence of the elder statesmen of America's synthetic gypsy movement meant something. It meant that the leaders of the booming psychedelic bohemia in the seminal city of San Francisco were their own men—and strangely serious men, indeed, for hippies. Ginsberg and Leary may be Pied Pipers, but they are largely playing old tunes. The young men who make the new scene accept Ginsberg as a revered observer from the elder generation; Leary they abide as an Elmer Gantry on their side, to be used for proselytizing squares, only.

The mountain symposium had been called for the extraordinary purpose of discussing the political future of the hippies. Hippies are many things, but most prominently the bearded and beaded inhabitants of the Haight-Ashbury, a little psychedelic city-state edging Golden Gate Park. There, in a daily street-fair atmosphere, upwards of fifteen thousand unbonded girls and boys interact in a tribal, love-free, free-swinging, acid-based type of society where, if you are a hippie and you have a dime, you can put it in a parking meter and lie down in the street for an hour's suntan (thirty minutes for a nickel) and most drivers will be careful not to run you over.

Speaking, sometimes all at once, inside the Sierra cabin were many voices of conscience and vision of the Haight-Ashbury—belonging to men who, except for their Raggedy Andy hair, paisley shirts, and pre-mod western Levi jackets, sounded for all the world like Young Republicans.

They talked about reducing governmental controls, the sanctity of the individual, the need for equality among men. They talked, very seriously, about the kind of society they wanted to live in, and the fact that if they wanted an ideal world they would have to go out and make it for themselves, because nobody, least of all the government, was going to do it for them.

The utopian sentiments of these hippies were not to be put down lightly. Hippies have a clear vision of the ideal community—a psychedelic community, to be sure—where everyone is turned on and beautiful and loving and happy and floating free. But it is a vision that, despite the Alice in Wonderland phraseology hippies usually breathlessly employ to describe it, necessarily embodies a radical political philosophy: communal life, drastic restriction of private property, rejection of violence, creativity before consumption, freedom before authority, de-emphasis of government and traditional forms of leadership.

Despite a disturbing tendency to quietism, all hippies *ipso facto* have a political posture—one of unremitting opposition to the Establishment which insists on branding them criminals because they take LSD and marijuana, and hating them, anyway, because they enjoy sleeping nine in a room and three to a bed, seem to have free sex and guiltless minds, and can raise healthy children in dirty clothes.

The hippie choice of weapons is to love the Establishment to death rather than protest it or blow it up (hippies possess a confounding disconcern about traditional political methods or issues). But they are decidedly and forever outside the Consensus on which this society places such a premium, and since the hippie scene is so much the scene of those people under twenty-five that *Time* magazine warns will soon constitute half our population, this is a significant political fact.

This is all very solemn talk about people who like to skip rope and wear bright colors, but after spending some time with these fun and fey individuals you realize that, in a very unexpected way, they are as serious about what they're doing as the John Birch Society or the Junior League. It is not improbable, after a few more mountain seminars by those purposeful young men wearing beads, that the Haight-Ashbury may spawn the first utopian collectivist community since Brook Farm.

That this society finds it so difficult to take such rascally looking types seriously is no doubt the indication of a deep-rooted hang-up. But to comprehend the psychosis of America in the computer age, you have to know what's with the hippies.

Ken Kesey—I
Games People Play, Merry Prankster Division

Let us go, then, on a trip.

You can't miss the Tripmaster: the thick-necked lad in the blue and white striped pants with the red belt and the golden eagle buckle, a watershed of wasted promise in his pale blue eyes, one front tooth capped in patriotic red, white, and blue, his hair downy, flaxen, straddling the incredibly wide divide of his high forehead like two small toupees pasted on sideways. Ken Kesey, Heir Apparent Number One to the grand American tradition of blowing one's artistic talent to do some other thing, was sitting in a surprisingly comfortable chair inside the bus with the psychedelic crust, puffing absentmindedly on a harmonica.

The bus itself was ambulatory at about fifty miles an hour, jogging along a back road in sylvan Marin County, four loudspeakers turned all the way up, broadcasting both inside and outside Carl Orff's *Carmina Burana*, and filled with two dozen people simultaneously smoking marijuana and looking for an open ice-cream store. It was the Thursday night before the Summit Meeting weekend and Kesey, along with some fifteen members of the turned-on yes men and women who call him "Chief" and whom he calls the "Merry Pranksters" in return, was demonstrating a "game" to a delegation of visiting hippie firemen.

Crossing north over the Golden Gate Bridge from San Francisco to Marin County to pay Kesey a state visit were seven members of the Diggers, a radical organization even by Haight-Ashbury standards, which exists to give things away, free. The Diggers started out giving out free food, free clothes, free lodging, and free legal advice, and hope eventually to create a totally free cooperative community. They had come to ask Kesey to get serious and attend the weekend meeting on the state of the nation of the hippies.

The dialogue had hardly begun, however, before Kesey loaded all comers into the bus and pushed off into the dark to search for a nocturnal ice-cream store. The bus, which may be the closest modern man has yet come to aping the self-sufficiency of Captain Nemo's submarine, has its own power supply and is equipped with instruments for a full rock band, microphones, loudspeakers, spotlights, and comfortable seats all around. The Pranksters are presently installing microphones every three feet on the bus walls so everybody can broadcast to everybody else all at once.

At the helm was the Intrepid Traveler, Ken Babbs, who is auxiliary chief of the Merry Pranksters when Kesey is out of town or incommunicado or in jail, all three of which he has recently been. Babbs, who is said to be the model for the heroes of both Kesey novels, *One Flew Over the Cuckoo's Nest* and *Sometimes a Great Notion*, picked up a microphone to address the guests in the rear of the bus, like the driver of a Grayline tour: "We are being followed by a police car. Will someone watch and tell me when he turns on his red light."

The law was not unexpected, of course, because any cop who sees Kesey's bus just about *has* to follow it, would probably end up with some form of professional D.T.s if he didn't. It is part of the game: the cop was now playing on their terms, and Kesey and his Pranksters were delighted. In fact, a discernible wave of disappointment swept across the bus when the cop finally gave up chasing this particular UFO and turned onto another road.

The games he plays are very important to Kesey. In many ways his intellectual rebellion has come full circle; he has long ago rejected the structured nature of society—the foolscap rings of success, conformity, and acceptance "normal" people must regularly jump through. To the liberated intellect, no doubt, these requirements constitute the most sordid type of game. But, once rejecting all the norms of society, the artist is free to create his own structures—and along with any new set of rules, however personal, there is necessarily, the shell to the tortoise, a new set of games. In Kesey's case, at least, the games are usually fun. Running around the outside of an insane society, the healthiest thing you can do is laugh.

It helps to look at this sort of complicated if not confused intellectual proposition in bas-relief, as if you were looking at the simple pictures on Wedgwood china. Stand Successful Author Ken Kesey off against, say, Successful Author Truman Capote. Capote, as long as his game is accepted by the system, is free to be as mad as he can. So he tosses the biggest, most vulgar ball in a long history of vulgar balls, and achieves the perfect idiot synthesis of the upper-middle and lower-royal classes. Kesey, who cares as much about the system as he does about the Eddie Cantor Memorial Forest, invents his own game. He purchases a pre-forties International Harvester school bus, paints it psychedelic, fills it with undistinguished though lovable individuals in varying stages of eccentricity, and drives brazenly down the nation's highways, high on LSD, watching and waiting for the cops to blow their minds.

At the least, Kesey's posture has the advantage of being intellectually consistent with the point of view of his novels. In *One Flew Over the Cuckoo's Nest*, he uses the setting of an insane asylum as a metaphor for what he considers to be the basic insanity, or at least the fundamentally bizarre illogic, of American society. Since the world forces you into a game that is both mad and unfair, you are better off inventing your own game. Then, at least, you have a chance of winning. At least that's what Kesey thinks.

Ken Kesey—II
The Curry Is Very Hot; Merry Pranksters Are Having Pot

There wasn't much doing on late afternoon television, and the Merry Pranksters were a little restless. A few were turning on; one Prankster amused himself squirting his friends with a yellow plastic watergun; another staggered into the living room, exhausted from peddling a bicycle in ever-diminishing circles in the middle of the street. They were all waiting, quite patiently, for dinner, which the Chief was whipping up himself. It was a curry, the recipe of no doubt cabalistic origin. Kesey evidently took his cooking seriously, because he stood guard by the pot for an hour and a half, stirring, concentrating on the little clock on the stove that didn't work.

There you have a slice of domestic life, February, 1967, from the swish Marin County home of attorney Brian Rohan. As might be surmised, Rohan is Kesey's attorney, and the novelist and his *aides de camp* had parked their bus outside for the duration. The duration might last a long time, because Kesey has dropped out of the hippie scene. Some might say that he was pushed, because he fell, very hard, from favor among the hippies last year when he announced that he, Kesey, personally, was going to help reform the psychedelic scene. This sudden social conscience may have had something to do with beating a jail sentence on a compounded marijuana charge, but when Kesey obtained his freedom with instructions from the judge "to preach an anti-LSD warning to teenagers" it was a little too much for the Haight-Ashbury set. Kesey, after all, was the man who had turned on the Hell's Angels.

That was when the novelist was living in La Honda, a small community in the Skyline mountain range overgrown with trees and, after Kesey invited the Hell's Angels to several house parties, overgrown with sheriff's deputies. It was in this Sherwood Forest setting, after he had finished his second novel with LSD as his copilot, that Kesey inaugurated his band of Merry Pranksters (they have an official seal from the State of California incorporating them as "Intrepid Trips, Inc."), painted the school bus in glow sock colors, announced he would write no more ("Rather than write, I will ride buses, study the insides of jails, and see what goes on"), and set up funtime housekeeping on a full-time basis with the Pranksters, his wife and their three small children (one confounding thing about Kesey is the amorphous quality of the personal relationships in his entourage—the several attractive women don't seem, from the outside, to belong to any particular man; children are loved enough, but seem to be held in common).

When the Hell's Angels rumbled by, Kesey welcomed them with LSD. "We're in the same business. You break people's bones, I break people's heads," he told them. The Angels seem to like the whole acid thing, because today they are a fairly constant act in the Haight-Ashbury show, while Kesey has abdicated his role as Scoutmaster to fledgling acid heads and exiled himself across the Bay. This self-imposed Elba came about when Kesey sensed that the hippie community had soured on him. He had committed the one mortal sin in the hippie ethic: *telling* people what to do. "Get into a responsibility bag," he urged some four hundred friends attending a private Halloween party. Kesey hasn't been seen much in the Haight-Ashbury since that night, and though the Diggers did succeed in getting him to attend the weekend discussion, it is doubtful they will succeed in getting the novelist involved in any serious effort to shape the Haight-Ashbury future. At thirty-one, Ken Kesey is a hippie has-been.

Ken Kesey—III
The Acid Tests—From Unitarians to Watts

Kesey is now a self-sufficient but lonely figure—if you can be lonely with dozens of Merry Pranksters running around your house all day. If he ever gets maudlin, which is doubtful, he can look back fondly on his hippie memories, which are definitely in the wow! category, because Ken Kesey did for acid roughly what Johnny Appleseed did for trees, and probably more.

He did it through a unique and short-lived American institution called the Acid Test. A lot of things happened at an Acid Test, but the main thing was that, in the Haight-Ashbury vernacular, everyone in the audience got zonked out of their minds on LSD. LSD in Pepsi. LSD in coffee. LSD in cake. LSD in the community punch. Most people were generally surprised, because they didn't know they were getting any LSD until it was too late. Later, when word got around that this sort of mad thing was happening at Acid Tests, Kesey sometimes didn't give out LSD on purpose, just so people wouldn't know whether they did or did not have LSD. Another game.

The Acid Tests began calmly enough. In the early versions Kesey merely gave a heart-to-heart psychedelic talk and handed LSD around like the Eucharist, which first happened at a Unitarian conference in Big Sur in August of 1965. He repeated this ritual several times, at private gatherings in his home in La Honda, on college campuses, and once at a Vietnam Day Committee rally at Berkeley. Then Kesey added the Grateful Dead, a pioneer San Francisco rock group, to his Acid Tests and, the cherry on the matzos, the light show atmospheric technique of projecting slides and wild colors on the walls during rock dances. This combination he called "trips." Trip is the word for an LSD experience, but in Kesey's lexicon it also meant kicks, which were achieved by rapidly changing the audience's sensory environment what seemed like approximately ten million times during an evening by manipulating bright colored lights, tape recorders, slide projectors, weird sound machines, and whatever else may be found in the electronic sink, while the participants danced under stroboscopic lights to a wild rock band or just played around on the floor.

It was a fulgurous, electronically orgiastic thing (the most advanced Tests had closed circuit television sets on the dance floor so you could see what you were doing), which made psychedelics very "fun" indeed, and the hippies came in droves. Almost every hippie in the Bay Area went to at least one Acid Test, and it is not exceeding the bounds of reasonable speculation to say that Kesey may have turned on at least ten thousand people to LSD during the twenty-four presentations of the Acid Test. (During these Tests the Merry Pranksters painted everything including themselves in fluorescent tones, and bright colors became the permanent in-thing in psychedelic dress.)

Turning so many unsuspecting people on to LSD at once could be dangerous, as the Pranksters discovered on a 1965 psychedelic road show when they staged the ill-fated Watts Acid Test. Many of the leading citizens of Watts came to the show, which was all very fine except that whoever put the LSD in the free punch that was passed around put in too much by a factor of about four. This served to make for a very wild Acid Test, and one or two participants "freaked out" and had a very hard time of it for the next few days.

After the California legislature played Prohibition and outlawed LSD on October 6, 1966, Kesey wound up the Acid Test syndrome with what was billed as a huge "Trips Festival" in San Francisco. People who regularly turn on say the Trips Festival was a bore: it embodied all the Acid Test elements except acid and, happily for the coffers of Intrepid Trips, Inc., attracted a huge crowd of newspapermen, narcotics agents, and other squares, but very few hippies. The Merry Pranksters slyly passed out plain sugar cubes for the benefit of the undercover agents.

Suddenly San Francisco, which for a grown-up city gets excited very easily, was talking about almost nothing but "trips" and LSD. Hippies, like overnight, had become fashionable.

If you are inclined to give thanks for this sort of thing, they go to the bad boy wonder of Psychedelphia, disappearing there over the horizon in his wayward bus.

Stanley Booth

The Killing Ground

It is late. All the little snakes are asleep. The world is black outside the car windows, just the dusty clay road in the headlights. Far from the city, past the last crossroads (where they used to bury suicides in England, with wooden stakes driven through their hearts), we are looking for a strange California hillside where we may see him, may even dance with him in his torn, bloody skins, come and play.

A train overpass opens in the sky before us; as we come out of it there is an unmarked fork in the road. The Crystals are singing "He's a rebel." The driver looks left, right, left again. "He don't know where he's going," Keith says. "Do you—are you sure this is the way?" Mick asks. Turning left, the driver does not answer. The radio is quite loud. "Maybe he didn't hear you." Mick closes his eyes. Certain we are lost, but so tired, with no sleep for the past forty hours, less able each moment to protest, to change direction, we proceed in a black Cadillac limousine into the vastness of space.

"Something up ahead here," the driver says. Parked by the road is a Volkswagen van, a German police dog tied by a rope to the back door handle. The dog barks as we pass. Farther on there are more cars and vans, some with people in them, but most of the people are in the road, walking in small groups, carrying sleeping bags, canvas knapsacks, babies, leading more big ugly dogs. "Let's get out," Keith says. "Don't lose us," Mick tells the driver, who says, "Where are you going?" but we are already gone, the five of us, Ron the Bag Man, Tony the Spade Heavy, the Okefenokee Kid, and of course Mick and Keith, Rolling Stones. The other members of the band are asleep back in San Francisco at the Huntington Hotel, except Brian, who is dead and, some say, never sleeps.

The road descends between rolling dry-grass shoulders, the kind of bare landscape where in 1950s science-fiction movies the teenager and his busty girlfriend, parked in his hot rod, receive unearthly visitors, but it is crowded now with young people, most with long hair, dressed in heavy clothes, blue jeans, army fatigue jackets against the December night air that revives us as we walk. Mick is wearing a long burgundy overcoat, and Keith has on a Nazi leather greatcoat, green with mold, that he will leave behind tomorrow or more accurately today, about sixteen hours from now, in the mad blind panic to get away from the place we are lightly swaggering toward. Mick and Keith are smiling, it is their little joke, to have the power to create this gathering by simply wishing for it aloud and the freedom to walk like anybody else along the busy barren path. There is laughter and low talking within groups, but little cross-conversation, though it seems none of us is a stranger; each wears the signs, the insignia, of the campaigns that have brought us, long before most of us have reached the age of thirty, to this desolate spot on the western slope of the New World.

"Tony, score us a joint," Keith says, and before we have been another twenty steps giant black Tony has dropped back and fallen into stride with a boy who's smoking and hands Tony the joint, saying "Keep it." So we smoke and follow the trail down to a basin where the shoulders stretch into low hills already covered with thousands of people around campfires, some sleeping, some playing guitars, some passing smokes and great red jugs of wine. For a moment it stops us; it has the dreamlike quality of one's deepest wishes, to have all the good people, all one's family, all the lovers, together in some private country of night. It is as familiar as our earliest dreams and yet so grand and final, campfires flickering like distant stars as far as our eyes can see, that it is awesome, and as we start up the hillside to our left, walking on sleeping bags and blankets, trying not to step on anyone's head, Keith is saying it's like Morocco, outside the gates of Marrakech, hear the pipes. . . .

The people are camped right up to a cyclone fence topped with barbed wire, and we are trying to find the gate, while from behind us the Maysles film brothers approach across sleeping bodies with blinding blue-white quartz lamps. Mick yells to turn off the lights, but they pretend to be deaf and keep coming. The kids who have been looking up as we pass, saying Hi, Mick, now begin to join us; there is a caravan of young girls and boys strung out in the spotlights when we reach the gate which is, naturally, locked. Inside we can see the Altamont Speedway clubhouse and some people we know standing outside it. Mick calls, "Could we get in, please?" and one of them comes over, sees who we are, and sets out to find someone who can open the gate. It takes a while, and the boys and girls all want autographs and to go inside with us. Mick tells them we can't get in ourselves yet, and no one has a pen except me, and I have learned not to let go of mine because they get the signatures and go spinning away in a frenzy of bliss and exhilaration, taking my trade with them. So we stand on one foot and then the other, swearing in the cold, and no one comes to let us in, and the gate, which is leaning, rattles when I shake it, and I say we could push it down pretty easy, and Keith says, "The first act of violence."

False Match

The first time I saw Shaw he was in a pose like the discus thrower's but more extreme, and in his hand instead of a discus was a dark green bottle with a burning rag in its mouth. He should have thrown it right away, but he paused a moment, looked around and saw me watching. He smiled. Then the bottle rose into the ice-colored dawn, returned to earth and burst into flame on the windshield of a U.S. Army Plymouth. Fire splashed across the glass and poured in through the windows. A minute later there was an explosion, and flame gushed out both ends of the car. When I glanced back to where the bottle had come from, Shaw was gone.

He had traveled fast and light in those days, involved in politics that were serious, full time and not at all distracted by the electoral process. He was also married, I eventually learned, one of those political couples who never had a roof or a car or a bed of their own, for whom children were unimaginable since there was hardly time or place to conceive, much less bear, nurse and raise. Their life consisted of borrowed rooms, meetings, mimeograph ink, coffee, gasoline, Benzedrine, theory, strategy, criticism, self-criticism and, at the end of the night, Mexican food and beer. There was also a big, faded purple Indian motorcycle that they both drove.

The only time I met Greta she was so fierce and implacable that even Shaw appeared sentimental by comparison. Their life had a function to which all else was subordinated, and a discipline that must have fed secret appetites. Instead of ropes and riding crops, perhaps, they competed to see who would sacrifice what the other could not, a calculus whose limit both must have seen coming, yet which neither chose to avoid. In the end who left whom? Maybe one night neither came back to wherever they were sleeping, and each, finding himself capable of doing without that, too, stayed away for weeks before learning that the other was also gone.

In any event, Greta took the motorcycle. Shaw heard that she had gone to Los Angeles and become involved in a group with PLO connections; later she disappeared. He did not expect to see her again. One day I met him on the street, and he asked if I knew of a place to stay. Jimmy and I had just rented this house and were looking for roommates. Shaw brought over his few things that afternoon.

In the year since, he has done almost nothing. Days he passes on the Avenue drinking coffee with a few former political friends; nights he reads long, dense texts of political and aesthetic theory, the syllabus of a graduate program he dropped out of three years ago. He sleeps very little. He isn't especially interested in women. When people talk about politics, Shaw rarely participates, or he will say something so oblique and impenetrable he seems to be making a joke at his own expense, the arcane syntax presumably an ironic comment on his current extreme passivity.

One evening last April, Shaw picked up Donna in the Café Med. She thought he was picking her up anyway. She'd gotten into a conversation he was having with some other people, Shaw had mentioned his dissertation ("Class Origins of the Modern American State," one-quarter completed, moldering in his closet), and Donna had said she'd like to see it. So he brought her back to the house, showed it to her, and they sat up talking until four in the morning. When she finally said she was sleepy, Shaw put her to bed alone on the sun porch.

She has been there ever since. For a while she kept after him. She was great looking and unembarrassed as only nineteen can be, and Shaw liked that, but he wouldn't sleep with her. Jimmy got jealous (though of whom and what it would be interesting to know), so Donna fucked him once, but that was all. After a few weeks it settled down, Jimmy got his editing job, and the three of us became four. Now every morning Jimmy drives off to work, Donna practices piano (rehearsals or gigs at night), Shaw does whatever it is he does, and I come up here to write. We pool our money and take turns cooking.

Tonight I made hamburgers, and, while we ate, Jimmy Wax read us a letter he had gotten today from his mother:

Dear Jimmy,

I'm not quite sure how to answer you, because although we have our wishes (and there's certainly no need to go over them), we respect your judgment and your right to lead your own life. I only wonder if "intuition" is the thing to trust with a decision like this when one's entire future is at stake.

We know that you love movies, "passionately" as you say, and that you have felt most fulfilled working on them. You ask us to support you in this choice, and we certainly want to. If we hesitate, it is only because it has seemed to take you so long to complete your projects. Unless I'm mistaken, you've made only two films in the three years you've been out in California, and both of them quite short. I should think a person would have to work a good bit faster if he wanted to make a go of it in filmmaking. I understand that it's a very competitive field and that a great many talented people want to get into it these days.

I confess that when you applied to medical school last year, we both hoped you might finish what Alan started, but you're right, you haven't any obligation to make up for our disappointments. I do trust at least that your decision is not irrevocable. I know you said it was, but so much that we think is final turns out to be anything but. Just to be safe, Dad called the admissions office, and Dick Wheeler assured him they would hold a place for you in next fall's class.

I suppose my real fear is that a lot of intelligent young men like yourself decide in their twenties that they are "totally committed to film," and wake up one morning to find themselves forty years old and living in a rented room. Perhaps there comes a time when we have to look life square in the eye and make hard decisions.

Much love,
Mother

P.S. We're delighted to hear about Lucy, and if she makes you half as happy as you say, she must be really special.

There followed a silence broken only by the faint ping of Shaw's cigarette tapping against the edge of his plate. Jimmy refolded the letter and put it in his pocket. He smiled at Shaw. "You like that?"

Shaw made a noncommittal gesture with the cigarette. Donna went into the kitchen and lit the burner under the coffee. One could feel it happen, the maneuvering around this widening hole. There was something Jimmy wanted from us, but God knew what. Say it was all right, maybe. It's all right, Jim, forget the bitch. Yet Jimmy just kept grinning as if the whole thing were a riot.

Shaw looked at me and raised his eyebrows.

Jimmy said, "What?"

Shaw shook his head.

"No, come on, what?"

Shaw smiled in astonishment: what was he talking about?

Jimmy waited for an answer while Shaw's smile curled outward at an infinitesimal rate. Finally he said a very quiet and direct, "Well, fuck you, man," got up and left the room.

Donna looked out from the kitchen and said, "What's with him?"

Shaw made another face: what did she think? She brought the coffee pot to the table and filled three cups. Shaw went into the kitchen for milk, and she called to him, "Get the milk," just as he was coming back through the door with it.

Donna did not like these scenes. Every so often one of us would be seized by a fit of despair over his prospects in life, and Donna would gawk as if she had no idea what the trouble was. Jimmy, for instance, what was his problem? He had a job editing a film ($400 a week and we were living like gentry), he had a new girlfriend, and if he had not quite gotten it completely together yet, he was at least collecting it all in one place. He could be anything he wanted this time around, Donna thought, and she did not like it when Shaw told her that that was not exactly true, that one's mother could set certain limits. . . .

"So big, fucking deal," Donna said. "My Mom's a cunt, too. I don't give a shit."

Though of course she did. Every time her fingers couldn't forget the years of classical piano and just improvise, Donna would feel her mother watching her practice, that fierce, handsome, stone-slab face yielding not a flicker of approval until Donna had gotten it right, right, right, every note, and who gave a shit for feeling. Donna never mentioned this, but we all heard it when she couldn't play and smashed the keys instead.

Shaw was trying to make her see that, saying, "Donna, listen . . ." But she wouldn't. He was talking about mothers or capitalism or technology (a different trip every night), and she was afraid that if she paid attention it would touch her life, she'd be sucked down into it and drowned. But standing back and refusing to listen, she knew that Shaw was wrong, at least for her. She was nineteen, you made your own, and hers was different.

She got up. He was still talking (softly, it seemed, she wasn't sure), and she interrupted, "Look, I've got rehearsal. Let's talk about it later." Shaw could not believe this. She went upstairs to get her stuff, but his impenetrable surface had been torn open, and she heard him back at the table screaming after her. Donna didn't understand that he wasn't trying to drown her, only show her his own predicament. His and hers and Jimmy's and mine; they were all one to Shaw.

Donna came back into the dining room with her music, but by then he had turned silent as ice. She put on her leather jacket, shook out her American hair. Jimmy was at the table again, drinking her coffee and reading the paper. Donna made a helpless gesture of apology, but Shaw would have none of it. Older brothers had bullied Donna as a kid, and now she had an edge much harder than necessary that was forever cutting things by accident. She felt bad about it, said, "You know I love you guys, but Jesus Christ . . ."

"You love him more," said Jimmy.

She laughed, relieved, but as Shaw's face did not alter, she finally just said, "Okay," and left.

Another silence. Ashes stuck in the grease on Shaw's plate, fluttered like water reeds in the breeze from the door. The sense of an ending. Now what? Then what? Rented rooms.

We adjourned to the living room and watched television, or, rather, watched and commented, our remarks sprinkled through the scenes like supplementary dialogue. We liked talking this way, at and about something external, the TV screen. When we spoke directly to each other, the immediacy inhibited us, we became clumsy, self-conscious and eventually fell silent. The television cured this, unstopped our speech and drew to itself remarks that were, at once, a conversation among the three of us and commentary on its passing text.

At the end of the night there was a film we had watched often, and I began to think (as we responded again to those moments we liked best) that what we share after all these years are the movies we have seen together and that we have agreed to love them instead of each other. Which is to say that I cannot love Jimmy or Shaw, nor can they love me, but that we may all feel for certain films of Don Siegel an affection far in excess of what they deserve. They have become like a trust into which our mutual love is invested and from which a small income is occasionally paid. It isn't a wholly satisfactory arrangement, but it is our own.

Donna came home about two with a guy from her band. She said, "This is Jerry," and we each took an eye from the screen long enough to tell him our names, but then blood was dripping on a black shoe, and we had to look back. The band was all black except for Donna, and Jerry was light black with very black clothes and a black music case in his hand. He stood watching the show because Donna did, and he waited on her word. After a minute she said, "Let's go up," and they went.

We hardly noticed. Lee Marvin had suddenly doubled over, and blood was coming through his shirt, but when the woman moved he mastered the pain and put the gun back on her. She said, No, wait . . . But he couldn't. Lady please, he said, I haven't got the time. A shot. Lee staggered out the front door holding the briefcase over his wound, but it was true, he didn't have the time. Halfway to the car his knees gave, he crumpled, died, and when the briefcase broke open, waves of gray money blew across the lawn. Pull back. End titles. Shaw turned it off.

And now, instead of going to sleep, we drifted out to the kitchen where the strange ritual of separating for the night was indefinitely postponed. We made toast, drank more coffee, glanced at each other furtively. Often it was difficult to understand why we were not going to bed together. When there was nothing left to occupy us, we went upstairs and reconvened at the bathroom door. More talk and amusement but finally each of us went into his room, shut his door, opened his book. Later, one by one, we turned out our lights and jerked off into our towels. I had been abstaining recently, but tonight permitted myself a leisurely session to the tune of this woman Jimmy cannot remember, yet who, like the angel she is, sang me to my sleep.

Lies

Yes, she said, trying to catch up to him. Every morning you go and sit in Burgerland with your fountain pen.

I'm writing, he said, do you hear?

But why are you the only one still using a fountain pen? she said. How come you haven't heard about the ballpoint revolution? How can you have such contempt for progress?

Khub iss bakokt, khub iss in drerd, he said, running, crossing streets unsafely.

By now, traffic had stopped. He turned around, with his arm high in the air, like Simón Bolívar on his horse.

You! You do nothing. You are fundamentally unserious. A nihilist, you hear? The desire for movies and restaurants has destroyed your talent, you hear? Each day I sit in the window of Burgerland and write social commentary, you hear?

I thought it was aphorisms, she said.

By then, she had caught up with him.

They're the same, he said. But I don't know what to do with these pieces, yes, that's the question, what to do with them.

Well, why don't you take them and mail them away somewhere?

I would do that, except the only thing that happens to me is I look at them, and they look like crap, he said.

But isn't that called . . . getting a skill? she said.

By then, they were at his place. Look, how would it be if I did this detox with you? she said.

I must have at least three gallons of poison in my small intestine, with all the Cokes I drank in my lifetime, he said. I must've had at least 10,000 Cokes, my prostate must be shot to hell. At least do something useful when I'm not around, read Kafka or Shakespeare, do the Sonnets. Then we'll have something to talk about next time we see each other. Then, at least we'll have a basis.

That really hurts my feelings, I thought we already had a basis.

Well, something to give it that little extra bit of richness. I phoned this herb store in the city today. I had this awful scene there with two people who own it about a year ago, but the older woman, she forgot about it. I called them and asked if they had Dr. Christopher's formulas. All of them, they said.

I wanna go on this detox with you, she said.

If you did, you'd be beautiful, he said. Years would fall off your face. The spots would disappear, anyone can see you're toxed.

But aren't you afraid you'll lose me if I get too beautiful?

I'll take my chances. Do you know how to give yourself an enema?

I'm afraid of enemas. My mother once tried giving me one when I was a kid.

Trust me. I could give you one to start off.

I'm afraid I couldn't do that, she said.

You're so fucking conventional, he said. You'd rather walk around toxed, pretending you're sexy, when there's a foul stench inside you. Your colon is loaded with shit, but you'd rather go to some restaurant and put more shit in there, and then to a movie, to put some more shit in your head, as if you don't have enough in there already. It's grotesque, your nihilistic priorities.

Well, you're one helluva difficult boyfriend to have, she said.

You! Once wasn't enough for you! You want the same damn rotten lies you had in your marriage, the same stinkin' rotten lies, only more so!!! he said, only more of the same, don't you??? Because you think there's nothing else! Am I sexy?? Did you like it???! A little jocko, a little *shtupo*, a little *il perverso*. And you're jealous of my writing because I want to make a break with everything. You're jealous because I want to get the shit out of my system. Yesterday I wrote some damned good social commentary. If you were serious, you'd be able to write too, but your head is so full of shit, you can't think.

It's not that I can't think, she croaked inside her heart, *I can't feel, which is ten times worse.*

If *you* were writing, you'd be ruthless with your time!

Oh, please! Stop attacking me, the woman said.

I haven't even started yet. Who else will tell you the truth? Your nihilist friends?

Okay, so I'd be ruthless.

You bring nothing but the philistine into my life. Fuck me, fuck me, do you love me? Do you want me? It's grotesque, a parody of intimacy.

After a certain amount of abuse, she took leave of him and went home. She was happy to be alone and gorged on food. Two weeks went by, and no call. Two weeks without a fuck.

Then the phone rang. It was a woman friend.

I've been two weeks without a fuck, she said to her friend.

Well, at least you've got somebody to fuck you sometimes. I can hardly even have a conversation with a man, let alone sex, the friend said. I'm jealous.

At first, he was just a talking friend. I couldn't wait for him to become my lover. Fuck me, fuck me, I cried, you're tantalizing me with your talk, your global mind.

It's global foreplay! said the friend.

But he keeps lecturing me on nihilism.

Oh, they do lecture, that's the male thing.

It's very frustrating.

It's for power, I suppose. They love coherence. It gives them the illusion of something. I couldn't be coherent if my life depended on it. I'm done with coherence, and trying to produce the illusion of coherence.

Would you say you were incoherent? said the woman.

I meditate. All I do is meditate. I can't take anybody's lectures. I can't absorb anybody's verbal output.

It *is* awful, said the woman.

No, it's wonderful for some people. But for me, I just can't stand it anymore, said the friend.

I said to him, how did you get to be so global?

I listen to my shortwave radio, he said. The BBC, you get global that way. Try shortwave, he said.

Darling, darling, I love your mind, I said.

Not only are you not global, you're not even regional, he said to me.

A typical male, typical, said the friend. Keep it up, you've got a good thing going. Does he want to marry you? I bet he wants to marry you already.

As a matter of fact, he talked about marrying, but it all turned out to be a four-hour lecture on the bestial media. *The media . . . in all its bestial nihilism . . .* it began.

You, you are a natural wonder, said the friend. To be able to listen to all that is no small thing. That takes stamina. Every day, I get up and run to the Tibetan temple on top of the hill, and I lay under the prayerwheel for hours, meditating. That way, I can escape people's verbal output. The wheel makes a lovely sound, I find it very soothing, I don't even know why. Then, in the evening, I go back again for evening meditation, from five to six. Silk flags are flying overhead, beautiful flowers and incense. *There's some very good energy there.* Yesterday, as I was lying down under the prayerwheel, a young woman came up to me. Did anyone ever give you instruction in how to lie under this prayerwheel? she said to me.

Instruction? No. I do it because I like it, a very good sound comes out of it, well, it is a little like fucking, as a matter of fact, it's like having a lover with no verbal output.

The two women started to laugh, and one nearly peed her pants.

As far as what they call global, the friend said, what they call global now will pass away. In one hundred years, all these global ideas will be replaced by other global ideas.

How I love being here with you and talking like this, the woman said. I love women for helping me find my bearings, I love my woman friends. The men, I only suffer them for a little physical warmth. I see them above me in the shadows, their testicles hanging down, their penis juggernauting towards me in the night, fuck me, fuck me, I cry, in my little nihilistic heart. Such a tight little pair of testicles, so dry and tight, wrapped as it were, in a bat skin, a bat skin I do not understand. No, I don't love his verbal output, I love his Champion Juicer. Two weeks ago, he told me about sentences. He's taken up writing, and suddenly, he's lecturing me on semicolons and Henry James. The story must move forward by sentences, he said. The story must go on. Not by digressions, but by forward-thrusting sentences.

How male!

He buys nothing. He knows how to live without money. Detox and didactics, that's what it's all about, he said.

Meanwhile, I am back in his apartment, and my twelve-year-old calls.

Mom . . . . ═ . . . . ! ! ! ! ! ! ! ! ! ! ! ! ! ! ! ! ! What are you doing there? *Are you fucking?*"

No, I'm just drinking carrot juice and listening to the radio.

You're lying!

Migrations

All the passengers . . . thronged with shining eyes upon the platform. At every turn we could look further into the land of our happy future. At every turn the cocks were tossing their clear notes into the golden air and crowing for the new day and the new country. For this indeed was our destination—this was the "good country" we had been going to so long.   R. L. STEVENSON

Raquel Scherr

La Japonesa

My mother, Juana Estela Salgado de Scherr, came home from her English class and said, in Spanish, "I had a very interesting conversation with a Japanese woman while I was waiting for the bus." Her eyes glistened with amusement and she cupped her mouth when she laughed. "The woman came up to me and started speaking Japanese. I told her in Spanish that I did not speak Japanese. She laughed too. She thought I was Japanese." I could understand why—my mother's black black eyes, their Indian slant, straight black hair, cinnamon-and-lemon colored skin, cheekbones tilted toward the sun. My father's Baltimore Jewish family, who had never seen a Mexican before, said my mother "looks like Madame Chiang-Kai-Shek."

In the 1950s, in Berkeley, foreign faces looked familial to me, rather like seeing an American in a Mexican town—an instantly familiar stranger. We lived in Albany's Codornices Village, on Sixth Street, a mostly Black neighborhood. My father, Max Scherr, often took me to the Piccolo, a popular coffee shop near the Berkeley campus where he'd meet his friends. They were mainly Jewish or Black. How different they seemed from college men with crewcuts slicked in vasoline, and college women in tight skirts, cashmere sweaters, and duck-tailed hair. I thought they all came from places like Modesto. My friend Judy Nikaido referred to them as "white people." She was born in a detention camp in California. After the war a young white couple helped ease the Nikai-dos' financial pressures by taking the youngest of seven children until things got better. When things got better, they refused to give her back. Nothing could be done because she didn't want to come back. Mrs. Nikaido cried in the corner of her living room which smelled strongly of incense, while Judy and I played Monopoly. Neither of our mothers spoke English.

I asked my mother how she was able to have a conversation with the woman at the bus stop. "A little Spanish, a little Japanese, a little English, and a lot of hands. We understood each other very well." She would always say this about the people in her classes. "We understand each other very well." She told me about her good friend, "el Peruano" (the Peruvian), who was putting himself through college and supporting his aunt and invalid mother by working at Larry Blake's restaurant, or about "la joven Pakistani" (the young Pakistani woman) who wanted to go back home, but her husband wanted to stay. There were also the Delgados, a Cuban family who came to California before the rev-olution. Their kids went to school with my brothers and me. They were the only "latinos," besides the Randalls' kids who were mixed like us, and my Mex-ican friend Gloria who insisted she was Spanish. In later years, my mother told me about "la Vietnames" whose husband was killed while carrying medical equipment in Saigon. She brought her son to the U.S., but left her small daugh-ter behind. "And your father writing about hippies," my mother said, meaning the *Berkeley Barb*, an underground newspaper my father started in 1965.

My mother kept going back to school to practice her English; not to learn it but to be with friends: "el Colombiano," "la Nicaraguense," "la Koreana," "el Panameño," "la Japonesa," "la China," "la Filipina."

She had been in her last year of medical school at the University of Mexico when she met my father, a young lawyer who rode the rails to California, then hitchhiked to Mexico. My mother had read the Classics. Octavio Paz had been her schoolmate. Her first few years in Berkeley she wore long handpainted Mexican skirts and thickly colored embroidered blouses. "The whole world comes to my English class," she'd say. "The whole world comes to California. We understand each other very well." I think of her talking to the woman at the bus stop, and it seems, thousands of years ago, my Mexican mother—part Az-tec, French, and Spanish—was Japanese.

— *Maya Angelou* —

I Know Why the Caged Bird Sings

In the early months of World War II, San Francisco's Fillmore district, or the Western Addition, experienced a visible revolution. On the surface it appeared to be totally peaceful and almost a refutation of the term "revolution." The Yakamoto Sea Food Market quietly became Sammy's Shoe Shine Parlor and Smoke Shop. Yashigira's Hardware metamorphosed into La Salon de Beauté owned by Miss Clorinda Jackson. The Japanese shops which sold products to Nisei customers were taken over by enterprising Negro businessmen, and in less than a year became permanent homes away from home for the newly arrived Southern Blacks. Where the odors of tempura, raw fish and *cha* had dominated, the aroma of chitlings, greens and ham hocks now prevailed.

The Asian population dwindled before my eyes. I was unable to tell the Japanese from the Chinese and as yet found no real difference in the national origin of such sounds as Ching and Chan or Moto and Kano.

As the Japanese disappeared, soundlessly and without protest, the Negroes entered with their loud jukeboxes, their just-released animosities and the relief of escape from Southern bonds. The Japanese area became San Francisco's Harlem in a matter of months.

A person unaware of all the factors that make up oppression might have expected sympathy or even support from the Negro newcomers for the dislodged

Japanese. Especially in view of the fact that they (the Blacks) had themselves undergone concentration-camp living for centuries in slavery's plantations and later in sharecroppers' cabins. But the sensations of common relationship were missing.

The Black newcomer had been recruited on the desiccated farm lands of Georgia and Mississippi by war-plant labor scouts. The chance to live in two- or three-story apartment buildings (which became instant slums), and to earn two- and even three-figured weekly checks, was blinding. For the first time he could think of himself as a Boss, a Spender. He was able to pay other people to work for him, i.e. the dry cleaners, taxi drivers, waitresses, etc. The shipyards and ammunition plants brought to booming life by the war let him know that he was needed and even appreciated. A completely alien yet very pleasant position for him to experience. Who could expect this man to share his new and dizzying importance with concern for a race that he had never known to exist?

Another reason for his indifference to the Japanese removal was more subtle but was more profoundly felt. The Japanese were not whitefolks. Their eyes, language, and customs belied the white skin and proved to their dark successors that since they didn't have to be feared, neither did they have to be considered. All this was decided unconsciously.

No member of my family and none of the family friends ever mentioned the absent Japanese. It was as if they had never owned or lived in the houses we inhabited. On Post Street, where our house was, the hill skidded slowly down to Fillmore, the market heart of our district. In the two short blocks before it reached its destination, the street housed two day-and-night restaurants, two pool halls, four Chinese restaurants, two gambling houses, plus diners, shoe-shine shops, beauty salons, barber shops and at least four churches. To fully grasp the never-ending activity in San Francisco's Negro neighborhood during the war, one need only know that the two blocks described were side streets that were duplicated many times over in the eight- to ten-square-block area.

The air of collective displacement, the impermanence of life in wartime and the gauche personalities of the more recent arrivals tended to dissipate my own sense of not belonging. In San Francisco, for the first time, I perceived myself as part of something. Not that I identified with the newcomers, nor with the rare Black descendants of native San Franciscans, nor with the whites or even the Asians, but rather with the times and the city. I understood the arrogance of the young sailors who marched the streets in marauding gangs, approaching every girl as if she were at best a prostitute and at worst an Axis agent bent on making the U.S.A. lose the war. The undertone of fear that San Francisco would be bombed, which was abetted by weekly air-raid warnings and civil-defense drills in school, heightened my sense of belonging. Hadn't I, always, but ever and ever, thought that life was just one great risk for the living?

Then the city acted in wartime like an intelligent woman under siege. She gave what she couldn't with safety withhold, and secured those things which lay in her reach. The city became for me the ideal of what I wanted to be as a grownup. Friendly but never gushing, cool but not frigid or distant, distinguished without the awful stiffness.

To San Franciscans "the City That Knows How" was the Bay, the fog, Sir Francis Drake Hotel, Top o' the Mark, Chinatown, the Sunset District and so on and so forth and so white. To me, a thirteen-year-old Black girl, stalled by the South and Southern Black life style, the city was a state of beauty and a state of freedom. The fog wasn't simply the steamy vapors off the Bay caught and penned in by hills, but a soft breath of anonymity that shrouded and cushioned the bashful traveler. I became dauntless and free of fears, intoxicated by the physical fact of San Francisco. Safe in my protecting arrogance, I was certain that no one loved her as impartially as I. I walked around the Mark Hopkins and gazed at the Top o' the Mark, but (maybe sour grapes) was more impressed by the view of Oakland from the hill than by the tiered building or its fur-draped visitors. For weeks, after the city and I came to terms about my belonging, I haunted the points of interest and found them empty and un-San Francisco. The naval officers with their well-dressed wives and clean white babies inhabited another time-space dimension than I. The well-kept old women in chauffeured cars and blond girls in buckskin shoes and cashmere sweaters might have been San Franciscans, but they were at most gilt on the frame of my portrait of the city.

Pride and Prejudice stalked in tandem the beautiful hills. Native San Franciscans, possessive of the city, had to cope with an influx, not of awed respectful tourists but of raucous unsophisticated provincials. They were also forced to live with skin-deep guilt brought on by the treatment of their former Nisei schoolmates.

Southern white illiterates brought their biases intact to the West from the hills of Arkansas and the swamps of Georgia. The Black ex-farmers had not left their distrust and fear of whites which history had taught them in distressful lessons. These two groups were obliged to work side by side in the war plants, and their animosities festered and opened like boils on the face of the city.

San Franciscans would have sworn on the Golden Gate Bridge that racism was missing from the heart of their air-conditioned city. But they would have been sadly mistaken.

A story went the rounds about a San Franciscan white matron who refused to sit beside a Negro civilian on the streetcar, even after he made room for her on the seat. Her explanation was that she would not sit beside a draft dodger who was a Negro as well. She added that the least he could do was fight for his country the way her son was fighting on Iwo Jima. The story said that the man pulled his body away from the window to show an armless sleeve. He said quietly and with great dignity, "Then ask your son to look around for my arm, which I left over there."

Gretel Ehrlich

Heart Mountain

Kai Nakamura lay across the bed with only a shirt on. It was late and it was raining again. After Li made love to him she rested her head on his stomach.

"You nervous. Everything noisy in there."

Kai shifted, laughing, and pulled one knee up. He reached over her hip and lit a cigarette. The room smelled of green vegetables and cooking oil. Li climbed off the bed.

"Here," she said, pinning a badge to his shirt. She kissed his chest where the shirt was open. His shoulders were big because he was on the Cal Berkeley swim team. He read the badge. It said, I AM CHINESE.

The noise of the city wallowed in the room, a mechanical gargling of horns, rain, music, and engines. On the fire escape the potted chrysanthemum he had given Li for her birthday tossed about in the wind. He ground out the cigarette until it looked like a pig's flared snout and clasped Li's head tightly in the crook of his arm. He thought her hair shone like the stalks of black bamboo. He rolled her from side to side. Locking his arms across the small of her back, he entwined his legs with hers until she wriggled from him. He grabbed her again and pinned her on her back with a wrestler's hold.

"Hello," he said.

Li smiled. She knocked at his shins with the tops of her feet, then went limp.

Kai dropped heavily to her side. He was thinking ahead, about the next day and the next, and a coolness had gone through him. Li examined his face.

"Who are you?" she said.

There was a knock on the door. Kai scrambled under the covers as Jimmy Wong, Li's older brother by twelve years, burst into their room. "No more Chinese women for you!" he announced, laughing. He handed Kai the *San Francisco Chronicle*. The headlines read, ALL JAPS MUST GO. Kai sat up propping himself against the wall. He leafed through the newspaper: ". . . it makes no difference whether the Japanese is theoretically a citizen. He is still a Japanese. Giving him a scrap of paper won't change him. I don't care what they do with them as long as they don't send them back here. A Jap is a Jap. . . ."

Jimmy sat on the edge of the bed and stared out the window. The building that housed the dumpling shop and mah-jongg room across the street was dark. A fire escape clung tentatively to its side and the green dragon—a symbol of vitality and long life—used in the New Year's parade where he had met Li lay unfurled against three upstairs windows.

Jimmy turned to Kai and whispered: "You stay here. Wear badge. Marry Li. Keep go to college. Change from great Japanese scholar to great Chinese scholar."

Kai laughed. "I'm not either. I'm just American boy with slant eyes. Chinese wouldn't have me," he said.

Li reentered the room with two bottles of Coke. She uncapped them with the bottle opener by the bed and handed one to Kai and the other to her brother. The rain intensified. It slapped hard at the one window. Against city lights the drops looked black and fog enclosed the streets of Chinatown like sea-lanes leading to places no one in that room knew.

Kai unpinned the badge and twirled it between his fingers. It pricked his thumb. A drop of blood appeared and Li licked it away. After, Kai flung his hand over his head in a mocking backstroke. He thought about swimming from this dank room so redolent with intimacy. He would swim backward from the trancelike, forward motion of time, starting in San Francisco Bay, doing the backstroke under the bridge, the crawl out into the channel, then float past the Farallon Islands into rough seas.

Li opened the window. A surge of wind rushed past the bed. She pulled the chrysanthemum, whose heavy blossoms were bent completely over, into the room.

"Look what's happened," she said.

Kai didn't look at the plant but at her. Perhaps this was the last time he would see her. In two days he would be evacuated. Whatever else happened he would remember her diminutiveness and the tart taste of her skin.

After he left Li on that last night of freedom, Kai waited for sunrise at an all-night upstairs teahouse where he was known by the waiters. It would have been dangerous for him to walk the streets because a curfew and a five-mile travel limit had been placed on "all persons of Japanese ancestry." Even the binoculars he used for baseball games had been confiscated. Evacuation notices were posted on power poles all over the city. He and his friends had read them and had taunted the man pasting them up. Now, he sipped black tea and waited for sunrise alone.

At eight he boarded the ferry for Richmond. He hadn't seen his parents for two years, though they lived less than ten miles apart. When he was twelve, Kai had been sent to an orphanage and, later, to live with a Caucasian professor and his wife to learn "the American Way." The American Way had brought him, at twenty-four, a Ph.D. candidacy in history.

The man at the ticket office, a Filipino, hesitated before giving Kai passage on the ferry, adding insult to injury because the Filipinos hated the Japanese as well.

Kai walked the streets of Richmond. Turning a corner, he saw his parents' tiny frame house. In the front yard, a cypress had been pruned into an odd, windblown shape, and a single vine crawled a trellis up one wall.

He knocked on the door. When Mr. Nakamura opened it, he did not recognize his son. "Who are you looking for?" he asked briskly.

Kai shoved his hands into his pockets and stepped back, chuckling.

"Pop, it's me," he said, but his father only stared uncomprehending.

He heard his mother. She pushed past her husband and let out a gasp. "Oh . . . it's you—come in."

"Don't mind him," she whispered, "it's just that you've changed," she said, smiling. She turned to Mr. Nakamura. "He has grown so big, *desu-ne?*"

Kai's father stood to one side and nodded yes.

The house was bare. All the furniture had been sold or stored for safekeeping. In the living room Mr. Nakamura sat on a packing crate and bent toward the big radio. It lit his face like a jack-o'-lantern.

Kai's mother called from the kitchen. She was stirring scallions into broth, shoyu, and sake, then eggs and eel.

"I don't eat this food very much anymore," Kai said.

"Oh, this is special for you. *Unagi donburi*. You always liked it," she said, though Kai could remember liking no such thing.

He looked at his mother. He resembled her in build and the shape of his face but he still wondered if these were his parents. When they spoke during the meal he could not understand what they said.

After lunch Kai and his father drove to Japantown. Mr. Nakamura wanted to show his son the store. On the way, he saw a sign in the morgue: I'D RATHER DO BUSINESS WITH A JAP, and a crudely handwritten one in the barber shop: FREE SHAVES FOR JAPS. NOT RESPONSIBLE FOR ACCIDENTS.

"How's business been going, Pop?"

Mr. Nakamura grunted. "No good now."

It was a Wednesday but Japantown was deserted. The noodle shop, the *mochi* shop, the restaurants were all closed. Mr. Nakamura pulled up in front of his hardware store and unlocked the door. It was housed in a triangular building at the end of a block flanked on two sides by narrow streets.

Inside Kai walked up and down the aisles. There were shelves of tools: planers and chisels and saws, garden tools and seed packets, and a ceiling-high stack of black twine rolled into balls. In another aisle were kitchen goods: bamboo steamers and water ladles, cast iron pots with wooden lids, chopsticks and scrub brushes, and a penny jar full of bubble gum.

Mr. Nakamura took his place behind the counter. When he came to America he worked as a laborer on a celery farm, a chicken-sexer, a flower grower, and now the owner of Japantown's only hardware store. Above his head was the business license he had framed austerely in black and next to it, a photograph of the Great Buddha at Nara.

"For God's sake, Pop, take that down," Kai said, pointing to the photo.

Mr. Nakamura stood motionless. Kai slid a penny into the gum machine and popped a jawbreaker into his mouth. His father turned away in disgust and struggled with a locked door. Kai helped him. Finally the door swung open. Instead of the street, there was a garden, no bigger than a closet, with stepping-stones, mossy banks, a stone water basin, three flowering shrubs, and, against a tall fence, a thicket of black bamboo.

"I sell business yesterday," Kai's father said solemnly. "Seven hundred dollar. The car too. But didn't show them this."

Kai spit the gum into his hand and stared at the massive block of stone under his feet. Already the moss had begun to grow beyond its borders. Across the street a gong in the Buddhist temple rang. Kai heard glass breaking. He turned around. His father had broken the picture frame and held a match to the photograph of the Buddha. The glossy paper lifted and curled toward him and became ash.

They locked the store and drove home in the Studebaker. Sometimes the horn stuck and Mr. Nakamura had to lift the hood and pinch a certain wire, but not today. They glided through empty streets. Their first night of evacuation would be spent at a racetrack in converted horsestalls. The idea amused Kai at first, and he thought of getting a rake from the store for the manure, but changed his mind.

"Seabiscuit, here we come," he said, though quietly, so his father would not hear.

The next morning Mrs. Nakamura swept the floors a last time though the house appeared to be spotless. Three large suitcases and a bulging duffle bag were set out at the front door. At the last moment Mr. Nakamura parted with his beloved possession: a potted bonsai he had grown from seed. The neighbors, who were Danish, were to care for it. Mr. Nakamura explained the strict watering and pruning schedule, then handed the tree to the sea captain.

"It is very beautiful, this little tree," Jan Carlson exclaimed. He was tall and in his big red hands the tree looked even smaller. "Don't worry; it will live longer than this damned war," he shouted. "It will be very healthy tree when you return. I will have it for you, sure."

Mr. Nakamura looked at the man, his eyes glazed with shame, then bowed deeply.

Two days later Kai and his parents were on a train. All through the cars he could see only black hair, dark eyes, the sound of a language his parents had forbidden him to learn. The journal he began keeping that day was a way of steadying himself against drastic change. Already, the lullaby rocking of the train felt deathly to him. He dreamed the tracks were his arms. He was holding Li. The heavy cars rolled over them.

Amy Tan

Jing-Mei Woo:
The Joy
Luck Club

My father has asked me to be the fourth corner at the Joy Luck Club. I am to replace my mother whose seat at the mah-jongg table has been empty since she died two months ago. My father thinks she was killed by her own thoughts.

"She had a new idea inside her head," said my father. "But before it could come out of her mouth, the thought grew too big and burst. It must have been a very bad idea."

The doctor said she died of a cerebral aneurysm. And her friends at the Joy Luck Club said she died just like a rabbit: quickly and with unfinished business left behind. My mother was supposed to host the next meeting of the Joy Luck Club.

The week before she died, she called me, full of pride, full of life: "Auntie Lin cooked red bean soup for Joy Luck. I'm going to cook black sesame seed soup."

"Don't show off," I said.

"It's not show-off." She said the two soups were almost the same, *cha bu-to*. Or maybe she said *bu-tung*, not the same thing at all. It was one of those Chinese expressions that mean the better half of mixed intentions. I can never remember things I didn't understand in the first place.

My mother started the San Francisco version of the Joy Luck Club in 1949, two years before I was born. This was the year my mother and father left China with one stiff leather trunk filled only with fancy silk dresses. There was no time to pack anything else, my mother had explained to my father after they boarded the boat. Still his hands swam frantically between the slippery silks looking for his cotton shirts and wool pants.

When they arrived in San Francisco, my father made her hide those shiny clothes. She wore the same brown-checked Chinese dress until the Refugee Welcome Society gave her two hand-me-down dresses, all too large, in sizes for American women. The Society was composed of a group of white-haired American missionary ladies from the First Chinese Baptist Church. And because of these gifts, my parents could not refuse their invitation to join the church. Nor could they ignore the old ladies' practical advice to improve their English through Bible Study Class on Wednesday nights and, later, through choir practice on Saturday mornings. This was how my parents met the Hsus, the Jongs, and the St. Clairs. My mother could sense that the women of these families also had unspeakable tragedies they had left behind in China and hopes they couldn't begin to express in their fragile English. Or at least, my mother recognized the numbness in these women's faces. And she saw how quickly their eyes moved when she told them her idea for the Joy Luck Club.

Joy Luck was an idea my mother remembered from the days of her first marriage in Kweilin, before the Japanese came. That's why I think of Joy Luck as her Kweilin story. It was the story she would always tell me when she was bored, when there was nothing to do, when every bowl had been washed and the formica table had been wiped down twice, when my father sat reading the newspaper and smoking one Pall Mall cigarette after another, a warning not to disturb him. This is when my mother would take out a box of old ski sweaters sent to us by unseen relatives from Vancouver. She would snip the bottom of a sweater and pull out a kinky thread of yarn, anchoring it to a piece of cardboard. And as she began to roll with one sweeping rhythm, she would start her story. Over the years, she told me the same story, except for the ending, which grew darker, casting long shadows into her life, and eventually, into mine.

"I dreamed about Kweilin before I ever saw it," my mother began, speaking Chinese. "I dreamed of jagged peaks lining a curving river, with magic moss greening the banks. At the tops of these peaks were white mists. And if you could float down this river and eat the moss for food, you would be strong enough to climb the peak. If you slipped, you would only fall into a bed of soft moss and laugh. And once you reached the top, you would be able to see everything and feel such happiness, it would be enough to never have worries in your life ever again.

"In China, everybody dreamed about Kweilin. And when I arrived, I realized how shabby my dreams were, how poor my thoughts. When I saw the hills, I laughed and shuddered at the same time. The peaks looked like giant fried fish heads trying to jump out of a vat of oil. Behind each hill, I could see shadows of another fish, and then another and another. And then the clouds would move just a little and the hills would suddenly become monstrous elephants marching slowly toward me! Can you see this? And at the root of the hill were secret caves. Inside grew hanging rock gardens in the shapes and colors of cabbage, winter melons, turnips, and onions. These were things so strange and beautiful you can't ever imagine them.

"But I didn't come to Kweilin to see how beautiful it was. The man who was my husband brought me and our two babies to Kweilin because he thought we would be safe. He was an officer with the Kuomintang, and after he put us down in a small two-story house, he went off to the Northwest, to Chungking.

"We knew the Japanese were winning, even when the newspapers said they were not. Every day, every hour, thousands of people poured into the city, crowding the sidewalks looking for places to live. They came from the East, West, North, and South. They were rich and poor, Shanghainese, Cantonese, Northerners, and not just Chinese, but foreigners and missionaries of every religion. And there was, of course, the Kuomintang and their army officers who thought they were top level to everyone else.

"We were a city of leftovers mixed together. If it hadn't been for the Japanese, there would have been plenty of reason for fighting to break out among these different people. Can you see it? Shanghai people with Northern water peasants, bankers with barbers, rickshaw pullers with Burma refugees. Everybody looked down on someone else. It didn't matter that everybody shared the same sidewalk to spit on and suffered the same fast-moving diarrhea. We all had the same stink, but everybody complained someone else smelled the worst. Me? Oh, I hated the American air-force officers who said habba-habba sounds to make my face turn red. But the worst were the Northern peasants who emptied their noses into their hands and pushed people around and gave everybody their dirty diseases.

"So you can see how quickly Kweilin lost its beauty for me. I no longer climbed the peaks to say, How lovely are these hills! I only wondered which hills the Japanese had reached. I sat in the dark corners of my house with a baby under each arm, waiting with nervous feet. When the sirens cried out to warn us of bombers, my neighbors and I jumped to our feet and scurried to the deep caves to hide like wild animals. But you can't stay in the dark for so long. Something inside of you starts to fade and you become like a starving person, crazy-hungry for light. Outside I could hear the bombing. Boom! Boom! And then the sound of raining rocks. And inside I was no longer hungry for the cabbage or the turnips of the hanging rock garden. I could only see the dripping bowels of an ancient hill that might collapse on top of me. Can you imagine how it is, to want to be neither inside or outside, to want to be nowhere and disappear?

"So when the bombing sounds grew farther away, we would come back out like newborn kittens scratching our way back to the city. And always, I would be amazed to find the hills against the blue sky had not been torn apart.

"I thought up Joy Luck on a summer night that was so hot even the moths fainted to the ground, their wings were so heavy with the damp heat. Every-place was so crowded there was no room for fresh air. Unbearable smells from the sewers rose up to my second-story window and the stink had nowhere else to go but into my nose. At all hours of the night and day, I often heard screaming sounds. I didn't know if it was a peasant slitting the throat of a runaway pig or an officer beating a half-dead peasant for lying in his way on the sidewalk. I didn't go to the window to find out. What use would it have been? And that's when I thought I needed something to do to help me move.

"My idea was to have a gathering of four women, one for each corner of my mah-jongg table. I knew which women I wanted to ask. They were all young like me, with wishful faces. One was an army officer's wife, like myself. An-other was a girl with very fine manners from a rich family in Shanghai. She had escaped with only a little money. And there was a girl from Nanking who had the blackest hair I have ever seen. She came from a low-class family, but she was pretty and pleasant and had married well, to an old man who died and left her with a better life.

"Each week one of us would host a party to raise money and to raise our spir-its. The hostess had to serve special dim-sum to bring good fortune of all kinds—dumplings shaped like plump silver ingots, long rice noodles for long life, boiled peanuts for conceiving sons, and of course, many good-luck or-anges for a plentiful, sweet life.

"What fine food we treated ourselves to with our meager allowances! We didn't notice that the dumplings were stuffed mostly with stringy squash and that the oranges were spotted with wormy holes. We ate sparingly, not as if we didn't have enough, but to protest how we could not eat another bite, we had already bloated ourselves from earlier in the day. We knew we had luxuries few people could afford. We were the lucky ones.

"After filling our stomachs, we would then fill a bowl with money and put it where everyone could see. Then we would sit down at the mah-jongg table. My table was from my family and was of a very fragrant red wood, not what you call rosewood, but *hong mu* which is so fine, there's no English word for it. The table had a very thick pad, so that when the mah-jongg *pai* were spilled onto the ta-ble, the only sound was of ivory tiles washing against one another.

"Once we started to play, nobody could speak, except to say *pung!* or *chr!*

when taking a tile. We had to play with seriousness and think of nothing else but adding to our happiness through winning. But after sixteen rounds, we would again feast, this time to celebrate our good fortune. And then we would talk into the night until the morning, saying stories about good times in the past and good times yet to come.

"Oh, what good stories! Stories spilling out all over the place! We almost laughed to death. A rooster that ran into the house screeching on top of dinner bowls, the same bowls that held him quietly in pieces the next day! And one about a girl who wrote love letters for two friends who loved the same man. And a silly foreign lady who fainted on a toilet when firecrackers went off next to her.

"People thought we were wrong to serve banquets every week, while many people in the city were starving, eating rats and later, the garbage that the poorest rats used to feed on. Others thought we were possessed by demons—to celebrate when even within our own families we had lost generations, had lost homes and fortunes, and were separated, husband from wife, brother from sister, daughter from mother. Hnnnh! How could we laugh, people asked.

"It's not that we had no heart or eyes for pain. We were all afraid. We all had our miseries. But to despair was to wish back for something already lost. Or to prolong what was already unbearable. How much can you wish for a favorite warm coat that hangs in the closet of a house that burned down with your mother and father inside of it? How long can you see in your mind arms and legs hanging from telephone wires and starving dogs running down the streets with half-chewed hands dangling from their jaws? What was worse, we asked among ourselves, to sit and wait for our own deaths with proper somber faces? Or to choose our own happiness?

"So we decided to hold parties and pretend each week had become the new year. Each week we could forget past wrongs done to us. We weren't allowed to think a bad thought. We feasted, we laughed, we played games, lost and won, we told the best stories. And each week, we could hope to be lucky. That hope was our only joy. And that's how we came to call our little parties Joy Luck."

My mother used to end the story on a happy note, bragging about her skill at the game. "I won many times and was so lucky, the others teased that I had learned the trick of a clever thief," she said. "I won tens of thousands of yuan. But I wasn't rich. No. By then paper money had become worthless. Even toilet paper was worth more. And that made us laugh harder, to think a thousand yuan note wasn't even good enough to rub on our bottoms."

I used to think her Kweilin story was a Chinese fairy tale, until the day she told me this new ending.

"An army officer came to my house early one morning and told me to go quickly to my husband in Chungking. And I knew he was telling me to run away from Kweilin. I knew what happened to officers and their families when the Japanese arrived. How could I go? There were no trains leaving Kweilin. My friend from Nanking, she was so good to me. She bribed a man to steal a wheelbarrow used to haul coal. She promised to warn our other friends.

"I packed my things and my two babies into this wheelbarrow and began pushing to Chungking four days before the Japanese marched into Kweilin. On the road I heard news of the slaughter from people running past me. It was terrible. Up to the last day, the Kuomintang insisted that Kweilin was safe, protected by the Chinese army. But later that day, the streets of Kweilin were strewn with newspapers reporting great Kuomintang victories, and on top of these papers, like fresh fish from a butcher, lay rows of people—men, women and children who had never lost hope, but had lost their lives instead. When I heard this news, I walked faster and faster, asking myself at each step, Were they foolish? Were they brave?

"I pushed toward Chungking, until my wheel broke. I abandoned my beautiful mah-jongg table of *hong mu*. By then, I didn't have enough feeling left in my body to cry. I tied scarves into slings and put a baby on each side of my shoulder. I carried a bag in each hand, one with clothes, the other with food. I carried these things until deep grooves grew in my hands. And I finally dropped one bag after the other when my hands began to bleed and became too slippery to hold onto anything.

"Along the way, I saw others had done the same, gradually given up hope. It was like a pathway inlaid with treasures that grew in value along the way. Bolts of fine fabric and books. Paintings of ancestors and carpenter tools. Until one could see girl babies with muddy tears and later still, even silver urns lying in the road, where people had been too tired to carry them for any kind of future hope. By the time I arrived in Chungking I had lost everything except for three fancy silk dresses which I wore one on top of the other."

"What do you mean by everything?" I gasped the first time she told me this ending. I was stunned to realize the story had been true all along. "What happened to the babies?"

She didn't even pause to think. She simply said in a way that made it clear there was no more to the story: "Your father is not my first husband. You are not those babies."

When I arrive at the Hsus' house where the Joy Luck Club is meeting tonight, the first person I see is my father. "There she is! Never on time!" he announces. And it's true. Everybody's already here, seven family friends in their sixties and seventies. They look up and laugh at me, always tardy, a child still at thirty-five.

I'm shaking, trying to hold something inside. The last time I saw them, at the funeral, I had broken down and cried big gulping sobs. They must wonder now how someone like me can take my mother's place. A friend once told me that my mother and I were alike, that we had the same wispy hand gestures, the same girlish laugh and sideways look. When I shyly told my mother this, she seemed insulted and said, "You don't even know little percent of me! How can you be me?" And she's right. How can I be my mother at Joy Luck?

"Auntie, uncle," I say repeatedly, nodding to each person there. I have always called these old family friends auntie and uncle, even though we are not related by family. And then I walk over and stand next to my father.

He's looking at the Jongs' pictures from their recent China trip. "Look at that," he says politely, pointing to a photo of the Jongs' tour group standing on wide slab steps. There is nothing in this picture that shows it was taken in China rather than San Francisco, or any other city for that matter. But my father doesn't seem to be looking at the picture anyway. It's as though everything is the same to him, nothing stands out. He has always been politely indifferent. But what's the Chinese word that means indifferent because you can't *see* any differences? That's how troubled I think he is by my mother's death.

"Will you look at that," he says, pointing to another nondescript picture.

The Hsus' house feels heavy with greasy odors. Too many Chinese meals cooked in a too small kitchen, too many once fragrant smells compressed onto a thin layer of invisible grease. I remember how my mother used to go in other people's houses and restaurants and wrinkle her nose, then whisper very loudly: "I can see and feel the stickiness with my nose."

I have not been to the Hsus' house in many years, but the living room is exactly the same as I remember it. When Auntie An-mei and Uncle George moved to the Sunset from Chinatown twenty-five years ago, they bought new furniture. It's all there, still looking mostly new under yellowed plastic. The same turquoise couch shaped in a semicircle of nubby tweed. The colonial end tables made out of heavy maple. A lamp of fake cracked porcelain. Only the scroll-length calendar, free from the Bank of Canton, changes every year.

I remember this stuff, because when we were children, Auntie An-mei didn't let us touch any of her new furniture except through the clear plastic coverings. On Joy Luck nights, my parents brought me and my sisters to the Hsus'. Since I was the oldest, I had to take care of all the children, so many children it seemed like there was always one baby who was crying from having bumped its head on a table leg.

"You are responsible," said my mother, which meant I was in trouble if anything got spilled, burnt, lost, broken, or dirty. I was responsible, no matter who did it. She and Auntie An-mei were dressed up in funny Chinese dresses with stiff stand-up collars and blooming branches of embroidered silk sewn over their breasts. These clothes were too fancy for real Chinese people, I thought, and too strange for American parties. In those days, before my mother told me her Kweilin story, I imagined Joy Luck was a shameful Chinese custom, like the secret gathering of the Ku Klux Klan or the tom-tom dances of TV Indians preparing for war.

But tonight, nearly twenty-five years later, the Joy Luck aunties are all wearing slacks, bright print blouses, and different versions of sturdy walking shoes. We are all seated around the dining room table under a lamp that looks like a Spanish candelabra. Uncle George puts on his bifocals and starts the meeting by reading the minutes:

"Our capital account is $24,825 or about $6,206 a couple, $3,103 per person. We sold Subaru for a loss at six and three quarters. We bought a hundred shares of Smith International at seven. Our thanks to Lin-do and Tin Jong for the goodies. The red bean soup was especially delicious. The March meeting had to be cancelled until further notice. We were sorry to have to bid a fond farewell to our dear friend, Li-Jun, and extended our sympathy to the Woo family. Respectfully submitted, George Hsu, president and secretary."

That's it. I keep thinking the others will start talking about my mother, the wonderful friendship they shared and why I am here in her spirit, to be the fourth corner and carry on the idea my mother came up with on a hot day in Kweilin.

But everybody just nods to approve the minutes. Even my father's head bobs up and down routinely. And it seems to me my mother's life has been shelved for the next item.

Auntie An-mei heaves herself up from the table and moves slowly to the kitchen to prepare the food. And Auntie Lin, my mother's best friend, moves to the turquoise sofa, crosses her arms and watches the men still seated at the table. Auntie Bing, who seems to shrink even more every time I see her, reaches into her knitting bag and pulls out the start of a tiny blue sweater.

The Joy Luck uncles begin to talk about stocks they are interested in buying. Uncle Jack, who is Auntie Bing's younger brother, is very keen on a company that mines gold in Canada.

"It's a great hedge on inflation," he says with authority. He speaks the best English, almost accentless. I think my mother's English was the worst, but she always thought her Chinese was the best. She spoke Mandarin slightly blurred with a Shanghainese dialect.

"Weren't we going to play mah-jongg tonight?" I whisper loudly to Auntie Bing, who's slightly deaf.

"Later," she says, "after midnight."

"Ladies, are you at this meeting or not?" says Uncle George.

After everybody votes unanimously for the Canada gold stock, I go in the kitchen to ask Auntie An-mei why the Joy Luck Club started investing in stocks.

"We used to play mah-jongg, winner take all. But the same people were always winning, the same people always losing," she says. She is stuffing won ton, one chopstick jab of gingery meat dabbed onto a thin skin and then a single fluid turn with her hand that seals the skin into the shape of a tiny nurse's cap. "You can't have luck when someone else has skill. So long time ago, we decided to invest in the stock market. There's no skill in that. Even your mother agreed."

Auntie An-mei takes count of the tray in front of her. She's already made five rows of eight won ton each. "Eighty won ton, eight people, ten each," she says aloud to herself and then continues stuffing. "We got smart. Now we can all win and lose equally. We can have stock market luck. And we can play mah-jongg for fun, just for a few dollars, winner take all. Losers take home leftovers! So everyone can have some joy. Smart-hanh?"

I watch Auntie An-mei make more won ton. She has quick, expert fingers. She doesn't have to think about what she is doing. That's what my mother used to complain about, that Auntie An-mei never thought about what she was doing.

"She's not stupid," said my mother on one occasion, "but she has no spine. Last week, I had a good idea for her. I said to her, Let's go to the consulate and ask for papers for your brother. And she almost wanted to drop her things and go right then. But later she talked to someone. Who knows who? And that person told her she can get her brother in bad trouble in China. That person said FBI will put her on a list and give her trouble in the U.S. the rest of her life. That person said, you ask for a house loan and they say no loan, because your brother is a Communist. I said, you already have a house! But still she was scared.

"Auntie An-mei runs this way and that," said my mother, "and she doesn't know why."

As I watch Auntie An-mei, I see a short bent woman in her seventies, with a heavy bosom and thin, shapeless legs. She has the flattened soft fingertips of an old woman. I wonder what Auntie An-mei did to inspire a lifelong stream of criticism from my mother. Then again, it seemed my mother was always displeased with all her friends and with me, my sisters, and even my father. Something was always missing. Something always needed improving. Something was not in balance. This one or that had too much of one element, not enough of another.

The elements were from my mother's own version of organic chemistry. Each person is made of five elements, she told me.

Too much fire and you had a bad temper. That was like my father whom my mother always criticized for his cigarette habit and who always shouted back that she should keep her thoughts to herself. I think he now feels guilty that he didn't let my mother speak her mind.

Too little wood and you bent too quickly to listen to other people's ideas, unable to stand on your own. This was like my Auntie An-mei.

Too much water and you flowed in too many directions, like myself, for having started half a degree in biology, then half a degree in art, and then finishing neither when I went off to work for a small ad agency as a secretary, later becoming a copywriter.

I used to dismiss her criticisms as just more of her Chinese superstitions, beliefs that conveniently fit the circumstances. In my twenties, while taking Introduction to Psychology, I tried to tell her why she shouldn't criticize my younger sisters who were still living at home and quite miserable as far as I could tell.

"There's a school of thought," I said, "that parents shouldn't criticize children. They should encourage instead. You know, people rise to other people's expectations. And when you criticize, it just means you're expecting failure."

"That's the trouble," my mother said. "You never rise. Lazy to get up. Lazy to rise to expectations."

"Time to eat," Auntie An-mei happily announces, bringing out a steaming pot of the won tons she was just wrapping. There are piles of food on the table served buffet style, just like the Kweilin feasts. My father is digging into the chow mein which still sits in an oversized aluminum pan surrounded by little plastic packets of soy sauce. Auntie An-mei must have bought this on Clement Street. The won ton soup smells wonderful with delicate sprigs of cilantro floating on top. I'm drawn first to a large platter of *cha-swei*, sweet barbecued pork cut into coin-sized slices, and then to a whole assortment of what I've always called finger goodies—thin-skinned pastries filled with chopped pork, beef, shrimp and unknown stuffings that my mother used to describe as "nutritious things."

Eating is not a gracious event here. It's as though everybody has been starving. They push large forkfuls into their mouths, jab at more pieces of pork, one right after the other. They are not like the ladies of Kweilin who I always imagined savored their food with a certain detached delicacy.

And then, almost as quickly as they started, the men get up and leave the table. As if on cue, the women peck at last morsels and then carry plates and bowls to the kitchen and dump them in the sink. The women take turns washing their hands, scrubbing them vigorously. Who started this ritual? I too put my plate in the sink and wash my hands. The women are talking about the Jongs' China trip, then move toward a room in the back of the apartment. We pass another room, what used to be the bedroom shared by the four Hsu sons. The bunk beds with their scuffed, splintery ladders are still there. The Joy Luck uncles are already seated at the card table. Uncle George is dealing out cards, fast, as though he has learned this technique in a casino. My father is passing out Pall Mall cigarettes, with one already dangling from his lips.

The room in the back was once shared by the three Hsu girls. We were all childhood friends. And now they've all grown and married and I'm here to play in their room again. Except for the smell of camphor, it feels the same—as if Rose, Ruth, and Janice might soon walk in with their hair rolled up in big orange juice cans and plop down on their identical narrow beds. The white chenille bedspreads are so worn, they are almost translucent. Rose and I used to pluck the nubs out while talking about our boy problems. Everything is the same, except now a mahogany-colored mah-jongg table sits in the center. And next to it is a floor lamp, a long black pole with three oval spotlights attached like the broad leaves of a rubber plant.

Nobody says to me, "Sit here, this is where your mother used to sit." But I can tell even before everyone sits down. The chair closest to the door has an emptiness to it. But the feeling doesn't really have to do with the chair. It's her place on the table. Without anyone telling me, I know her corner on the table was the east.

The East is where things begin, my mother once told me, the direction from which the sun rises, where the wind comes from.

Auntie An-mei, who is sitting on my left, spills the tiles onto the green felt tabletop and we all start washing them, swirling them with our hands in a circular motion. They make a soothing swishing sound bumping into one another.

"Do you win like your mother?" asks Auntie Lin across from me. She is not smiling.

"I only played a little in college with some Jewish friends."

"Annh! Jewish mah-jongg," she says in disgusted tones. "Not the same thing." This is what my mother used to say, although she could never explain exactly why.

"Maybe I shouldn't play tonight. I'll just watch," I offer.

Auntie Lin looks exasperated, as though I am a simple child: "How can we play with just three people? Like a table with three legs, no balance. When Auntie Bing's husband died, she asked her brother to join. Your father asked you. So it's decided."

"What's the difference between Jewish and Chinese mah-jongg?" I once asked my mother. I couldn't tell by her answer if the games were different or just her attitude toward Chinese and Jewish people.

"Entirely different kind of playing," she said in her English explanation voice. "Jewish mah-jongg, they watch only for their own tile, play only with their eyes."

Then she switched to Chinese: "Chinese mah-jongg, you must play using your head, very tricky. You must watch what everybody else throws away and keep that in your head as well. And if nobody plays well, then the game becomes like Jewish mah-jongg. Why play? There's no strategy. You're just watching people make mistakes."

These kinds of explanations made me feel my mother and I spoke two different languages, which we did. I talked to her in English, she answered back in Chinese. Here at Joy Luck I remember the frustration: that my mother and I never really understood one another. We translated each other's meanings and wound up with mixed intentions. She was right about one thing: I didn't even know "little percent" of her.

"So what's the difference between Chinese and Jewish mah-jongg?" I ask Auntie Lin.

"Aii-ya," she exclaims in a mock scolding voice. "Your mother did not teach you anything?"

Auntie Bing patted my hand. "You a smart girl. You watch us, do the same. Help us stack the tiles and make four walls."

I follow Auntie Bing, but mostly I watch Auntie Lin. She is the fastest, which means I can almost keep up with the others by watching what she does first. Auntie Bing throws the dice and I'm told that Auntie Lin has become the East wind. I've become the North wind, the last hand to play. Auntie Bing is the South and Auntie An-mei is the West. And then we start taking tiles, throwing the dice, counting back on the wall to the right number of spots where our chosen tiles lie. I rearrange my tiles, sequences of bamboo and balls, doubles of colored number tiles, odd tiles that do not fit anywhere.

"Your mother was the best, like a pro," says Auntie An-mei while slowly sorting her tiles, considering each piece carefully.

Now we begin to play, looking at our hand, casting tiles, picking up others at an easy, comfortable pace. The Joy Luck aunties begin to make small talk, not really listening to each other. They speak in their special language, half in broken English, half in their own Chinese dialect, which no one else can understand. Auntie Bing mentions she bought yarn at half price, somewhere out in the Avenues. Auntie An-mei brags about a sweater she made for her daughter Ruth's new baby. "She thought it was store-bought," she says proudly.

Auntie Lin explains how mad she got at a store clerk who refused to let her return a skirt with a broken zipper. "I was *chi-se-la*," she said still fuming, "mad to death."

"But Lin-do, you are still with us. You didn't die," teases Auntie Bing and then as she laughs, Auntie Lin says *pung!* and *mah-jongg!* and then spreads her tiles out, laughing back at Auntie Bing while counting up her points. We start washing tiles again and it grows quiet. I'm getting bored and sleepy.

"Oh, I have a story," says Auntie Bing loudly, which startles everybody. Auntie Bing has always been the weird auntie, someone lost in her own world. My mother used to say Auntie Bing is not hard of hearing; she is hard of listening.

"Police arrested Mrs. Emerson's son last weekend," Auntie Bing says in a way that sounds like she's proud to be the first with this big news. "Mrs. Chan told me at church. Too many TV set found in his car."

Auntie Lin quickly says, "Aii-ya, Mrs. Emerson good lady," meaning Mrs. Emerson didn't deserve such a terrible son. But now I see this is also said for the benefit of Auntie An-mei, whose own youngest son was arrested two years ago for selling stolen car stereos. Auntie An-mei is rubbing her tile carefully before discarding it. She looks pained.

"Everybody has TVs in China now," says Auntie Lin, changing the subject. "Our family there all has TV sets—not just black and white, but color and re-mote! They have everything. So when we asked them what we should buy them, they said nothing, it was enough that we would come to visit them. But we bought them different things anyway, VCR and Sony Walkmen for the kids. They said, no, don't give it to us, but I think they liked it."

Poor Auntie An-mei rubs her tiles ever harder. I remember my mother telling me about the Hsus' trip to China three years ago. Auntie An-mei had saved two thousand dollars, all to spend on her brother's family. She had shown my mother the insides of her heavy suitcases. One was crammed with See's Nuts & Chews, M & Ms, candy-coated cashews, instant hot chocolate, and miniature marshmallows. My mother told me the other bag contained the most ridicu-lous clothes, all new: bright California style beachwear, baseball caps, cotton pants with elastic waists, bomber jackets, Stanford sweatshirts, and crew socks.

My mother had told her, "Who wants those useless things? They just want money." But Auntie An-mei said her brother was so poor and they were so rich by comparison. So she ignored my mother's advice and brought the heavy bags and their two thousand dollars to China. And when their China tour finally ar-rived in Hangzhou, the whole family from Ningbo was there to meet them. It wasn't just Auntie An-mei's little brother, but also his wife's stepbrothers and stepsisters, and a distant cousin, and that cousin's husband and that husband's uncle. They had all brought their mothers-in-law and children, and even their village friends who were not lucky enough to have overseas Chinese relatives to show off.

As my mother told it, "Auntie An-mei had cried before she left for China, thinking she would make her brother very rich and happy by Communist standards. But when she got home, she cried to me that everyone had their palm out and she was the only one who left with an empty hand."

My mother confirmed her suspicions. Nobody wanted the sweatshirts, those useless clothes. The M & Ms were thrown in the air, gone. And when the suitcases were emptied, the relatives asked what else the Hsus had brought.

Auntie An-mei and Uncle George got shaken down, not just for two thousand dollars worth of TVs and refrigerators, but a night's lodging for twenty-six people in the Overlooking the Lake Hotel, for three banquet tables at a restaurant that catered to foreign high prices, for three special gifts for each relative, and finally, for a loan of five thousand *yuan* in foreign exchange to a cousin's so-called uncle who wanted to buy a motorcycle, but who later disappeared for good along with the money. When the train pulled out of Hangzhou the next day, the Hsus found themselves depleted of some nine thousand dollars' worth of good will. Months later, after an inspiring Christmastime service at the First Chinese Baptist Church, Auntie An-mei tried to recoup her loss by saying it truly was more blessed to give than to receive, and my mother agreed, her longtime friend had blessings for at least several lifetimes.

Listening now to Auntie Lin bragging about the virtues of her family in China, I realize that Auntie Lin is oblivious to Auntie An-mei's pain. Is Auntie Lin being mean, or is it that my mother never told anybody but me the shameful story of Auntie An-mei's greedy family?

"So, Jing-mei, you go to school now?" says Auntie Lin.

"Her name is June. They all go by their American names," says Auntie Bing.

"That's okay," I say and I really mean it. In fact, it's even getting fashionable for American-born Chinese to use their Chinese names.

"I'm not in school anymore though," I say. "That was more than ten years ago."

Auntie Lin's eyebrows arch. "Maybe I'm thinking of someone else daughter," she says but I know right away she's lying. I know my mother probably told her I was going back to school to finish my degree, because somewhere back, maybe just six months ago, we were again having this argument about my being a failure, a "college drop-off," about my going back to finish.

Once again I had told my mother what she wanted to hear: "You're right. I'll look into it."

I had always assumed we had an unspoken understanding about these things: that she didn't really mean I was a failure, and I really meant I would try to respect her opinions more. But even if that's not what we meant, I know she had told Auntie Lin I was going back to school.

Auntie Lin and my mother were both best friends and arch enemies who spent a lifetime comparing their children. I was six months older than Waverly Jong, Auntie Lin's prized daughter. From the time we were babies, our mothers compared the creases in our belly buttons, how shapely our earlobes were, how fast we healed when we scraped our knees, how thick and dark our hair, how many shoes we wore out in one year, and later, how smart Waverly was at playing chess, how many trophies she had won last month, how many newspapers had printed her name, how many cities she had visited.

I know my mother resented listening to Auntie Lin talk about Waverly when she had nothing to come back with. At first, my mother tried to cultivate some hidden genius in me. She did housework for an old retired piano teacher down the hall who gave me lessons and free use of a piano to practice on in exchange. When I failed to become a concert pianist, or even an accompanist for the church youth choir, she finally explained that I was late-blooming, like Einstein who everyone thought was retarded until he discovered a bomb.

Now it is Auntie Bing who wins this hand of mah-jongg, so we count points and begin again.

"Did you know Lena move to Woodside?" asks Auntie Bing with obvious pride, looking down at the tiles, talking to no one in particular. She quickly erases her smile and tries for some modesty. "Of course, it's not best house in neighborhood, not million dollar house, not yet. But it's good investment. Better than paying rent. Better than somebody putting you under their thumb to rub you out."

So now I know Auntie Bing's daughter Lena told her about my being evicted from my apartment on lower Russian Hill. Even though Lena and I are still friends, we have grown naturally cautious about telling each other too much. Still, what little we say to one another often comes back in another guise. It's the same old game, everybody talking in circles.

"It's getting late," I say after we finish the round. I start to stand up, but Auntie Lin pushes me back down into the chair.

"Stay, stay. We talk a while, get to know you again," she says. "Been a long time."

I know this is a polite gesture on the Joy Luck aunties' part—a protest when actually they are just as anxious to see me go as I am to leave. "No, I really must go now, thank you, thank you," I say, glad I remembered how the pretense goes.

"But you must stay! We have something important to tell you, from your mother," Auntie Bing blurts out in her too-loud voice. The others look uncomfortable, as if this is not how they intended to break some sort of bad news to me.

I sit down. Auntie An-mei leaves the room quickly and returns with a bowl of peanuts, then quietly shuts the door. Everybody is quiet, as if nobody knows where to begin.

It is Auntie Bing who finally speaks. "I think your mother die with an important thought on her mind," she says in halting English. And then she begins to speak in Chinese, calmly, softly.

"Your mother was a very strong woman, a good mother. She loved you very much, more than her own life. And that's why you can understand why a mother like this could never forget her other daughters. She knew they were alive and before she died she wanted to contact her daughters in China."

The babies in Kweilin, I think. I was not those babies. The babies in a sling on her shoulder. Her other daughters. And now I feel like I'm in Kweilin amid the bombing and I can see these babies lying on the side of the road, their red thumbs popped out of their mouths, screaming to be reclaimed. Somebody took them away. They're safe. And now my mother's left me forever, gone back to China to get these babies. I can barely hear Auntie Bing's voice.

"She had searched for years, written letters back and forth," says Auntie Bing. "And last year she got an address. She was going to tell your father soon. Aii-ya, what a shame. A lifetime of waiting."

Auntie An-mei interrupts with an excited voice: "So your aunties and I, we wrote to this address," she says. "We say that a certain party, your mother, want to meet another certain party. And this party write back to us. They are your sisters, Jing-mei."

My sisters, I repeat to myself, saying these two words together for the first time.

Auntie An-mei is holding a sheet of paper as thin as wrapping tissue. In perfectly straight vertical rows I see Chinese characters written in blue fountain pen ink. A word is smudged. A tear? I take the letter with shaking hands, marveling at how smart my sisters must be to be able to read and write Chinese.

The aunties are all smiling at me, as though I had been a dying person who has now miraculously recovered. Auntie Bing is handing me another envelope. Inside is a check made out to June Woo for $1200. I can't believe it.

"My sisters are sending *me* money?" I ask.

"No, no," says Auntie Lin with her mock exasperated voice. "Every year we save our mah-jongg winnings for big banquet at fancy restaurant. Most times your mother win, so most is her money. We add just a little, so you can go Hong

Kong, take a train to Shanghai, see your sisters. Besides, we all getting too rich, too fat." She pats her stomach for proof.

"See my sisters," I repeat numbly. I am awed by this prospect, trying to imagine what I would see. And I am embarrassed by the end-of-the-year banquet lie my aunties have told to mask their generosity. I am crying now, great gulping sobs, seeing but not understanding this loyalty to my mother.

"You must see your sisters and tell them about your mother's death," says Auntie Bing. "But most important, you must tell them about her life. The mother they did not know, they must now know."

"See my sisters, tell them about my mother," I echo, nodding. "What will I say? What can I tell them about my mother? I don't know anything. She was my mother."

The aunties are looking at me as if I have become crazy right before their eyes.

"Not know your own mother?" cries Auntie An-mei with disbelief. "How can you say? Your mother is in your bones!"

"Tell them stories of your family here. How she became success," offers Auntie Lin.

"Tell them stories she told you, lessons she taught, what you know about her mind that has become your mind," says Auntie Bing. "Your mother very smart lady."

I hear more choruses of "tell them-tell them" as each auntie frantically tries to think what should be passed on.

"Her kindness."

"Her smartness."

"Her dutiful nature to family."

"Her hopes, things that matter to her."

"The excellent dishes she cooked."

"Imagine, a daughter not knowing her own mother!"

And then it occurs to me. They are frightened. That in me, they see their own daughters, just as ignorant, just as unmindful of all the truths and hopes they have brought to America. They see daughters who get impatient when their mothers talk in Chinese, who think they are stupid when they explain things in fractured English. They see that joy and luck do not mean the same to their daughters, that to these closed American-born minds "joy luck" is not a word, it does not exist. They see daughters who will bear grandchildren, born without any connecting hope passed from generation to generation.

"I will tell them everything," I say simply, and the aunties look at me with doubtful faces.

"I will remember everything about her and tell them," I say more firmly. And gradually, one by one they smile and pat my hand. They still look troubled, as if something is out of balance. But they also look hopeful, that what I say will become true. What more can they ask? What more can I promise?

They go back to eating their soft boiled peanuts, saying stories among themselves. They are young girls again, dreaming of good times in the past and good times yet to come. A brother from Hangzhou who makes his sister cry with joy when he returns nine thousand dollars plus interest. A youngest son whose stereo and TV repair business is so good, he sends leftovers to China. A daughter whose babies are able to swim like fish in a fancy pool in Woodside. Such good stories. The best. They are the lucky ones.

And I am sitting at my mother's place at the mah-jongg table, on the East, where things begin.

One Thing after Another

On days when the mind wakes up it's possible to see that very little connects or can be reasoned out, like checkers or a quick hand of poker. Very little makes sense, especially in our lives. This seems curious. Last night, for instance, I was reading Montaigne, not in bunches, but in single paragraphs and sentences for he sometimes is a burden and goes on and on when he should be quiet. One idea leapt up in my mind and stayed there, like a blue flame.

We do not correct the man we hang; we correct others through him. I do the same. I relished the seemingly comic posture: Montaigne on a scaffold with his hair full of eager wind and some poor guy on his knees, a slack halo of rope descending over his bowed head. Then I read the idea as a bit of spoken wisdom and liked it even more: that through punishment of one guy we scare the hell out of other guys.

I read this master last night. This morning I got up and ran my index finger down the classified ads in search of a Pontiac Grand Prix, something with a tilt steering wheel and cruise control. I found a 1982 for $7,000, and drove to the suburban town of San Pablo where, at Accurate's body and fender, I sat tilting the wheel up and down. I adjusted the seat and the mirror that showed a piece of the sky. I checked the seats for tears or oily stains. A fender man in overalls came over and raised the hood. I pulled out the dip stick and plucked the belts and stared at the engine as if some oily part was going to do magic.

OK, now how did I get from reading a great essayist to wanting to buy a car. What brain cell said, "Pontiac"? What brain cell said, "Let's read, Gary"? I'm not sure. And I'm not sure why later that afternoon after this business with the car, I spent a half an hour with a secretary talking about Puerto Rico and still later I hurried over to a luncheon honoring Paul S. Taylor, a Professor Emeritus at Berkeley, who is, in spite of his Anglican birth, the first Chicano historian, or so I would like to think of him. He's a remarkable man, and a sad one, for he is nearing ninety and is in ill health; his arms are thin, his skin blotched, his eyelids held open with scotch tape. When he talks you have to tilt an ear in the direction of a weak voice. We felt for this man, our first Chicano scholar, when he said over and over that he was happy to be presented a plaque. Tired, half-smiling, he held it up with two hands for us to see. The bronze plaque winked a flashing light and then went dark when he laid it in his lap.

From there I returned home troubled because it hurt to see a man in his failing years. When it is all over, is this who we become? A man with a plaque, with scotch tape holding open the eyes to see just a little more of the world? I gave my wife a hug, called my daughter "knucklehead," and went outside to the garage-turned-study until dinner time.

After dinner I lay on the couch, belly full and groaning when my daughter, a play doctor, gave me a shot in the head and asked if I felt better. I said yes. She lined her brow, looking worried as a real doctor, and said there were tiny holes on my nose. She gave me a shot for every hole and two long ones for my nostrils.

I got up with a start before she had finished my treatment when I remembered that the Mancini-Chacon fight was that night. If I can read Montaigne, mull over a car, and praise a great man all in less than twenty-four hours, then why not see the fight of the year? It was as good an entertainment as anything I could think of for the night. I called to Carolyn who was finishing the dishes to get dressed because we were going to see the fight. A light came on in her eyes as she hurried to the bedroom to dress and remake her face for the evening. I drove our daughter to my sister's place—my sister, a fight fan from the year one, pounded a fist into her palm and wished Chacon all the luck. When I returned home Carolyn was sitting cross-legged on the couch in her thrift shop fur, waiting.

We drove to the Ivy Room in Albany, a bar with cable television. When we walked in the patrons on barstools looked up from their drinks to show us veined noses and eyes like red scribbling. They looked tired and heavy in their heavy coats. Biker types were playing shuffleboard, whooping it up when one knocked the other's puck over the edge. The bartender, with his shirt sleeves rolled up, dipped glasses into soapy water, shook them until he thought they were clean, and then immersed them in clear water. We took a seat near the television, which was on with the sound turned down, ordered a beer for myself and a Calistoga for Carolyn, and talked about our recently purchased house, money, family, and our daughter the would-be doctor, as we waited for the fight to start. We then went quiet, looking around. It was a strange place, this redneck bar. I snuggled my face into her neck and asked if she was having fun. She raised her eyebrows and said, "You sure know how to treat a girl to a swell time." She took a long and hard swig of her Calistoga as she looked at me with eyes big as they could get.

When the fight started, two heavy guys moved their beers and themselves closer to the television. One looked drunkenly at Carolyn as he passed and sat down with a grunt in his chair. He looked up in silence at the screen. "Ching chong," he then started in. "Let's get some ching chong food." He turned to his friend. "What do you say, Dickie babe?" His friend, whose eyes were on the television and the first round that had Chacon against the ropes, said, "What the hell are you talkin' about?"

"Ching chong food."

His friend turned stiffly to his friend, "You're a crazy gook."

I was uneasy about their talk. Knowing Carolyn was Asian, they were being insulting and largely stupid. I tried to ignore them as it was the second round and Chacon was against the ropes again, gloves up and sliding away from Mancini's pitbull tenacity. But the heavy guys continued with the madeup words of "chow wow bow wow" and "ching ga ge cho cho." I'd had enough. I started with an Okie drawl with "Beans and weenies, taters to gobble up 'cause I got to pay for my fuckin' Ford." Carolyn pinched my arms for me to shut up. And I did. Not because of them but because Chacon was in trouble. Mancini had him in the corner, sticking hard and deep into his face. Stay up, little man, I said to myself. Don't go down. But Mancini pumped hard and Chacon pumped back slowly as he slid along the ropes. Then it was over. Tony Perez, the referee, stepped between them to stop the fight.

I forgot the heavy guys and they forgot me because Chacon, *our* Mexican, our California kid, our baby-faced boy wonder, was on one knee and not getting up. We watched the replay of the third round: the overhand right, then the stiff left, then the right again. A leg buckled. Blood sprayed like glass from his face and his smile of the early rounds turned to a wince. We watched the replay again, then a third time, before I chugged my beer and led Carolyn to the door, thanking the bartender as we walked past the long, almost empty, bar counter. In the night air I was still troubled. How could he lose? He was on our side, I told Carolyn as we crossed the street against a red light. He couldn't lose. He was one of us.

We hurried across the street to Captain Video and, even though we didn't own a video recorder, scanned with other couples through the movie selections. It didn't make sense, our being there. But neither did Chacon's loss. He was our blood, a genius of the heart, and no way could he go down without getting up. We looked around for a while and then trotted back across the street for another drink to see if his loss made sense.

Ishmael Reed

My Oakland, There Is a There There

On New Year's Eve, famed landscape architect John Roberts accompanied me on my nightly walk, which takes me from Fifty-third Street to Aileen, Shattuck, and back to Fifty-third Street. He was able to identify plants and trees that had been imported from Asia, Africa, the Middle East, and Australia. On Aileen Street he discovered a banana tree! And Arthur Monroe, a painter and art historian, traces the "Tabby" garden design—in which seashells and plates are mixed with lime, sand, and water to form decorative borders, found in this Oakland neighborhood and others—to the influence of Islamic slaves brought to the Gulf Coast.

I won over my neighbors, I think, after I triumphed over a dozen generations of pigeons that had been roosting in the crevices of this house for many years. It was a long and angry war, and my five-year-old constantly complained to her mother about Daddy's bad words about the birds. I used everything I could get my hands on, including chicken wire and mothballs, and I would have tried the clay owls if the only manufacturer hadn't gone out of business. I also learned never to underestimate the intelligence of pigeons. Just when you think you've got them whipped, you'll notice that they've regrouped on some strategic rooftop to prepare for another invasion. When the house was free of pigeons and their droppings, which had spread to the adjoining properties, the lady next door said, "Thank you."

Every New Year's Day since then our neighbors have invited us to join them and their fellow Louisianans for the traditional Afro-American good-luck meal called Hoppin' John. This year the menu included black-eyed peas, ham, corn bread, potato salad, chitterlings, greens, fried chicken, yams, head cheese, macaroni, rolls, sweet potato pie, and fruitcake. I got up that morning weighing 214 pounds and came home from the party weighing 220.

We've lived on Fifty-third Street for three years now. Carla's dance and theater school, which she operates with her partner, Jody Roberts—Roberts and Blank Dance/Drama—is already five years old. I am working on my seventh novel and a television production of my play *Mother Hubbard*. The house has yet to be restored to its 1906 glory, but we're working on it.

I've grown accustomed to the common sights here—teenagers moving through the neighborhood carrying radios blasting music by Grandmaster Flash and Prince, men hovering over cars with tools and rags in hand, decked-out female church delegations visiting the sick. Unemployment up, one sees more men drinking from sacks as they walk through Market Street or gather in Helen McGregor Plaza on Shattuck and Fifty-second Street, near a bench where mothers sit with their children waiting for buses. It may be because the bus stop is across the street from Children's Hospital (exhibiting a brand-new antihuman, postmodern wing), but there seem to be a lot of sick black children these days. The criminal courts and emergency rooms of Oakland hospitals, both medical and psychiatric, are also filled with blacks.

White men go from door to door trying to unload spoiled meat. Incredibly sleazy white contractors and hustlers try to entangle people into shady deals that sometimes lead to the loss of a home. Everybody knows of someone, usually a widow, who has been deceived into paying thousands of dollars more than the standard cost for, say, adding a room to a house. It sure ain't El Cerrito. In El Cerrito the representatives from the utilities were very courteous. If they realize they're speaking to someone in a black neighborhood, however, they become curt and sarcastic. I was trying to arrange for the gas company to come out to fix a stove when the woman from Pacific Gas and Electric gave me some snide lip. I told her, "Lady, if you think what you're going through is an inconvenience, you can imagine my inconvenience paying the bills every month." Even she had to laugh.

The clerks in the stores are also curt, regarding blacks the way the media regard them, as criminal suspects. Over in El Cerrito the cops were professional, respectful—in Oakland they swagger about like candidates for a rodeo. In El

Cerrito and the Berkeley Hills you could take your time paying some bills, but in this black neighborhood if you miss paying a bill by one day, "reminders" printed in glaring and violent typefaces are sent to you, or you're threatened with discontinuance of this or that service. Los Angeles police victim Eulia Love, who was shot in the aftermath of an argument over an overdue gas bill, would still be alive if she had lived in El Cerrito or the Berkeley Hills.

I went to a bank a few weeks ago that advertised easy loans on television, only to be told that I would have to wait six months after opening an account to be eligible for a loan. I went home and called the same bank, this time putting on my Clark Kent voice, and was informed that I could come in and get the loan the same day. Other credit unions and banks, too, have different lending practices for black and white neighborhoods, but when I try to tell white intellectuals that blacks are prevented from developing industries because the banks find it easier to lend money to Communist countries than to American citizens, they call me paranoid. Sometimes when I know I'm going to be inconvenienced by merchants or creditors because of my Fifty-third Street address, I give the address of my Berkeley studio instead. Others are not so fortunate.

Despite the inconveniences and antagonism from the outside world one has to endure for having a Fifty-third Street address, life in this neighborhood is more pleasant than grim. Casually dressed, well-groomed elderly men gather at the intersections to look after the small children as they walk to and from school, or just to keep an eye on the neighborhood. My next-door neighbor keeps me in stitches with his informed commentary on any number of political comedies emanating from Washington and Sacramento. Once we were discussing pesticides, and the man who was repairing his porch told us that he had a great garden and didn't have to pay all that much attention to it. As for pesticides, he said, the bugs have to eat, too.

There are people on this block who still know the subsistence skills many Americans have forgotten. They can hunt and fish (and if you don't fish, there is a man who covers the neighborhood selling fresh fish and yelling "Fishman," recalling a period of ancient American commerce when you didn't have to pay the middleman). They are also loyal Americans—they vote, they pay taxes— but you don't find the extreme patriots here that you find in white neighborhoods. Although Christmas, Thanksgiving, New Year's, and Easter are celebrated with all get-out, I've never seen a flag flying on Memorial Day, or on any holiday that calls for the showing of the flag. Blacks express their loyalty in concrete ways. For example, you rarely see a foreign car in this neighborhood. And this Fifty-third Street neighborhood, as well as black neighborhoods like it from coast to coast, will supply the male children who will bear the brunt of future jungle wars, just as they did in Vietnam.

We do our shopping on a strip called Temescal, which stretches from Forty-sixth to Fifty-first streets. Temescal, according to Oakland librarian William Sturm, is an Aztec word for "hothouse," or "bathhouse." The word was borrowed from the Mexicans by the Spanish to describe similar hothouses, early saunas, built by the California Indians in what is now North Oakland. Some say the hothouses were used to sweat out demons; others claim the Indians used them for medicinal purposes. Most agree that after a period of time in the steam, the Indians would rush en masse into the streams that flowed through the area. One still runs underneath my backyard—I have to mow the grass there almost every other day.

Within these five blocks are the famous Italian restaurant Bertola's, "Since 1932"; Siam restaurant; La Belle Creole, a French-Caribbean restaurant; Asmara, an Ethiopian restaurant; and Ben's Hof Brau, where white and black senior citizens, dressed in the elegance of a former time, congregate to talk or to have an inexpensive though quality breakfast provided by Ben's hardworking and courteous staff.

The Hof Brau shares its space with Vern's market, where you can shop to the music of DeBarge. To the front of Vern's is the Temescal Delicatessen, where a young Korean man makes the best po'boy sandwiches north of Louisiana, and near the side entrance is Ed Fraga's Automotive. The owner is always advising his customers to avoid stress, and he says good-bye with a "God bless you." The rest of the strip is taken up by the Temescal Pharmacy, which has a resident health adviser and a small library of health literature; the Aikido Institute; an African bookstore; and the internationally known Genova Deli, to which people from the surrounding cities travel to shop. The strip also includes the Clausen House thrift shop, which sells used clothes and furniture. Here you can buy novels by J. D. Salinger and John O'Hara for ten cents each. (Of all the establishments listed here, only the Siam restaurant, the Aikido Institute, and the Genova Deli remain.)

Space that was recently occupied by the Buon Gusto Bakery is now for rent. Before the bakery left, an Italian lady who worked there introduced me to a crunchy, cookielike treat called "bones," which she said went well with Italian wine. The Buon Gusto had been a landmark since the 1940s, when, according to a guest at the New Year's Day Hoppin' John supper, North Oakland was populated by Italians and Portuguese. In those days a five-room house could be rented for forty-five dollars a month, she said.

The neighborhood is still in transition. The East Bay Negro Historical Society, which was located around the corner on Grove Street, included in its collection letters written by nineteenth-century macho man Jack London to his black nurse. They were signed, "Your little white pickaninny." It's been replaced by the New Israelite Delight restaurant, part of the Israelite Church, which also operates a day-care center. The restaurant offers homemade Louisiana gumbo and a breakfast that includes grits.

Unlike the other California neighborhoods I've lived in, I know most of the people on this block by name. They are friendly and cooperative, always offering to watch your house while you're away. The day after one of the few whites who lives on the block—a brilliant muckraking journalist and former student of mine—was robbed, neighbors gathered in front of his house to offer assistance.

In El Cerrito my neighbor was indeed a cop. He used pomade on his curly hair, sported a mustache, and there was a grayish tint in his brown eyes. He was a handsome man, with a smile like a movie star's. His was the only house on the block I entered during my three-year stay in that neighborhood, and that was one afternoon when we shared some brandy. I wanted to get to know him better. I didn't know he was dead until I saw people in black gathered on his doorstep.

I can't imagine that happening on Fifty-third Street. In a time when dour thinkers view alienation and insensitivity toward the plight of others as characteristics of the modern condition, I think I'm lucky to live in a neighborhood where people look out for one another.

A human neighborhood.

Willkommen Castro

Wayne Friday carefully held Harvey Milk's legs in case the car had to make a sudden lurch forward. As she drove slowly toward the City Hall rally site, Anne Kronenberg kept retracing the routes to the nearest hospital in case it happened. Less than a year ago, Anne had walked into Castro Camera to volunteer for some campaign work because she didn't have anything better to do; now, she was driving one of the nation's most famous gay leaders, bracing herself for the sound of gunfire. So much had happened so fast. And it had only begun.

Harvey and Frank Robinson had prepared one of the dramatic pieces of oration Harvey loved so much for that day. Maybe the assassination threats had made him think of Martin Luther King, because he quoted King freely during the speech, even calling for a march on Washington for the next July 4. Few politicians in American history got the chance to directly address a crowd the size of the one stretched out before him and Harvey wanted to make the best of it.

"My name is Harvey Milk—and I want to recruit you. I want to recruit you for the fight to preserve democracy from the John Briggs and Anita Bryants who are trying to constitutionalize bigotry.

"We are not going to allow that to happen. We are not going to sit back in silence as 300,000 of our gay sisters and brothers did in Nazi Germany. We are not going to allow our rights to be taken away and then march with bowed heads into the gas chambers.

"On this anniversary of Stonewall, I ask my gay sisters and brothers to make the commitment to fight. For themselves, for their freedom, for their country. Gay people, we will not win our rights by staying quietly in our closets. We are coming out. We are coming out to fight the lies, the myths, the distortions. We are coming out to tell the truths about gays, for I am tired of the conspiracy of silence, so I'm going to talk about it. And I want you to talk about it. You must come out. Come out to your parents, your relatives. I know that it is hard and that it will hurt them, but think of how they will hurt you in the voting booths.

"Jimmy Carter, you talk about human rights. You want to be the world's leader for human rights. There are fifteen to twenty million gay people in this nation. When are you going to talk about *their* rights?

"If you do not speak out, if you remain silent, then I call upon lesbians and gay men from all over the nation, your nation, to gather in Washington one year from now, on that very same spot where over a decade ago, Dr. Martin Luther King spoke to a nation of his dreams, dreams that are fast fading, dreams that to many in this nation have become nightmares rather than dreams. I call upon all minorities and especially the millions of lesbians and gay men to wake up from their dreams, to gather in Washington and tell Jimmy Carter and their nation: Wake up. Wake up, America. No more racism. No more sexism. No more ageism. No more hatred. No more. And to the bigots, to the John Briggs, to the Anita Bryants, and all their ilk: Let me remind you what America is.

"Listen carefully:

"On the Statue of Liberty, it says, 'Give me your tired, your poor, your huddled masses yearning to be free . . .' "

"In the Declaration of Independence, it is written: 'All men are created equal and they are endowed with certain inalienable rights . . .'

"And in our national anthem, it says: 'Oh, say does that star-spangled banner yet wave o'er the land of the free.'

"For Mr. Briggs and Ms. Bryant, and all the bigots out there: That's what America is. No matter how hard you try, you cannot erase those words from the Declaration of Independence. No matter how hard you try, you cannot chip those words off the base of the Statue of Liberty. And no matter how hard you try, you cannot sing the 'Star Spangled Banner' without those words.

"That's what America is.

"Love it or leave it."

The sight of the hundreds of thousands gathered in front of the stately City Hall, overflowing from the large Civic Center plaza, flashed on television sets across the nation that night. The press had a field day with human-interest side stories to the event. One white-haired, seventy-four-year-old woman, for example, told reporters about her two gay sons who were both teachers. "My older son committed suicide when his local school board found out he was gay and made moves to fire him," she said. "My other son is afraid to be here today because of that S.O.B. Briggs and what he wants to do to teachers. I lost one son to the likes of Mr. Briggs and I don't intend to lose another one."

Also granting interviews that day was Supervisor Dan White, who stood grimly on the sidelines of the parade as the thousands marched by. White was the only supervisor who had voted against closing Market Street for the annual parade. "This is our only opportunity to approve or disapprove of what goes on in our streets," he said. "The vast majority of people in this city don't want public displays of sexuality."

Anita Bryant asked Christians to pray for San Francisco on that Sunday.

Harvey was ecstatic about the response to his speech. As usual, he never mentioned the assassination fears once the imminent threat had passed. Instead, he spoke enthusiastically about the crowd and carefully handed out copies of his speech to every reporter he could buttonhole. Already, he could imagine the tens of thousands walking by the White House next year, assembling under the shadow of the Washington Monument. Such good theater.

Bienvenidos Castro. Willkommen Castro. Bienvenue Castro. In seven languages, the large canvas banner festooned over the intersection of Eighteenth and Castro spoke to the new role the Castro neighborhood now fulfilled in the homosexual collective conscious. The corner had been dubbed the crossroads of the gay world, and by the summer of 1978, the neighborhood had become an international gay tourist mecca. Thousands more were moving to the neighborhood, prompting gay politicos to speculate not *if* gays would become a numerical majority of San Francisco adults, but when. A new gay chauvinism ran rampant, complete with a lexicon of pejoratives. Heterosexuals became known as breeders—"Today's breeders, tomorrow's cows," went one slogan— and the game of spotting heterosexuals on Castro Street replaced the old heterophile game of picking out queers.

The neighborhood represented less a trend than a bona-fide sociological phenomenon. An entire Castro life-style evolved, fixed squarely on machismo. A gym membership became a prerequisite to the neighborhood's social life. Solid pectorals and washboard stomachs were highly valued for their aesthetic benefits during the ritualistic tearing off of sheer tank tops during the sweaty nights on the disco dance floor. The milieu was more macho than anything in heterosexual life and early settlers were disquieted by a profound shift in the neighborhood. No longer was the area a social experiment in the throes of creation; the life-style had solidified. Gays no longer came to the Castro to create a new life-style, they came to fit into the existing Castro Street mold. The summer of '78 seemed the Castro gays' equivalent of the Haight-Ashbury hippies' summer of love eleven years earlier; like its predecessor, the hot sunny days marked the end of an epoch as well as the beginning.

The continuing influx of gays from across the country strained housing stock and once distinct neighborhoods adjacent to the Castro soon became "Castroized," as Harvey called it. The renovating gay immigrants bought up tract after tract of century-old Victorians, often at extravagant prices. Housing prices skyrocketed further because of the high demand—and the real estate speculators, who were taking advantage of the boom to quickly buy and sell the homes. The rate of real-estate transactions jumped 700 percent between 1968 and 1978, according to one federal study of the Duboce Triangle neighborhood a few blocks off Castro. The gay immigrants bought heavily into neighboring black and Latino areas, whose low-income minorities could not compete economically. Black leaders were especially vocal in asserting that gays were shoving minorities out of the city. By the end of 1978, gay neighborhoods dominated roughly twenty percent of the city's residential expanses.

No single strip in San Francisco felt the pinch of the inflated real-estate values like the two-block core of the Castro district. Leases rose dramatically, killing marginal businesses to make way for establishments oriented toward the high-profit services needed by tourists and the increasingly affluent residents. A few hundred feet from the Willkommen Castro banner was another sign that spoke as meaningfully of the changing Castro. In the window of Castro Camera: "We need a new home."

Thom Gunn

The J Car

Last year I used to ride the J CHURCH Line,
Climbing between small yards recessed with vine
—Their ordered privacy, their plots of flowers
Like blameless lives we might imagine ours.
Most trees were cut back, but some brushed the car
Before it swung round to the street once more
On which I rolled out almost to the end,
To 29th Street, calling for my friend.
    He'd be there at the door, smiling but gaunt,
To set out for the German restaurant.
There, since his sight was tattered now, I would
First read the menu out. He liked the food
In which a sourness and dark richness meet
For conflict without taste of a defeat,
As in the Sauerbraten. What he ate
I hoped would help him to put on some weight,
But though the beer and crusted pancakes drew him
They never seemed to make much difference to him,
And I'd eat his dessert before we both

Rose from the neat arrangement of the cloth,
Where the connection between life and food
Had briefly seemed so obvious if so crude.
Our conversation circumspectly cheerful,
We had sat here like children good but fearful
Who think if they behave everything might
Still against likelihood come out all right.
　　But it would not, and we could not stay here:
Finishing up the Optimator beer,
I walked him home through the suburban cool
By dimming shape of church and Catholic school,
Only a few white teenagers about.
After the four blocks he would be tired out.
I'd leave him to the feverish sleep ahead,
Myself to ride through darkened yards instead
Back to my health. Of course I simplify.
Of course. It tears me still that he should die
As only an apprentice to his trade,
The ultimate engagements not yet made.
His gifts had been withdrawing one by one
Even before their usefulness was done:
This optic nerve would never be relit;
The other flickered, soon to be with it.
Unready, disappointed, unachieved,
He knew he would not write the much-conceived,
Much-hoped-for work now, nor yet help create
A love he might in full reciprocate.

Theodora Kroeber

Ishi: The Last of His Tribe

Blurred memories came back to him: of the Monster, a trolley car, a ferryboat, seagulls, foghorns. *The City—this is the City, the museum-watgurwa. But where is my friend?*

There was a knock at the door; it was Majapa. *He makes no sign that he smells my fear.*

His friend asked if he had slept well; if he was hungry. "It is breakfast time," he said.

They went down a long hall and downstairs to the museum dining room where several museum men were already gathered around the table. They shook hands with Ishi and repeated the words, "Welcome, welcome to the museum."

Ishi answered, "Welcome, welcome!" And one of the men patted his shoulder and said, "Good, very good!"

For breakfast, there was oatmeal mush. They asked Ishi if it was as good as acorn mush. He nodded politely. "Haxa—it is good with a little salt. The milk of the cow spoils it." There was also the muddy saldu drink, coffee; and bread, bacon and eggs.

Do they have to go far to find the nests with the eggs? Perhaps it would not be a polite question.

The museum men did not stare at his hair or his bare feet. They knew a few words of Yahi and they listened closely when he spoke. "It is as in the Old Days when my grandfather sat at the firepit of neighbors; friendly and courteous people speaking a different tongue," said Ishi to Majapa.

The museum men do not press in upon me; their voices are quiet.

After breakfast, Majapa took Ishi to his office, and then to a room where there were many bows and arrows. He opened the cases in which the bows were kept and motioned Ishi to take them out if he wished. One by one, Ishi examined each bow. Some were made of juniper or other wood he knew; some of wood which was strange to him. He felt their grip, their weight, and he held them in position to string and bend. Some of the bows were of great age; Ishi knew they would break if they were to be strung and bent. Majapa explained that they had lain in caves or been buried in the ground for many moons.

I could make arrows fly from these bows. But the Peoples who made them are not known to me: Algonquin, Comanche, Navajo, says Majapa; and Persian, Scythian, Macedonian; the names sing as the singing of my lost bow. Aii-ya! To shoot, to shoot the bow again! To see arrows flying from these warrior bows!

"You have no Yahi bow here."

"I have never seen one."

"They are different from these. I could make a Yahi bow for you, but I have no tools."

"We shall see. Perhaps we can find the tools."

We talk more words today than yesterday. My friend's Yahi words are sometimes not right. But he listens when I speak. And always he makes more of the bird tracks on the white bark which he keeps in his pocket. Then he says the words over to me, many times until he says them in the true Yahi way. It is as when I make a fine arrowpoint, using smaller and finer flaking tools, the way Katsuna would do it.

Ishi repeated over and over the saldu names: train, trolley car, ferryboat. He listened to the talk of the museum men and soon knew the names of the different foods which came to the museum dining table. He learned the saldu names of the furniture in his room: bed and chair and table and lamp. And he learned the name of each person he met, repeated it and remembered it. He was beginning to speak the saldu tongue.

A Kuwi, a Doctor, came to the bow room with his young son to meet Ishi. They were friends of Majapa. Ishi smiled at the boy, saying to his father, "This is a fine wanasi. Is he to be a hunter, or will he have power over certain pains?"

The Doctor shook his head. "Who knows?" he said. "He is a dreamer, this one."

They went outside where Majapa smoked his pipe and Ishi and the Kuwi smoked cigarettes. The smoke was light and sweet, like sacred tobacco; it drifted away toward Outer Ocean while they talked a little of hunting with the bow. They went down the high museum steps, past the rows of white houses, to the forest Ishi had seen from his window and which the saldu called a park. It was quiet there, with trails leading into the brush, and ponds with ducks and geese and swans, and an open hillside with buffalo and antelope.

So passed Ishi's first day in the museum-watgurwa. After dinner, in the evening, Majapa came to Ishi's room. Ishi's few clothes, his treasure bundle, and whatever other articles he owned were neatly put away on shelves. A pot of tea was on the table and Ishi and one of the museum men were sitting, drinking tea.

Majapa motioned around the room. "You like? Aizuna—It is your own."

Ishi smiled. "Wowi aizuna, wowi aizuna." My own home.

He waved goodnight to Majapa and turned back to his visitor who was telling him about fishing in Outer Ocean. That much of the story was clear to Ishi. For the rest, he understood only a word here and there, but he knew fishing stories, and he was sure this was a good one. *When I know more saldu talk I will tell this museum man a fishing story.*

Said Ishi to Majapa the next day, "This watgurwa is bigger than the whole village of Wowunupo."

"Will you take me to visit Wowunupo in the time of the spring salmon?"

Ishi shook his head. "It is a dead world."

"I think it is not dead. You remember it, and I remember it."

Does this Friend own a Power Dream which takes him upstream with the salmon? How else could he remember the Yahi World? Sometime I think he may tell me his Dream.

The next day, Majapa took Ishi to a room where there were baskets, nothing but baskets. Said Majapa, "These baskets do not come from across the ocean as do some of the bows. They are all from Peoples like the Yahi who lived on the land before the coming of the saldu."

Ishi nodded, then turned to the baskets, looking at them shelf by shelf, row by row, until he came to a certain row where he stopped.

"These are the baskets of my People." He spoke then almost in a whisper, "But how is it the Museum-watgurwa has these baskets?" He pointed to two, side by side.

Majapa looked at the two baskets. "They are Yahi, are they not?"

"These baskets were made by my Cousin. She made them in Wowunupo." Ishi sat down on a bench. There was a weakness in his legs; his heart pressed against his chest; slow tears formed in his eyes.

These are the Little One's baskets—but this kind saldu, my Friend, was not among those who came to Wowunupo. I saw their faces; I heard their voices; his was not one of them. How do these baskets come here?

Majapa had put the two baskets beside him on the bench; Ishi did not touch them. "My Friend, you speak sometimes as if you were once in the Yahi World, I know not whether on a Dream journey or a waking one. It was not you who found these baskets?"

"No, no! I saw no baskets in the Yahi World. . . . You remember the saldu who came to Wowunupo?"

"Haxa."

"There was one who spoke to your mother?"

"Haxa. I remember that one."

"He did not steal from Wowunupo?"

"He took nothing. He spoke with courtesy to my mother."

"And he returned the next day and tried to find your mother?"

"Haxa."

"This one came to the City, to the museum-watgurwa to tell me about finding your village and about the Old One there who had a sickness in her legs. As soon as I could—it was not until the end of the heat moons, a long time—I went to the Great Valley, and he and I made our way into Wowunupo. For the length of a moon we searched for you . . . for your mother. We found nobody, nothing. . . ."

"Why did you wish to find her?"

"We knew she could not be alone, and that whoever was with her was without tools or blankets. . . . We hoped we could help. . . . We were too late. . . ."

Ishi's thoughts went back to two saldu he had swum away from, after Mother was gone, and of other saldu he had seen from time to time. _Majapa was not one of them. He must have come to Wowunupo while I was looking for the Lost Ones in Upper Meadow._

But Majapa was speaking. "Someone in the sheriff's village sent these baskets to the museum, two moons ago. I put them with other baskets most like them. . . . Here. . . . They are yours. . . ."

Majapa picked up one and started to remove the museum label, but Ishi stopped him, waving his hand, palm out, back and forth. "Let the museum mark stay. My cousin's baskets are part of this watgurwa of treasures." He took the basket which Majapa held out to him, and picked up the second one, bringing them to his face, smelling them. "Aahh! The smell of the cave, of Wowunupo, is in them!" He traced with a finger the design woven into one of them. "This is a fern stem. It came from Round Meadow. This is iris. The Little One and I found it across the creek, high up. . . . Su! The Little One becomes part of the Saldu World, even as I."

Spirits

The California cult of the self has nothing to do with the Classical cult of the self.   MICHEL FOUCAULT

The Events in California

"Who knows, maybe this continent was not destined for the white man, and it might have been better to leave it alone," said a European friend to me. I would have agreed with his divining in those mountains and deserts the powerful presence of vengeful demons with whom only the Indians knew how to maintain alliances. But in California those demons seemed to evince no good will even to the Indians, allowing themselves to be placated only because the Indians remained on the lowest level of civilization, without agriculture or the use of metal. I am also always puzzled why the white man steered clear of California for so long, though word of it had reached him through the accounts of sailors. But, after all, those were unfavorable reports: a foggy ocean, parched cliffs, impenetrable forests, thorny brushwood. No one could have foreseen the citrus and orange plantations, the cultivated valleys irrigated artificially, the factories producing airplanes and rockets for interplanetary travel. In California, prehistory, millennia of generations passing without chronicle, leaving no other traces than the flint arrowheads found in the clay, collided with the nineteenth century—not the nineteenth century of revolutionaries and poets, but that other, rougher nineteenth century where every man had an equal right to lust for gold.

There was, however, a brief interlude. It is doubtful whether a great project for the organization of human society can be inferred from the teaching of St. Francis, but one Franciscan, Father Junípero Serra, born in Majorca, believed that he was faithful to the patron of his order. When he set out northward on muleback from Mexico in 1769, he was not guided by a desire to increase his own wealth or glory; he was probably not concerned about the interests of the crown of Spain either, although Spain, fearing the encroachments of the Russians on its nominal possessions, had a division of soldiers accompany him. Junípero wanted to save the souls of those who had never been reached by the Gospel. He was harsh to himself and his assistants and his eventual achievement would perhaps not have met with the full acceptance of the saint from Assisi, but it was the result of a deliberate plan that took into account the frailty of human nature, and especially the childish mentality of the Indians for whose salvation he was responsible. Baptized, taught farming and crafts, they were supposed to remain strangers to the greed for possessions. And so they tilled the soil together and placed the fruits of their labor in common storehouses from which every family received portions according to their need. Modesty in manners and dress, strict monogamy, participation in religious rites, and obedience to their superiors were obligatory, enforced by flogging for the slightest disobedience. Their earthly way thus mapped out, they could expect to spend the years allotted them by the Creator without great temptations. Neither were the arts to be neglected if they served the glory of God, and the more talented were trained in sculpture and painting; one example of their work is the interior of the Mission Church at Santa Barbara, where imitations of the marble dear to Spanish monks were hewn from wood by Indian artists.

Father Junípero's cell in the Carmel Mission has been preserved in its original state; his narrow makeshift bed beneath an iron crucifix is a touching sight—no larger than a board, it was there he allowed himself a few hours of sleep each night, no doubt deploring that he had to thus forbear the body. The gilded spines of the volumes in his library in the next cell I found even more of an inducement to silent meditation. Though Serra had wandered there from a Europe which, at that time, was reading Voltaire, he had remained indifferent to such impious, passing novelties. With the help of theological treatises, he intended to organize the little society he ruled so that it would be linked to the changeless, eternal order established by Providence. But the defeat of his enterprise was already being prepared in the domain he held in contempt, that of movement, light-minded slogans, and struggles. Europe had been infected by a kind of progress not to the liking of the great landowners of Mexico, of which California was the most remote province. Aided by the Church (the greatest landowner), they revolted against the King of Spain in 1821 and declared their independence; by that time, word of the extremely rich mission communal farms had long been circulating among them. So they grabbed the farms at once, scrambling for them among themselves, turning the small number of meek Indians who had not fled into farmhands. The great project had come to nothing, and, fortunately for him, Father Junípero had by that time been in his grave in the courtyard at the Carmel Mission for more than twenty years. He had left behind a dozen odd mission buildings made of stone and unfired brick, a road that linked them from south to north—the King's Highway, El Camino Real—and the name given to the hamlet by the bay initially mentioned in the chronicles of exploration as Yerba Buena. Until the Christians pointed out the inherent indecency of the body, the inhabitants of that region had walked about naked and dealt with the problem of the cold ocean mist in their own fashion—at night they smeared themselves with mud, which would crumble off in the heat of the day. In what later became the city of San Francisco, the impulse to bare oneself was to be the sole sign of fidelity to those spirits; other than that, the city had no concern for any of its heritage, least of all the precepts of voluntary poverty.

To undertake a project, as the word's derivation indicates, means to cast an idea out ahead of oneself so that it gains autonomy and is fulfilled not only by the efforts of its originator but, indeed, independently of him as well. Perhaps every project concerning human societies contains an element of self-sacrifice on behalf of those who will live after us. The triumph of California was, however, the result of crass appetites, the brazen arrogance of the ego not ashamed to proclaim that it cared only for itself; there is no hint of old Faust's dreams here. Taking a walk around the reconstruction of Fort Ross, not far from the mouth of the Russian River, I tried to imagine the ponderous Russians who once lived there settling around the samovar in the post commander's wooden house (so unlike anything American, it might have been brought from Siberia), or praying in their small wooden church. As to their diplomacy, the Russians did not make war on the Indians, whose realm began beyond the palisade, or try to convert them, preferring to carry on trade with them, but their cannons on that coast suggest that the outline of a project existed in their heads. In fact, the Russians had been drawn from Alaska to California by the abundance of seals and by a small animal whose coat was the most valuable of all, the sea otter; their ships were primarily instrumental in the near extermination of the still rare sea otter. At Fort Ross I indulged in historical fantasies, asking myself what would have happened if, on a certain December day on the military parade ground in St. Petersburg, the revolutionary officers had been victorious, not Tsar Nicholas I. In all Russia, the Decembrists alone seemed to have appreciated the role of overseas expansion and probably would not have abandoned the fort so easily. A dozen or so years later it was sold to the greatest landholder in those parts, Johann August Sutter, an adventurer from Basel, and sold without profit, for the convoy with the money from the transaction was ambushed. We may assume, for lack of evidence to the contrary, that Sutter was innocent.

Can Manifest Destiny, calling and compelling Americans to march west, as far as the shores of the Pacific, be termed a project? But they were on their way before that slogan was invented; fascinated by virgin nature, its endless potential, its promise, they were extending a flight which had already placed an ocean between them and their old countries. But here even the plural is deceptive, because each person was a separate case, every man played for his own stakes. Fenimore Cooper's *The Pathfinder*, with its internal contradictions: to move ever farther away, as long as it was farther from the constraints of civilization, into the primeval, the unnamed; but others would immediately begin advancing along the trail he had blazed, and once again he would have to curse what he had unwillingly brought about. Both Manifest Destiny and the war of conquest with Mexico, which put the entire Far West, including California, into American hands, were thus the consequences, the fruit, the sanctioning of an elemental urge, and not the realization of an intention established at the outset. Neither did anyone impose on those pushing west the idea of the extermination of the Indians as the highest, noblest task and mission. Passion drove them to it; the revulsion of the fair-skinned and fair-haired for the dark-skinned and the dark-haired was so strong it excluded the Indians from the ranks of the human, and a God-fearing patriarch mindful of the morality of his sons and daughters was proud to kill Indians, certain that he was ridding the earth of vermin. And many people were killed, not just Indians. Once again, the Christianity assimilated by the peoples of Europe had been revealed in all its relativity. Assuming that a Christian believes in hell, he ought rather to perish than risk his soul to eternal punishment only in order to eat, drink alcohol, and sleep with women for a laughably short spell on earth. So the image of hell was probably never able to supplant certain vague popular suspicions—that the image belonged to a ceremonial and highly necessary ritual that connected the members of a community in exaltation and dread, but was separate from daily labors and struggles, just as children's seriousness about games and their terror at fairy tales do not disturb the boundary between the real and the make-believe.

The wars—but they were wars only for the Indians defending themselves. For the white men they were police actions against criminals whose guilt was proven in advance because they hindered the immigrants in acting freely on territories that they, without hesitation, maintained belonged to no one. The conquest, in fact, preceded the project for conquest, and in their fervor the conquerors did not make much of a search for pretexts. The last independent Indian tribe in California, the Modoc, could no longer have been a threat to anyone in 1867. They were pursued, until, retreating higher and higher up rocky mountain ridges, they all took refuge with their women and children in a mountain fortress of caves. A siege ensued: rifles and cannons against bows and slings. But the Indians were remarkable bowmen, and it was only after several months that they succumbed to starvation. This could have served as a theme for an epic poem, but it will never be written, because the fall of that fortress signified the end of that tribe and its language.

Call it delusion, but a demonic presence can be felt on this continent whose apparent concern is that Christian man see his own nature revealed and that he unleash all his brutality. Something nameless is concerned with destroying ideology in him and, thus far, has rewarded him not for possessing ideology but for not possessing any. Despite all his Pharisaism, a person aware of all this tends to relate with a certain indifference to the violence men do each other. Complaining of the horrors of their own wars and totalitarian systems, Europeans can never understand this, for in their legends America is always only a picturesque adventure.

Journey to Nowhere

Feminism, ecology, pseudo mysticism, communalism, psychic hygiene, philanthropy mixed with commerce, half-baked messianism: Kerista was an eccentric, recycled ragbag of many of the temptations characteristic of the New Age. They were absurd, these men and women; they were also, most probably, quite harmless—as harmless as the germs that go to make up a common cold. But a common cold, given a suitable twist of fate, can turn into bronchial pneumonia. In this hothouse atmosphere of pampered self-consciousness, ideas—or what passed for ideas—floated like viruses. They were a disease you caught; a contamination of the intellect.

I walked on down the line of booths.

"An Idea Whose Time Has Come," announced a bold banner.

It was the stall of the World Hunger Project. I had heard a little about this body, which had set itself the task of ending hunger on the planet by 1997. It was an offshoot of the highly successful consciousness-raising est (Erhard Seminars Training) organization.

"Hi!" A teenage girl, name tag pinned to her breast, smiled beatifically at me. "Would you like to make a donation?"

I asked her to tell me something about the World Hunger Project.

"We plan to rid the world of hunger by 1997. The ending of hunger is an idea whose time has come."

"That's nice to know. But what does the World Hunger Project actually do?"

"It makes each person realize that he or she can make a difference."

"What does that mean?"

"It means that if you decide you want to end world hunger you can."

"I still don't understand. How does my deciding I want to see world hunger end make world hunger end?"

The beatific smile was becoming edged with impatience. "I'll get someone who can explain it better," she said.

She went off, found a young man and brought him to me.

"Hi!" The young man grinned and shook my hand. "What's the problem?"

"I can't get him to understand the idea behind the World Hunger Project," she said.

The young man laughed pleasantly. He looked into my eyes. "What's your name, sir?"

I told him.

"Quite simply, Shiva, we feel it's an idea whose time has come."

"I'm aware of that. What I'd like to know is how you plan to implement that idea."

"Well, Shiva, if you and millions of other people like you want to see world hunger end, you can make it happen."

"All I have to do is *want* world hunger to end? Nothing else?"

"That's about the size of it, Shiva."

"But what does the World Hunger Project itself do with all the millions of dollars it has collected? Has it actually helped to feed anyone?"

"You're missing the point, Shiva," he said gently. "It's not our aim to actually feed anyone."

"Then why do you need to collect money?"

"Our job, Shiva, is to spread the good news. That's what we use the money for, Shiva."

"What good news?"

He too was beginning to show signs of impatience. "The good news that hunger can be ended by 1997 if millions of people like you decided that they wanted it to end. We collect signatures, Shiva, of people who have made that commitment. We spread the idea—the good news."

"I must say it's a very elusive idea."

He signaled over another—and older—man.

"I'm experiencing some difficulty explaining the World Hunger Project to my friend Shiva," the young man said.

"Hi, Shiva! That's an interesting name you've got there. Like it! Like it!" The newcomer beamed at me. "What aspect of the World Hunger Project is troubling you?"

"All aspects."

He did his best. Since the beginning of time there had been hunger. The attitude throughout the ages had always been that it was inevitable. Malthusian economic doctrine had helped to reinforce that fatalistic attitude. The World Hunger Project was reversing that traditional pessimism. It was saying that where there was a will, there was a way. Using modern technology, the planet could produce enough to satisfy the needs of four billion people. If the majority of people wanted to end starvation, starvation would be ended.

We had been joined by a third man.

"Can I share Shiva with you?" he asked.

It was agreed that I could be shared.

"You see, friend Shiva, it's all about commitment," he began. He spoke of Karl Marx, the French Revolution, the Russian Revolution, the program to land a man on the moon, the campaign to eradicate smallpox. Those had all been acts of will, acts of commitment. The Hunger Project was in the same mold. It had been praised by the Indian Government and by the United Nations. True, they were not ending hunger as such. What they were doing was creating a *context* in which hunger could be ended.

He put a hand on my shoulder. "I can see you're a pretty negative type, Shiva," he said, gazing compassionately into my face. "You're hung up on logic and all that kind of bullshit. To understand the Hunger Project, Shiva baby, you've got to forget everyday logic. For some of us, I know, that's difficult. It took me about a year to get the hang of it. But, man, when I finally did, it just sort of blew my mind, you know?"

"How about a donation?" the girl asked.

"I think I'll get the hang of it first," I said. "Wait for the idea to blow my mind."

"Sure, friend Shiva. Sure. Take your time. Let it sink in. That's okay by us. Nobody's forcing you to do anything."

Looking around, I discovered another devotee of the Project, a woman of pensionable age, on the point of persuading my five-year-old son to commit himself. I seized the enrollment card he was holding. "The Hunger Project is mine completely," it said. "I am willing to be responsible for making the end of starvation an idea whose time has come. As an expression of my participation, I will do the following: (1) I will fast on the 14th of ——; (2) I will enroll another individual or individuals in the Hunger Project; (3) I will donate the following amount to the Hunger Project: $10, $25, $50, $100, or more . . . ; (4) I will create my own form of participation."

"He's five years old," I said. "How do you expect him to create his own form of participation?"

The woman apologized and retreated.

Fatigued by the chimeras of the New Age, I went out into the gloomy San Francisco afternoon.

They often call it the twenty-first century. California, in this view of things, is something more than merely the richest and most populous state of the Union, the first among equals. It is a state of mind; a state of being. The dogma has it that what California is doing today, the rest of the United States will be doing tomorrow; and, of course, whatever the United States is doing tomorrow, the whole world will be doing the day after. According to one of its devotees, it is a seminal ground for new ideas, one vast laboratory of the human spirit. Californians are the ultimate pioneers, a chosen people living in a golden land flowing with milk and honey, whose precocious self-consciousness makes them more than ordinarily human.

It is not accidental that its Governor, Jerry Brown, should have a sophisticated spiritual life replete with a cortege of Zen gurus, should talk of "planetary realism" and should have an amateur's enthusiasm for the colonization of outer space. (In California, to avoid confusion, one must always make clear the kind of space that is being referred to—inner or outer.) But the legend does not stop there. It is not simply a matter of adventurousness fueled by great wealth, of people playing with privilege. Land and man, we are further invited to believe, are bonded together in a mystical unity. California is uniquely what it is because the land itself is magical. Its vibrations enter into the soul and irrevocably alter it.

". . . After a while," write the editors of a book typically titled *The California Dream*, "one notices something different about otherwise familiar objects. Colors are deeper, metals are shinier, the air is cleaner and the brilliant California sun seems to jump from every surface. Before long, everyday scenes begin to look like Technicolor scenes." Sometimes the worship takes on a more aggressive tone, as in an essay by the Los Angeles–based writer John Gregory Dunne. A defector from New York, Dunne expresses himself with all the vehemence of a convert. His essay is aimed at the supercilious Eastern seaboard. "I do not think that anyone in the East," he wrote, "truly understands the importance of this idea of space in the West. The importance of that emptiness is psychic. We have a sense out here . . . of being alone, of wanting more importantly to be left alone, of having our own space, a kingdom of self with a two-word motto: 'Fuck Off.' " Dunne hymns the "narcosis" to be found on the free-ways. He contemplates with rapture the arabesques formed by off-ramps, on-ramps, and intricate lane interchanges, emblems of a mobility that is both physical and spiritual. He is entranced by the subtle tricks played on him by the subtropical light. For him, refineries gleam and glitter like extraterrestrial space stations. "It is the end of the line. It is the last stop. Eureka! I love it."

Such an attitude lends itself to extremism, to frenzy: we often become vic-tims of our legends. For many, California is indeed the last stop; the end of the line. The triumphant cry of Eureka! must wither and die on a multitude of lips every day. Heightened consciousness, heightened expectation can aggravate as well as liberate. A girl brings a gun to her high school and shoots several of her fellow pupils dead; a man finds his parking place usurped and he too goes on a murderous rampage. Californian crimes tend to have a spectacular qual-ity. That is only to be expected. If colors are deeper and metals are shinier, so, in proportion, are the derelictions of failure and madness more vividly ex-pressed than elsewhere. They stand out starkly in that clean, golden air. "Here," an acquaintance said to me, "you either reach for the stars or you crack up and run amok with a chain saw."

But that is overstating the case, an excessively romantic extension of the leg-end. California, it has to be admitted, has its fair share of outwardly normal people. You see them by the hundreds in a suburb like Sunnyvale, not many miles south of San Francisco. On weekends, mothers and fathers herd their children to the Little Leagues of soccer and baseball and football. From the sidelines they exhort and criticize, instilling the orthodox reflexes of compe-tition. These mothers and fathers are conservative and patriotic and hate big government. They are fearful that the presence of too many blacks in the neigh-borhood will drive house prices down. One woman I met mentioned with em-barrassment that her first marriage had ended in divorce. She was fearful that if her marital history became widely known in the community it might cause her neighbors anxiety.

Conformity was the first prerequisite of happiness in Sunnyvale. It was un-thinkable that a child should not be an enthusiastic member of one Little League team or another. A man whose work kept him at home—a writer, for instance—would be regarded with suspicion. The people of Sunnyvale are really no different from those you meet in Des Moines, Iowa. They would eat the same convenience foods (Americans hardly seem to cook anymore), watch the same mass-audience television programs, read the same syndicated col-umnists. In Des Moines, as in Sunnyvale, American flags will grace neat front lawns. Perhaps the lawns are neater and the flags more plentiful in Des Moines, but at bottom, all belong to that vast, featureless prairie of well-nourished, clean-thinking humanity known as Middle America, whose chief cultural monuments are the self-contained shopping plaza and the cavernous discount store. Middle Americans, whether Californian or Iowan, are as alike as Chinese. "I resent the energy crisis," I overheard a middle-aged San Franciscan saying. "Do you know why I resent it? I resent it because I am an American. I resent it because as an American I have a right to do as I like." His audience did not disagree. A remark like that takes one several light-years away from planetary realism and the New Age.

But that having been said, it is also to be conceded that California is unique. The legend does have its effect, creating its own special lure and vulnerabilities. Iowa does not, as a rule, attract the vagrant and the restless. Its neat farms and lush meadows discourage fantasy. America's wilder dreams have always rolled to the Far West. Fantasies flourish best in a warm, sensual climate. In 1967, during the summer of love and flower-power, the hippies rolled west to San Francisco's Haight-Ashbury district and Golden Gate Park. Charles Manson, cradling his murderous dreams, rolled west from Cincinnati, Ohio. The colonies of trailer homes, harboring an anonymous population of adventurers, have rolled instinctively west and come to a halt, face to face with the Pacific Ocean. America's homosexuals, rolling west in search of fulfillment, have laid siege to San Francisco. Predicting a nuclear holocaust, Jim Jones and a handful of disciples rolled west from Indiana in 1965.

"I would say without hesitation," a woman in New York said to me, "that it was the more unstable members of my family who chose to settle in California."

She may have had a point. In San Francisco I ran into a couple of her cousins. One, a mild, soft-spoken creature, had joined a Zen sect. He had, he said, become a Buddhist in reaction to the hypocrisy he saw in society. For a while, he had been moderately active in behalf of progressive political causes. But he had come to the conclusion that it was no good doing anything about anything. Whatever happened did so of its own accord, when the time was ripe for that thing to happen. His only aim in life now was to empty his mind. The other cousin was involved in a cult of (I believe) Indonesian origin. But he would not talk to me about it. What about the girl, a disciple of an Indian guru, who claimed she was following his teachings by working as a dancer in one of San Francisco's topless bars? "My guru says everything is holy, everything comes from God. It doesn't matter what you do. Everyone must follow his own path. I dedicate my sexuality to God." Would her family in Wisconsin have understood that?

Some are driven to desperation, like the "cocktail waitress" from New Jersey who had rolled west to San Francisco to make her fortune and had ended up as a common streetwalker. She had offered me her services for a mere fifteen dollars.

"Why so cheap?" I asked.

"I just want to get out of this place," she said. "All I want is the bus fare *out*. They're all as crazy as hell." She started to weep. "I don't even know who's a man or who's a woman anymore. It's crazy."

I looked around the bar. "It seems fairly easy to tell," I said.

"That's what you think. But most of the women you see in here are really men. They've had that operation. And a lot of the men are women. It's crazy, I tell you. A normal girl like me can't make a living in this town."

California sucks in America's loose ends. It twists and tangles them in a hundred different ways.

The legend crops up in some of the most unlikely places. I was being driven around Los Angeles by a black journalist, a man who, all so typically, had migrated west from New York after his marriage had broken up and he had begun to feel that his life was falling apart. He had discovered that California—Southern California—was the paradise for which he had always been unconsciously yearning.

"This sun! This sun! I worship it. It does things to you, man. It melts you down. It loosens you up. You have to experience it yourself to truly understand how people who live here feel about this place."

We drove into Watts, the ghetto that had been the scene of some of the most violent black rioting in the 1960s. Traces of that violence could still be seen in the many empty lots once occupied by businesses that had never been rebuilt. From Watts, the hills of Hollywood are plainly visible, the name etched out in giant letters on a hillside: HOLLYWOOD. Those who lived up on those hills would have seen the glow of the fires raging on the asphalt plains below. But on that bleak, if light-filled, Southern California morning, my companion's thoughts roamed far from memories of insurrection.

Did Watts, he wanted to know, conform to my preconception of a ghetto? He pointed out the streets of neat bungalows, the trim lawns. Was this anything like Harlem? Chicago? Boston? Compared with those, Watts was anything but a slum. Even misery acquired a gloss in Southern California. The weather made everything possible. Cars lasted longer. Houses remained in better repair. You spent next to nothing on heating. Every harsh winter in the Northeast brought in new floods of refugees—you could tell what was going on by the number of out-of-state license plates that suddenly appeared. His paean broadened its scope. Southern California had managed to create a genuinely open society. Everything was new. There were no rigid traditions about anything. It was a free-form, extemporaneous universe in which nothing was sacred and everything was possible to those who dared.

We passed a Mercedes-Benz without a license plate.

"That means *new*," he pointed out helpfully. "That Benz is probably fresh from the showroom. Somebody has just made his pile and he's letting the world know. That's how it goes in L.A. Maybe six months from now he'll have blown it all and be back in a Ford subcompact. That's how it goes in L.A. too. Easy come, easy go."

It was different in San Francisco. Money there was hidden, used more discreetly. It was an older town, with a long-established aristocracy. San Francisco was another ball game. His California, his magic kingdom, was unambiguously southern in complexion. John Gregory Dunne, in the essay already referred to, is also anxious to make the distinction between the two cities. "Perhaps it is easier to define Los Angeles by what it is not. Most emphatically, it is not Eastern. San Francisco is Eastern . . . Yankee architecture and Yankee attitudes boated around the Horn and grafted on to the Bay . . . Small wonder Easterners feel comfortable there. They perceive an Atlantic clone; it does not threaten as does that space-age Fort Apache five hundred miles to the south."

Again, there is exaggeration. The uniqueness of Los Angeles (Southern California) can be as overplayed as the uniqueness of California itself. How different is Los Angeles from the pride of Texas—Houston? Houston too might describe itself as a space-age Fort Apache. With justification: it is the headquarters of NASA, the National Aeronautics and Space Administration. It has all the un-Eastern virtues that Dunne admires. Consider the introduction I was given to Houston by the publicity brochure I picked up in my hotel:

> Houston is a Boston Brahmin's nightmare. It's got hundreds of miles of freeways, a gas station on every block, countless cars, no buses, subways or trains, a brash attitude that won't be put in its place. . . . Houston has got what everybody else in the world wants: money, guts, untold prosperity, vitality. . . . If Ulysses had had a choice of Houston or the sirens, he'd have picked Houston. *That's* how strong the lure is. It's even stronger for an American, born and bred on the ideals of the West. Free men. No nonsense. Don't waste time. Don't tread on me. Liberty or death. Don't fence me in. If you don't like it where you are, move on. . . . If there's any city that seems to have a monopoly on the American Spirit, that city has got to be Houston. . . .

This apocalyptic vulgarity is shared by Los Angeles.

That San Francisco does have more orthodox pretensions to sophistication and refinement is undeniable. One need penetrate no further than the all-male preserve of the Bohemian Club with its impeccably dressed clubmen, its wood-paneled walls and its elective exclusivity to understand that. But San Francisco, while it may not be a Boston Brahmin's nightmare, is also the city that pioneered topless bars, est, and the hippie movement. Marin County outside San Francisco is as laid-back, as mellow and as experimental as anywhere in the cosmos. Los Angeles and San Francisco offer different versions of the California legend. In the latter, Eastern sensibilities are refracted into the more inward-looking neuroses of the New Age. The languages are different, but they spring from a common root—the California "dream." In the south, that dream, turning into nightmare, spawned Charles Manson and his Family; in the north, it spawned Werner Erhard, the synthesizer of salesmanship and Zen, upon whom Enlightenment descended as he drove across the Golden Gate Bridge.

That common, legendary root goes even deeper—to America itself, to the New World dream of rebirth and self-realization in a spacious land uncontaminated by memory, tradition, and restraint. California became, as it had to, the New World's New World, its last repository of hope. In California, you come face to face with the Pacific and yourself. There is nowhere else to go. Just as both Los Angeles and San Francisco are, in their separate ways, recognizably Californian, so is California recognizably American. All that California does is magnify what is brought to it; and often, under the strain of magnification, there occurs a sea change. It seems that those whom the gods wish to destroy they first send to California.

They come from everywhere—from Pittsburgh, New York, Chicago, South Dakota. Enraptured by their good fortune, they expect you to be enraptured too. The demand for admiration is tinged with totalitarianism. Go to any party. Once it is discovered that you are a stranger, the conversation turns to California and its wonders. Isn't it just too marvelous for words? All those years spent in Pittsburgh seem like a punishment now. How could they ever have tolerated it? Heads shake in perplexity. Those Chicago winters! That New York rat race! That South Dakota tedium and nothingness! You walk out on the sun deck. The sky is flawless blue; the vegetation shines with a hard, precise sparkle. In the distance is the blue expanse of San Francisco Bay, lazily alive with the colorful sails of pleasure craft. California wine foams into your glass. Sun-soaked flesh glows. Languid eyes gaze at the red towers of the Golden Gate.

Isn't it just too marvelous for words? How can you bear the thought of having to return to London? If you are rash enough to keep silent or even, God help you, murmur a few words of mild dissent, you are done for. Conversation lags. Your hosts become remotely polite. It is unlikely that another invitation to participate in the splendor of it all will ever be received. To be reticent about California is to insult your hosts and their friends. Their individuality, their identity, has been absorbed by the sun, the space, the color. Their lives and their life-styles are one. They are incestuously bound up with the land and its legend. That seductive view from the sun deck is, at bottom, a narcissistic projection, a mirror of the imagined self. When they look at it, they are looking at their alter egos; when they adore it, they are adoring themselves; when they invite you to praise it, they are inviting you to praise them. The California dream cannibalizes the personality and ends by taking its place.

"One meets here," observed William Brewer in the 1860s (he was a member of the California Survey), "people apparently out of their station." The remark was prompted by his meeting with a raggedly dressed prospector in a rough mining town. Their conversation revealed that the man had come from a solid middle-class background in the East. A graduate of the U.S. Naval Academy, he was well traveled and cultivated: a Boston Brahmin. However, he had lost his fortune and come out to California in the hope of remaking it—and remaking himself. Hardly unusual in 1860. What is remarkable is that the impulse to seek regeneration in California has persisted with such strength.

"I left my home in Georgia," sang Otis Redding in the 1960s, "and headed for the Frisco Bay/I had nothing to live for . . ." One continues to run into people who, literally and metaphorically, are out of station. California is thronged not only with seekers of fame and fortune but seekers of new selves who have deliberately severed their ties with the past. It is a vagrancy that knows no class barriers: it can be discerned in the doctor who threw up a lucrative practice and came west to paint and dabble in Zen; in an academic like Timothy Leary who turned to the chemical ecstasy of LSD and made himself an outcast; in the young waitress from New York who now called herself a radical lesbian; in the businessman who turned to consciousness raising and took up full-time work with est; in the kind of tramp about whom Otis Redding sang. The out-of-station are to be met with at every twist and turn.

Away from the East, it is said, restraint seems to fall away. The gravitational force exerted by tradition weakens. Life, to use the fashionable word, becomes unstructured. Men and women become ripe for conversion; ripe for revelation. Culturally, the California atmosphere is lunar. Insecurely anchored by that weak gravitational field, one finds it all too easy to float off into absurdity and extremism. The nuts and bolts of the personality are loosened, and a certain promiscuity of thought and practice becomes endemic.

One comes across Sears, Roebuck–type catalogues catering exclusively to seekers of the exotic. A publication titled *Common Ground* is one of these—"a directory," it proclaims itself, "of growth, healing and spiritual experiences in

the Greater Bay Area." It lists in alphabetical order over two hundred organizations. You can, through the Accelerated Personal Growth Program (forty
dollars for one and half hours), achieve rapid personal transformation and
growth in self-awareness and self-integration. This will involve body work,
"clearing," dream work, and participation in group processes. The program
will transform the way in which you perceive your reality by freeing you from
the past and putting you in present time, thereby releasing your infinite abilities. Actualism (no price supplied) will actualize your untapped potential for
creative self-expression and enable you to communicate joyfully with all forms
of life by awakening the inner light-fire. And so on and on through the pages of
the catalog. These organizations are not the inventions of unfriendly fabulists
or satirists. They exist; they have hourly rates. One must assume that to some
extent, supply mirrors demand. Intellectual and spiritual adventurousness becomes indistinguishable from intellectual and spiritual collapse.

It is a sobering thought that in 1974 six and a half thousand predominantly
white, middle-class people paid forty dollars each for the privilege of attending
a seminar set up by the est group in San Francisco's Civic Auditorium. The
theme: Making Relationships Work. Six and a half thousand people listening
raptly to the words of a former encyclopedia salesman! Six and a half thousand
people in search of a revelation. Six and a half thousand of the most affluent and
privileged humans in the world willing to be taught how to live. More recently
(in 1978 and 1979), thousands of whites from the Bay Area were attracted to a
sect called the Church of Hakeem, founded by Hakeem Abdul Rasheed (alias
Clifford Jones), a handsome and enterprising black from Detroit. "I feel good!
I feel great! I feel terrific!" his disciples chanted. Hakeem said he was in touch
with the World Mind and that diseases like cancer and tuberculosis were the
results of negative thinking. "Wow!" responded his listeners. "Amen!" The
Church of Hakeem also promised wealth: donations made to its "Dare To Be
Rich" program would, because of divine intercession, be multiplied fourfold
and, in this enhanced state, be restored to the donors. When Hakeem finally
came to court, one of his unrepentant disciples recited her version of the
Twenty-third Psalm: "Rasheed is my shepherd. I know what I want, he maketh
me to lie down in pastures that are crisp, green and clean."

Theodore Roszak, a bright star in California's intellectual firmament, has
written a book titled *Person/Planet*—a fusion, as the title implies, of ecology
and self-discovery. He advocates "the open, organic textures of small towns,
rural hamlets, agrarian cooperatives and family homesteads. . . . What
yearns to be big in us, to be vast beyond reckoning, is the adventure of self-
discovery. The larger that grows, the more lightly will human society rest upon
the earth." Education, in the new order, will be largely introspective, a coming

to terms with the inner motions of mind, body, and soul. We must develop a sense of kinship with all things; a religious respect for the earth.

The ideas float like ghosts. So do the men and the women who cling to the ideas. A swirling vapor of assorted "idealisms"—ecology, feminism, heightened consciousness—clouds the brain. The gurus wait with open arms. You can get a good deal at the Anubhava School of Enlightenment: room, board and Illumination all for one hundred dollars. "Authentic enlightenment experiences occur for some and mental, physical and emotional barriers to the truth are cleared, enabling one to make swift spiritual progress. Recommended for seekers of truth."

James D. Houston

The Hip Plumber

The hip plumber is underneath my sink, squeezed in between the flung-wide cabinet doors, working with his wrench to unscrew the trap so he can unplug the drain.

"Sometimes," he says, "when I am up under here all by myself, in the shadows with the pipes and the smells, I think what the hell am I doing in a situation like this? And then I just relax and say to myself, It's okay. It's okay to be here. This is where I am *supposed* to be. If I wasn't supposed to be here, I wouldn't be here. You know what I mean? What I am saying is, I surrender to that place and that time, and then I am at peace with it, I become one with it. Hand me that flashlight now, so I can see what the hell is *in* here."

I hand him the flash and he peers around at the stuccoed underbelly of the sink, the chalky corrosion stains.

"I don't take any of this seriously," he says. "I mean, it has to be fun. I have to enjoy it. I go out on one of these big jobs, where some contractor calls me in to do the whole kitchen and bathroom, and these other guys are out there, the roofers, the sheetrock guys. They're glum. They're walking around doing what they do, but they can't wait for the day to end. And me? I'm singing, I'm smiling. They say, Hey, you don't have any right to smile, doing this kind of shitwork. In their view, see, anybody who smiles must not know what he's got himself into. They think something is wrong with me because I really do enjoy what I'm doing. But hey, it's all one, isn't it? Work is worship. That's what I tell them out there on the big construction jobs. I say, Work is worship. They just look at me."

Now he has the pipes loose, and he is feeding the snake-cable down into the long drain, a few inches at a time, feeding, cranking the spool handle ferociously, then feeding a few more inches of cable.

"You see, I am just a puppet. This came to me nine years ago. I saw that what I had to do was surrender myself to . . . whatever you want to call it. God. Brahman. The Great Force. The Oversoul. You name it. I call it God. But you know what I mean. You surrender to it. You are a puppet, and it works through you. Each morning I wake up, and I think to myself, Okay, what is important. Feel good. That is the first thing. Then, Share it. Share what you feel. And surrender to whatever comes your way. Look at this snake. You know what it's doing? It's flopping around down there at the bottom of your pipe where all the gunk has accumulated. There is nothing wrong with your drain pipe, by the way—although I might re-plumb this trap for you one of these days, if you're into that. You have about a ten-inch loop here, and all you need is four, otherwise you have water standing on both sides of ten inches, plus these two extra fittings you really don't need. Who installed this stuff anyhow?"

I tell him it came with the house. He inspects the loop, eyes wide in the half-dark. He shifts his position. He gives the handle another crank, with another smile, the funlover's grin, playful, a prankster.

"What I'm saying is, the drain pipe is innocent. The drain just does what it has to do, which is be a pipe for the water. And the water does what it has to do, which is swirl as it descends, so that over the years it coats the inside of the pipe with all the little pieces of stuff that come down out of the sink, and this makes a kind of doughnut inside the pipe, a doughnut with a hole through the middle that gets a little bit smaller year by year. The doughnut gets bigger, and the hole gets smaller and smaller and smaller, until it is down to a very fine point—which is just like meditation, you see. But then one day, bip, the little hole closes. The drain stops draining, and the snake goes down there and opens it up, like the kundalini snake of breakthrough perception! And whammo, a channel is cleared and the water is flowing again!"

Leo E. Litwak

Getting It

I interviewed Werner Erhard, est's founder, in his plush Franklin House head-quarters in San Francisco in 1976. He has honed his system of response so that it has few holes. He is never caught off base. His vocabulary runs the gamut from very lofty to very profane. Though he expresses affinities with Plato, L. Ron Hubbard, D. T. Suzuki, Alan Watts, Lenny Bruce, Swami Muktananda, he says est cannot be understood simply as a blend of the teachings and disciplines he has studied. The origin of est, he says, was a life-transforming experience he underwent on a California freeway.

"To relate what I experienced to time is a true lie. It did not happen in time. It didn't happen in some place. I wasn't on the freeway in my wife's car on the way to the city. Yet to put it in the language I must locate it for you. But that does damage to it. There were no words attached to it. No feelings, no attitudes, no body sensations."

What Erhard experienced he calls "getting it." "It" is an experience of the world as it is without the intercession of the human understanding. He started est, he says, to share this experience with others. His problem was that the experience, being ineffable, couldn't be communicated by ordinary means.

Erhard doesn't look the way I imagine a man who has received enlighten-ment ought to look. In fact, with his Hollywood handsomeness, charm and nerve, he looks like someone I should keep my eye on. He goes all out for what he wants. My inclination was to close my heart and guard my pockets.

Erhard is not unaware of his effect. It is an effect he has incorporated into the very heart of the est training. He knows the trainee wrestles with the possibility that slickers are trying to con him out of $250 and afterwards suck him into an organization which will take over his mind and milk him dry. And if, because of the urging of friends and phone calls from est "assistants," and because you are not getting the satisfactions from life that you want—you may even be depressed and have insomnia—you have plunked down your money and now suspiciously await a definitive sign that est is conning you so that you can grab it back and run, you are exactly where Erhard wants you to be. You have assumed the role that will, he believes, make the training work.

"An enormous amount of what makes us inhuman," Erhard says, "comes out of our fear of being conned. Until you know that you can't be conned, your life is run by the fear of being conned. In judo any motion that stops becomes a position. The instant your opponent takes a position he is vulnerable. The man who has no position is invulnerable. The same is true in the training. In order to reveal people to themselves, you need them to take a position. And essentially the position that you can almost predict people are going to have is, 'YOU'RE NOT PULLING ANY WOOL OVER MY EYES! NO! NO! YOU'RE NOT GOING TO GET ME!' We call that 'the unwillingness to get off it.' Everybody takes that position. That's why the training works with everybody eventually." Erhard laughs gleefully.

"The thing to do is to make that position so blatantly obvious to people that they begin to see that it is that very position that makes them comical."

Erhard calls est's technique "mind-boggling." One boggles the mind by understanding its machinery. His intention, he says, is to shake people loose from deadening positions. He uses paradox in the fashion of the Zen master who gets students "to give up their system of epistemology—the way that they have of knowing—so that they can know the stuff in an entirely different way."

Erhard isn't anything like a Zen master. He has no air of detachment nor has he renounced the material things of the world. He has a valet, a chef and a chauffeur, a limousine and a leased Cessna airplane. He is shod and coiffed and garbed, albeit in a casual collegiate style reminiscent of the late fifties, early sixties. His voice is loud and brazen, and his fluency is that of a first-rate salesman. . . .

Werner Erhard's own story doesn't clarify these disparate elements. Though he claims he hides nothing, media exposés constantly plague him.

No stranger to aliases, Werner Erhard was born John Paul Rosenberg in Philadelphia, where his father—a convert to the Episcopal church—still operates a restaurant. After finishing high school, he married his high-school sweetheart and, using the pseudonym of Jack Frost, ran an automobile dealership. In 1960, at the age of twenty-five, he abandoned his wife and their four children and, with a woman he eventually married, fled west. Discarding his identity, he found a new one in *Esquire* magazine. He took "Werner" from an article on Werner Heisenberg and "Erhard" from an article on the German chancellor of the exchequer. He meant to be untraceable.

On the West Coast, he trained encyclopedia salesmen for *Parents Magazine*'s Cultural Institute and subsequently joined the Grolier Society, whose business is educational materials, as a division manager. He became what he calls "a discipline freak," avidly studying and practicing such "disciplines" as Dale Carnegie, Scientology, Subud, Gestalt, encounter, Rogerian nondirective counseling, Yoga, Zen, and Mind Dynamics. And for a time he was on the staff of Mind Dynamics—before the Government, in 1972, charged it with misrepresentation and practicing medicine without a license.

After his enlightenment experience, he ended his eleven-year flight from his family and made amends for old derelictions. Three children from his first marriage now live with him and his second wife. Both wives, several children, his parents, and brothers have all gone through the est training. Erhard says he accepts his family and they accept him.

"I have done evil things," he says. "Leaving a wife and four children is a lot more evil than any of the others—that comes up in any of the articles."

But Erhard distinguishes the Self from the story of the Self. In the system he has designed, history is given short shrift. He esteems the here and now. According to Werner Erhard, he has completed his past.

The training I took began at 8:30 on a Saturday morning. At the door of a large meeting room of a convention hotel in the San Francisco financial district we trainees were given tags bearing our first names in large block letters. Greeting us with cheery smiles—"Hi, Mike. Hi, Lily. Hi, Stanley. Hi, Ted."—an unflappably courteous staff led us to our folding chairs where 250 of us were seated flank by flank around a small platform. On the platform were a lectern, two stools, a microphone, and two greenboards. Reminding me of somewhat less straight Disneyland attendants, the est staff manned tables at the rear of the hall. From there, they operated sound equipment, transmitted messages to the trainer, and carried portable microphones to any trainee who wished to speak.

Erhard assured us that we were safe in this room. We could say anything and feel anything and no one would intrude. If we were attacked by lions, he said, the est staff would offer themselves first.

An assistant trainer barked out the ground rules of the training. In a drill sergeant's voice, he went over the simple instructions with a painstaking clarity that would have been suitable for an audience of naughty schoolchildren. He meant to get under our skins.

No eating except at times specified. Is that clear? No one leaves his seat without permission. Is that clear? If you are sitting next to a friend, change seats. All timepieces surrendered. All pens and pencils surrendered. No notes. Beneath our chairs was an agreement we were to sign. There was a pencil there, too. The agreement was that we would not violate the "confidentiality" of the training. No names were to be revealed. We could reveal our own experience of the training. We were urged to do so. In the course of the training it would be valuable to share what we were experiencing with others. We need only stand and we'd be given a mike. . . .

Erhard was taunting, pedantic, loud. He wore shiny, buckled loafers, a sporty jacket; his shirt collar was open and spread. We were instructed to applaud any trainee who rose to share his experience of the training.

The preamble over, Erhard read the est statement of purpose—vague, awkward prose about "transforming your ability to experience living," etc. It seemed banal to me but Erhard dealt with the statement as intensely as if it were gospel. He offered dictionary definitions of key words, subjecting each notion to careful scrutiny. And trainees prolonged the tedium by asking questions. Turkeys! I choked with boredom. I had no sense of how much time had elapsed. I yearned for a break. Erhard showed no sign of fatigue. He moved from greenboard to greenboard, scrawling words like "experience" and "non-experience" on one board, "knowledge" and "belief" on another.

An outraged trainee got up and took the mike. "You," he shouted at Erhard, "are the —— hole! You are an —— hole! A Talmudist! And a bore!"

Erhard applauded him. "Thank you, Walter." Strong applause from us who share Walter's sentiments. Erhard yelled at us. "You turkeys! Everything I've said is lies! Walter has the guts to share how he feels about this. I'm a liar!" he shouted. "Only an —— hole would try to understand lies!"

He then resumed the lecture. I felt the boredom as aches and pains. My head ached. My back and seat ached. I was hungry. Erhard continued, his voice abrasive.

A man stood up, received the mike. "I got to go to the bathroom so bad I can't pay attention to what you're saying. When do we get a break?" Applause.

Are we no more than tubes, Erhard asked. Is this all there is to our lives, eating and eliminating? Wasn't the issue our being alive? Jammed tight together, no relief in sight, facing hours and hours of this pedestrian philosophy, I shared the outrage that now came hot and heavy from all quarters. He was denounced as a fascist.

"Thank you."

"All I'm getting out of this is boredom!" Applause.

"Thank you."

The lecture resumed. There was no escape. When the break came, I discovered we'd been at it for ten hours. (The procedure has since been changed to allow for breaks every four hours.)

Braced against boredom, I forced my eyes open, I wiggled, I pressed my feet on the floor, I squeezed against the seat. It was a struggle not to go under. My mind raced with unexpressed scorn for myself, Erhard and all the turkeys. My interior voice spoke faster and faster, going over and over the same outrage. I mourned my vanishing $250.

Then the tape stopped. Somewhere toward the end of that first day, I no longer resisted my boredom and it disappeared. With the disappearance of my boredom came the possibility that, if experienced, various other unwanted attitudes and feelings—fear, sadness, etc.—could also be made to vanish. Erhard had found a way of illuminating familiar wisdom. . . .

A volunteer, suffering what he reported as an excruciating headache, went through a "process" with Erhard. Sitting with eyes closed, concentrating on the pain, he was asked: "Where precisely is your pain?" Erhard wanted to know the pain's exact shape, its size, its quality, if the headache were drained, how much of a cup it would fill. The questions were repeated. The pain was experienced without analyzing its causes or its consequences.

Headaches and backaches vanished throughout the room. . . .

Essentially the message of Erhard's est training goes something like this: The mind imposes judgments on a neutral world. In reality there are no "good" or "bad" experiences. To gain the satisfaction that comes from "real" experience we have to discard the fabrications of the mind and accept the world as it is. The mind, however, maintains grim control. We sacrifice our lives, says Erhard, trying to be right. His favorite analogy is to a rat, locating a tunnel containing cheese. If the cheese is withdrawn, the rat eventually gets the idea and abandons the tunnel. We, however, would rather be right than have cheese and we remain stuck in cheeseless tunnels, running the course again and again without reward. We spend our lives proving our cases against father, mother, sister, brother, wife, husband, child, friend and foe. We try to establish that they have made us what we are. They're to blame. THEY caused the war. THEY ruined our childhood. THEY destroyed our chances for happiness. Or else circumstance is blamed for the deficiency of one's own character. The mind grinds out excuses that bind us in a chain of causation, leaving us no space in which to act.

The fact is, says Erhard, the world doesn't distinguish victim from victor, raped from rapist, murderer from murdered, the bomber pilot from the exploded child. What is, is. Erhard cupped his hands around his mouth to make a megaphone. "There's nothing out there. No one cares. Do you get it?"

Jonathan Lieberson

Escape from Esalen

Pushing aside a complimentary tray of passion-fruit slices, I threw myself down on the bed of my room in the inn, reputedly the most luxurious hotel in Big Sur, and asked myself how so banal a conjunction of circumstances could have soured a holiday trip. The flight from New York had been marred by my seatmate, a California business executive of enormous girth, whose buttresses of bacon spilled over the armrest onto me, and who, after marinating himself in Scotch, fell into a deep sleep, punctuated by slurred off-color dream phrases, during the projection of a James Bond thriller. We were seated to the extreme left of the screen, and almost under it, so that I could view the screen only by craning my neck and looking past him. Unfortunately, near the climax of the film, he turned in his sleep with a protracted gurgle, and now faced me so closely that our noses would have touched—they did once—had I not leaned far to my left. In order to see the film, I had to run the risk of his awakening to find me staring directly into his massive face. Apart from this circumstance, and although the airline staff behaved, contrary to the implication carried by the name of the carrier, in a thoroughly disorganized fashion, the rest of the flight was without incident. Indeed, the biggest nonevent of all was the non-arrival of my luggage in San Francisco, a trifling affair I had to neglect in order to sprint the length of the airport to make a connecting flight to Monterey. A picturesque surprise greeted me when I ran panting onto the runway to catch it, for what I saw was not a plane at all, but what looked like a laundry basket held in the beak of a listless pterodactyl. Stepping into the contraption, I saw that in fact it was an ancient reconnaissance six-seater, in the charge of two teenagers, one of whom was boning up on an airway manual held upside down. The flight operations—an absurd description of the fiddling they did with the knobs, buttons, and pedals at their disposal—certainly sent color into the cheeks of the passengers. For some forty minutes the plane passed through a series of nauseating lurches and abrupt descents into air pockets, each of which was accompanied, as in a church responsory, by moans from the passengers as pitiful as those in the "Dies Irae" of Verdi's *Requiem*.

The inn (really a cluster of fancy dormitories perched on a hill), where I arrived a gibbering wreck some hours later, had been described to me as surpassing in luxury any similar institution in northern California. How wildly irresponsible this speculation was came home to me with peculiar force after my first interview with the desk clerk, a pretty blonde whose empty eyes and toneless manner of speech suggested a lifetime spent strung out on hypnotic drugs among the Frisbee crowd. She told me that I would be able to pay for my room only by credit card, provided that I furnish identification in the form of a driver's license together with information about the make and year of my automobile. When I explained to her that I neither used credit cards nor drove a car, but offered to pay by personal check backed up by my passport, she unconvincingly suppressed a giggle at my antiquated preference for impeccable New York banks and official government documents over so-called "credit" cards, symptoms of all that is misguided in our economic way of life.

In any case, the matter disposed of after a half-hour debate that drew attention from other guests by its ferocity and invective, I went on to explain that my luggage had been orphaned. "I have no fresh changes, you see," I said airily, "so will you send the presser or the room boy for the clothes I am wearing, and also the waiter, as I'll be dining in my room tonight in about an hour. . . ." Interrupting me curtly, the clerk said that the inn had no presser, no room boy, no laundry services of any kind, and no room service; if I wished, some slices of passion fruit or a jug of spring water could be sent to my room, but for a meal I would have to go to the hotel restaurant. "There it is," she said, pointing out the window to a speck on the top of the next mountain range and easily a forty-minute walk away, "but it won't be open for another two hours and since it's Saturday night, you won't get a reservation there for another two hours after that." I subsisted the rest of the afternoon by clawing open bananas pilfered from the hotel lobby.

At eight that evening, smoothing down my disheveled city clothes, I set out on the "scenic" walk the hotel had constructed to the restaurant. It proved to be an endlessly long and winding path through a forest, with funny little fake dead ends and rickety bridges over dried-up streams. The deeper I went into the forest the more each step I took grew palpable with tension. I imagined the ghosts of murderous lumberjacks whose trade had been displaced when the hotel was built leering at me through broken branches; at every turn in the path I saw the outline of a puma ready to dispatch me. When I reached the restaurant, a glass-and-wood affair typical of Northern California, I was spooked, compulsively dusting pine needles off my shoulders and disengaging burrs from my trouser legs, which may explain why the headwaiter seated me in a distant corner of the room, under a giant wooden beam and near the source of the inevitable recorded harp arrangements of Ravel and Satie. So fearful was I of not securing another reservation for the next 24 hours that I spent many hours in this seat, alarming other guests by my gluttony and stuffing buns and rolls into my jacket. It was pleasant enough, save for one irritating feature of the place. Each waiter I encountered there had cultivated the same strange fear of making an assertion. No matter how trivial the information that I requested, it was conveyed to me in an interrogative. I would ask, "How is the veal cooked?" and I would be told, "On the barbecue?" "Where is the bar?" would be answered by "Down the hall?" I have since learned that this curious affectation has been superseded in some parts of California by the practice of responding to a question by repeating it, so that the answer to "Where is the wine list?" is "Where is the wine list?" thus ensuring that no information whatsoever is passed.

After my first day at the inn, I wearied of writing letters home and wearing earplugs at the swimming pool to drown out the laughter of debauched singles gamboling in the hot tubs nearby, and decided it was time to explore the countryside. I had planned to rent a bicycle, but no service of this kind existed in Big Sur. I next considered a car and driver. This, too, appeared unavailable until after much effort I discovered a limousine service in distant Santa Clara. The car I was provided with, however—an immense silver Cadillac with circular portholes—was not ideally suited to the rustic terrain of Big Sur or its pockmarked roads, and when I was driven in it to places of interest such as state parks or nearby towns I was ogled by passersby. Perhaps, noting my rumpled suit and distracted look, they assumed that I was a presidential candidate who had lost his way, but as that sight must be fairly common to them, the explanation could not be a complete one.

My first call in the Cadillac was at a celebrated local hangout called Nepenthe, a restaurant where I settled myself into a crowd of T-shirted, bearded cats with potbellies and their women, many of whom took after Boadicea in appearance. We all sat there munching carrots and scooping up garbanzo beans, for the most part in silence, although occasionally a recording of bell music would be played or some comment from one of the couples, like "Play it cool, Goldilocks," would be heard. Everyone was exceedingly gentle, and even the bee that circled my ambrosiaburger retreated gracefully when he realized that I would not share it willingly. And the Druid wearing large amounts of wooden jewelry and a Navaho blanket who approached me and softly inquired whether I was a member of "the healing community" begged off on her own initiative when I replied that I subscribed in every detail to the therapeutic approach of Fritz Kunkel.

The next day we drove to Carmel—a show town with expensive stores selling, it seemed, mostly bread—and then on to Monterey, which, if possible, appeared to have surpassed its earlier efforts to ensnare tourists. Within moments of alighting from the car, I was swept into a noisome sea of corpulent psychiatrists and unreconstructed bohemians on Fisherman's Wharf. We inspected (as if with a group mind) little clay lobsters, scrimshaw work, and statues of bullwhackers; smiled idiotically at a flea-bitten trained monkey snatching dollar bills from us; threw tidbits to jaded performing sea lions and pelicans; stared at piles of bug-eyed rock cod and dried blowfish. Although one can tire rapidly of bleached wood, sandpipers, and flattened cypresses, the Seventeen-Mile Drive outside Monterey and more generally the coastline highway from it to Big Sur struck me as splendid as ever. As one leaves Monterey, with its mansions and golf courses, the road takes one through large, brilliantly green fields that stretch almost to the water line, and everywhere there is light and color and the smell of the sea. Then the road climbs and passes through more green fields, some of them thick with horses and sheep, which overlook a turbulent sea out of which huge piles of rock rise abruptly; the effect is rather like that of the western Irish coast. As it nears Big Sur, the road climbs even more and soon is nothing but a thin strip of pavement cut into the rock of the mountain, with high cliffs on one side and bottomless pits on the other, marked by diabolical twists and hairpin turns, giving the motorist frightening and startling views of tremendous expanses. I regret to say that amidst all this beauty I was torn by the conflicting impulses to throw myself out the window, on the one hand, and on the other to press myself to the door of the car nearest the inside of the road. And in addition, a disquieting suspicion arose within me that my driver, who had already displayed difficulties in driving the Cadillac through the twists in the road, was slowly becoming hypnotized by the vast expanses ahead of him and would soon plunge the car into the sea. To ensure that he was on the ball, I periodically shouted at him at the top of my voice to ignore the passing spectacles.

If I was afflicted with vertigo that afternoon, a more complicated strain of the same condition affected me the following day. I had always dreamed of visiting Esalen, the famous "human potential" institute located nearby my hotel. Unfortunately, on ringing up I was told that a rockslide blocked the road linking me to it, and that if I wished to visit, I could only do so between six at night and six in the morning, when the highway workers repairing the road were not at their posts, and that I should then have to cross the slide by foot, a distance of about a mile. My enthusiasm to see Esalen suffocated the voices of reason, and I arranged with my driver to drop me at my end of the slide at 6 A.M. and with an official of the institute to meet me at the other end shortly thereafter.

It was still dark when I started my way across the slide the next day. At first, I inched along, hugging the mountainside, every so often coming with a start against a bulldozer or a road sign warning of danger. Twice I took the wrong path and walked perilously close to the edge of a cliff, leaping back when I heard the sound of waves hundreds of feet below me. Midway across, my ears picked up something that turned my blood to ice. The wind had dislodged a handful of pebbles from the mountainside above me, and they skipped down over the larger rocks. As I was for all purposes blind in the darkness, I had no way of checking my immediate conjecture that this signified the beginning of another, more extensive and devastating rockslide. Electrified by fear, I doubled my efforts to reach the other side and began to scurry across the path in little steps like a Chinese peasant, my body bent almost double and my hands tracing the ground to ensure my safety. In doing all this, however, I neglected to consider what effect the previous night's dense fog might have had on the consistency of the soil at the places where the workers had plowed it with their bulldozers. At one point I sank with a piercing yell to my knees in mud and imagined that I was about to drop all the way down the mountain into Davy Jones's locker. Fortunately, the light had begun to break and I made out a tree root, which I used to help me reach firmer soil, where I lay for a few minutes recovering my strength. Then, in the dimness, I saw a shape that lightened my heart: Another human being was crossing the slide in the same direction as I was going. Except that he was an old, white-haired man who carried some sort of staff, I shall never know who he was, for despite my friendly cries he took no notice whatsoever of me; perhaps, as was later suggested to me, he was a Zen monk walking to the Tassajara monastery down the coast. In any case, despite his cold reception, I followed him and made it to the other side, where I met my contact from Esalen. Within minutes after I stepped into her car, we drove through the gate of the institute, a compound of houses located on a strip of land between the Santa Lucia Mountains and the sea.

To describe Esalen as devoted to research into "human potential" utterly fails to convey the staggering number and variety of its activities. For this one must turn to a document that was placed in my hand on arrival, and which is one of the most absorbing I have ever read: the Esalen catalogue of January– June 1984. According to it, just a few of the methods for exploring the central questions of life offered by Esalen are: "psychosynthesis," "holonomic integration" (which employs "evocative music, controlled breathing, facilitative body work, and mandala drawing"), "the hypnotic approaches of Dr. Milton H. Erickson," "hypnosis for health maintenance," "bioenergetics," "group rituals," "Hawaiian Huna" (an ancient mystical teaching of Polynesia), "modern kundalini research," "singing Gestalt therapy," "hot seat" encounter groups, "neo-Reichian emotional release," and ways "to get release from chronic pain and tension" such as "Moshe Feldenkrais's awareness work, Lauren Berry's joint work, deep tissue as taught by Ida Rolf, and the trigger point work of John St. John." One can visit the Esalen hot springs on a weeknight (open, however, I was told, to the public only from 1 to 5 A.M.), or attend a weekend seminar, or stay for longer periods of time as a resident or student.

Although once one has been exposed to the Esalen catalogue it is difficult to put down, the descriptions in it of courses offered by the institute present some unusual problems of interpretation. One weekend course, entitled "Exorcising the Demon 'Should,' " is described in part as follows: "Within each of us there lives a demon—our own personal critic—whose greatest joy comes from criticizing, denigrating, and destroying every experience we have. This demon, who commands us to be who we aren't in order to satisfy someone we can never satisfy, is the demon that we will seek to exorcise during the weekend." The price is $230, quite a bargain in light of the far greater price paid in similar efforts by Rimbaud or the Marquis de Sade. The promises made by other courses are not as easy to pin down. A course, also carrying the price tag of $230, called "Zen and the Art of Fly Fishing," is described as "a combination of practical instruction, visualization, physical exercise, and guided fantasy"; it argues that "there is a focus and subtlety of movement in fly fishing akin to Eastern meditative disciplines. The possibility always exists of entering the trout's world. In fly fishing, the trout are the teachers," a claim which suggests underwater tutorials, taught by Disney-like professor fishes wearing spectacles.

Pitiless Teutonic rigor is implied in the following course, entitled "Polarity Massage" ($230): "The Esalen mineral baths will be the classroom for exploring and learning by experience the basic concepts of polarity body work through the medium of massage. Emphasis will be on the dynamics of living anatomy and polarity energy balancing methods as implemented in the course of complete, full-body massage." And one course that would seem to require a stern hand if it is not to degenerate into hanky-panky claims to introduce "a new way of seeing the body, using eyes, nose, throat, hands, ears, and *hara*," the last-named being "an energy center located two fingers below the navel." The course description that sent thought balloons with question marks in them gliding over my head was "Shamanic Healing, Journeying, and the Afterlife Experience: Basic and Intermediate Shamanic Practice" ($680). In it, "with the aid of traditional sonic-driving and dancing methods, the group will engage in archetypical exercises and rituals practiced by North and South American Indian shamans to awaken dormant human capabilities and forgotten connections with the powers of nature. Practice will include shamanic journeys to both the Lower- and Upper-worlds for knowledge and power, work with animal and plant powers, divination, clairvoyance, and shamanic methods of healing." In addition, "there will be an introduction to the Ghost Dance method and to shamanic ways of exploring the afterlife experience"; participants are invited to "bring drums and rattles." The faculty conducting these seminars and workshops contains many unusual personalities, including a specialist in "personal applications of video," the founder of the "Gestalt Fool Theater Family of San Francisco," a writer "with earlier careers as homemaker and fiber artist," and someone called "Hareesh," crisply described as "interested in alternative nutritional programs." A tenure-track faculty member is Jezariah Canyon Munyer, who teaches a course entitled "Miracles of Infancy" ($230) with his parents; he is one year old.

Inflamed by expectations of witnessing some of these activities during my visit to Esalen, I was distressed to find that none of them were being currently offered, and that because of the rockslide I was doomed to spend twelve hours in what can only be described as a peculiar mixture of a singles resort and a lunatic asylum. This impression was suggested to me by my first sight of residents at the institute, a wiry, bearded old man out of John Brown's gang jogging painfully down a hillside path in the company of two laughing young women wearing waist-length hair and feather earrings, and it was confirmed by my encounters with others, equally arresting: a tall, head-nodding man who had just been to Findhorn, in Scotland, a "community" where he had been taught to speak with affection to cabbages and roses in order to make them grow, and where, he assured me, astonishing results had occurred; an earnest, bespectacled woman who had vowed never to use the word "I," and who hugged whomever she was with before taking leave; two elderly ladies in jumpsuits, sitting motionlessly and staring pop-eyed at the sea, then vigorously stripping off the suits and surrendering themselves to the sun; a woman who skipped down a hill singing coloratura exercises in half-voice, and then stopped, took a breath, and erupted into some deafening spectacular high notes; a man who said, "I have too many cars in my emotional garage."

I attended lunch in the mess hall of the institute in a crowd full of saintly faces and uplifted voices; declining an offer of some malodorous organic stew, I confined myself to a stubby glass of low-fat milk, until I observed that the glass was caked with filth and in a lightning move surreptitiously bleached a nearby cactus plant with the tainted liquid. After lunch, I elected to take a massage near the hot springs from one of Esalen's celebrated massage team. The scene that greeted me when I arrived there did not differ appreciably from that found in a typical fifties nudist-colony brochure: a number of senior citizens (including some Wagnerian Rhinemaidens with braids) frolicking in outdoor stone tubs and tossing medicine balls back and forth, splendidly unashamed of their liver spots, giant bellies, and floppy udders. It would have been instructive to take a leisurely survey of the behavior but the sulfurous odors rising from the springs forced me to turn away.

My masseuse I guessed to be in her mid forties, a vigorous apostle of health, who wore only a pair of sunglasses and a towel around her waist. To my delight, she posed not a single question to me and set to work immediately. Midway through the massage, however, while I was lying face down, I noticed to my surprise that her towel had crumpled to the floor below me. Thinking that her devotion to her work made her forgetful of such details, I was about to inform her when I felt my own towel gently disengaged from my body and tossed to the floor, so that both of us were fully exposed to the meditating grandmothers I had seen earlier on the cliff above the bathhouse. Her soothing fingers soon made me semiconscious, however, and I would have remained so were it not for an unforeseen incident. A masseur who had been working over a mountain of flesh of indeterminate sex on the next sunning table decided to take this time to retail his spiritual autobiography in a voice that could be heard at San Simeon some fifty miles down the coast. At first I tried to dismiss him as a mere phenomenon in space and time, of no enduring significance, but I was unable to sustain this attitude and began to listen. It seemed that he had recently discovered through painful self-analysis that he had never really been born. As he pounded and remolded the creature beneath him, he told us that he was following a new "discipline" called "rebirthing therapy," moreover of the "wet" sort that involved his being dragged in large basins of warm water and then, with great ceremony, lifted like a neonate into the world. He subscribed, he continued, to a rigorous retraining of his character and each day would write on his wrist a guiding thought like "purify yourself," and his teachers had assigned him exercises to test his powers of forming and re-forming "relationships," one of which required that he spend exactly sixty minutes in a bar with a woman. No doubt in a desperate effort to cut him off, the entity under his care stirred to life and twisted helplessly about on the mat. "Shhhhh," the masseur cooed, firmly holding him down, "muscles have memories. My deep tissue work may be reviving them. I may touch your foot and a memory of your childhood may return. You may cry, you may get angry. Here is a pillow to scream into." When my own massage was over, and I was leaving, I looked back at him: He was now violently kneading the flesh of his client, whose face was buried in the pillow, and repeating the words, "Externalize! Verbalize! Externalize! . . ."

According to the catalogue's scarcely intelligible description, Gestalt practice is "a form—nonanalytic, noncoercive, nonjudgmental—evolving out of the work of Fritz Perls, relating that work to ways of personal clearing and development both ancient and modern," and one of the highlights of my visit was that of attending a Gestalt encounter group led by one of Esalen's founders, Richard Price. A "hot seat" session, in which Price "facilitated" the catharsis of whoever chose to sit on a designated pillow near him, it was one of the very silliest events I have ever seen. The pillow was immediately occupied by a Texan woman of about twenty. Within a minute, as if on cue, she released a thin, low wail, which I took to be a malfunction of the air-conditioning unit until it changed suddenly into an ear-splitting shriek. This in turn subsided and the low wail, suggestive of the smoke-intoxicated cries of the Pythian priestess at Delphi, returned. Then she began to mutter: "No, Daddy, no! Find someone your own age to play with!" words of unmistakable significance that electrified the fraternity sitting cross-legged around her. When she then shouted these words fortissimo for about ten minutes thereafter, Price intervened and asked her what "age-space" she was "in." "Six," she snapped back, eliciting gasps of admiration and envy from her audience, many of whom were eager to follow her in the hot seat and were perhaps less skilled at pinpointing the date of traumatic memories. "Tell Daddy you are afraid of him," Price suggested, and she did. "Now tell Daddy you need and want him," and she did. "And now alternate, experiment: Say to Daddy, 'I want you,' 'I hate you,' 'I need you,' 'I don't need you,' 'I hate you.' " Then he placed his forearm against her knees (which at this stage were brought up to her chin in the manner of one of the inmates at Charenton) and asked her to "externalize" her predicament by first pushing his arm away and then drawing it close to her. In time, she produced a library of memories of such staggering dullness that it gradually became clear as day that her original complaint against Daddy had just been thrown in for glamor and that the real bone she wanted to pick with him was that he failed to adopt a "nonjudgmental" approach to her academic studies. Sensing that I had been taken in by a consummate con artist (or two) and noting with delight that the dials on my watch nearly signified the hour of my departure, I stood up to leave; as I did so, the Texan woman was reciting on Price's instruction pat little phrases like "I can get attention from you without feeling pushed" to the men in the room, each by turn, and was presently murmuring it coquettishly to a young man who, I had heard earlier, had recently been the target of a missile of hot food thrown by a man with whose wife he had been dallying. Soon I was being driven through the institute compound on the way back to the rockslide, and was once more ankle-deep in mud as I journeyed to meet the Cadillac on the other side. The moment I was out of view of the delegation that had driven me to the slide, I hurled the handfuls of promotional literature they had pressed on me into the sea with a sobbing laugh. Funny how one can summon the full force of one's personality to get things done without the aid of juice fasts or afterlife experiences.

Ishmael Reed

Ground Zero

You discover that living in an area in which a crack den, smokehouse, or in the language of the police, problem house is in operation, is like living under military rule. Your neighborhood is invaded at all times of the day or night by armed men and women—death squads—who carry the kinds of weapons that are employed in small wars all over the world. People are trapped in their homes, intimidated by rival drug armies who on more than one occasion have caused the murder of innocent men, women, and children as they fight over the spoils. A policeman's comment to the press that only if you live in this kind of area are you likely to become a statistic, is not reassuring. The couriers, usually teenagers, ride bicycles; the suppliers drive Japanese pickup trucks or unlicensed Broncos; and the assassins ease by in BMWs, or in noisy, dilapidated hotrods with two people riding shotgun in the back and two up front. When their menacing sentries stand about on the lookout for cops, people don't dare come out of the house.

The retired people, single-parent families, and widows who used to take so much pride in the neighborhood stay indoors. The lawns are still kept up and the repairs done, but the mood is one of trepidation. You dread coming home because you never know when a car full of unsavory characters might be parked in front of your house, or a drug dealer's pit bull, "a dangerous weapon," might be running up and down the street unleashed and terrorizing the neighborhood children. The streets are quiet during the day, an improvement over the situation in June, but at night it sounds like troop movements. You think of the song, "The Freaks Come Out At Night." This must be how it is in Haiti under the Duvaliers, which is the kind of regime that comes to mind when you see the hoodlums milling about on your street. They have all of the charm of the Tonton Macoutes and wear the same kind of sunglasses. Robberies occur; within one month, four auto break-ins and four burglaries, as The Living Dead attempt to steal radios or anything that will finance their habit.

The patrolman who arrives after the second break-in of your car within the month of October says that the Oakland police can't cover all of the posts, and that stopping the cocaine epidemic is like stopping sand; Chief Hart says that his forces are "stretched thin," and that there should be more concentration on education; the people you see involved in the drug trade have been out of school for a long time. You hear this from most of the people you interview: the drug war is over and the bad guys have won. The chief of police cites all of the arrests that he's made, only to conclude that "the problem is getting worse. It's horrible." He tells this to the newspaper, a remark that is in sharp contrast to the conclusion of howdy-doody optimism reached by the Oakland Inter-agency Council on Drugs, November 1986: "there is a 'sense of containment' of the problem, and a perceived response from a previously protesting community of residents that progress is being made." On the other hand, Councilman Leo Brazile credits the agency with having successfully driven the street operations indoors where arrests are easier to make.

This crack stuff is cheap and highly addictive, and so some of the addicts come into your neighborhood three or four times during the night. They belong to the kind of armies that don't clean up after themselves, and so the morning after a night of cars arriving and departing every ten minutes or so, all of which seem to have bad engines and worse mufflers, your neighborhood sidewalks and streets are filled with the kind of dreck you find on the grounds of a drive-in theater the morning after a horror movie has played. The kind of people who seem to want to advertise the fact that they drink Wild Irish Rose and Night Train.

The horror-movie metaphor is apt because the customers for this brain-scrambling stuff resemble cadavers as they wander in zombielike, some barefoot and wearing pajamas under overcoats. Some are obviously into prostitution to support their habit, and you read that in Chicago a woman sold her child for cocaine. In Oakland, another woman hid in the closet so her mother wouldn't share her profits. She was making one hundred dollars per day. So that her child wouldn't cry and her position be given away, she smothered the child to death.

A next-door neighbor said that he complained to the police about "that house" but nothing was done. People say that they call the Oakland police and the police don't arrive, and when they do arrive they complain about how they're undermanned, and how budget cuts have harmed the force, and later you hear from Bill Lowe, a man who confronts drug dealers regularly with non-violent techniques, that there have been no budget cuts.

The children are receiving an education about how low some adults can become. On the way to school they may have to step over some drug creep lying on their lawns, cracked into insensibility. You read about the effects of the drug operation on the psychological well-being of the children in Oakland. You really don't have to read; your daughter and the children on the block have nightmares about it. Drug dealers show up in their poetry.

No matter what you've done to maintain your house, your property value is reduced because who wants to buy a house in a neighborhood that has become a skid row, which is what can happen to a formerly decent neighborhood overnight, especially on the first and on the fifteenth when the welfare and Social Security checks are received.

This scene is spreading throughout Oakland. No matter what the people in the Junior League, the Lakeview Club, the ballet and symphony boosters may say about image, Oakland is in a state of war against drug fascists, and for the time being the drug fascists have gained the upper hand.

When you hear that the Oakland cocaine operation is a sort of take-out center for people in some of the more exclusive neighborhoods of Berkeley and Oakland, you wonder how many of the people in these exclusive neighborhoods have "Out of Nicaragua" bumper stickers on their Volvos, but are perfectly willing to tolerate drug fascists who prey upon the decent citizens of Oakland. You wonder how many agreed with a reporter for an alternative East Bay newspaper who just about drooled on his copy as he recorded the lurid activities of a heroin street dealer, making out as though this man were Robin Hood, or with another talented writer who made Felix Mitchell appear to be some sort of Mother Teresa—a man who headed an operation that took $50 million per year out of poor neighborhoods, enough to employ thousands of teenagers during the summer. Anybody who praises a person who is trafficking in cocaine and heroin, when intravenous drug use may wipe out one third of the black population—something that even the segregated regimes of the South and all of American racists combined haven't been able to accomplish— must be sick, and the admiration that some blacks have for these people must be the kind of twisted, perverted affection that a dog feels toward a master who sadistically tortures him.

What's hip about somebody who does errands for multinational drug Caesars for the peanut end of the take? What's hip about somebody who puts blacks and Latinos in a position where they're spending billions of dollars on hard drugs, and in doing so financing the economies of Third World and Western countries; a sort of Marshall Plan whose bills are paid by the destitute? What's hip about somebody who doesn't have the sense to funnel his underground profits into community projects like the ethnic gangsters of the past, but sends money to the white suburbs because of his clownish, brazen lifestyle, which demands BMWs and gold-trimmed Rolls-Royces?

What's hip about drug dealers whose infamous activities attract bad media coverage and dissuade investors from coming into Oakland, therefore losing thousands of jobs for Oaklanders? George Williams tells you that some investors won't come into Oakland because they are afraid that their safety can't be guaranteed. What's so hip about crack merchants who, according to a theory proposed by Bill Lowe, chairperson of the North Oakland District Community Council, have joined with unscrupulous realtors to scare the black elderly out of town, and make room for regentrifiers? Books such as Jonathan Kwitny's *The Crimes of Patriots* claim that the contras are financing their despicable operations by dumping drugs into the poor neighborhoods of America, so what's hip about somebody who puts poor blacks and Latinos into a position where they're financing a foreign policy they might not approve of?

In Oakland, there are two governments, the legally elected representative government and the government of crackers who can make decisions about how your neighborhood should operate without calling public hearings, which is the way things are managed by their fellow fascist governments. As you think about all of this, you've worked yourself into a state of anger, and you feel like Paul Muni in *The Last Angry Man*. On July 1 you read that a sixty-year-old man living in what is described as a quiet black neighborhood near the Berkeley border is caught in crossfire between some drug fascists and is paralyzed from the neck down.

When you attend a meeting of the Oakland Arts Council the next day, you say that this place is becoming like Beirut, and a couple of women who look like the Piedmont types who seem to rule over Oakland society and culture look at you as though you're crazy. They don't live at Ground Zero.

Apocalypse

California is a tragic land—like Palestine, like every
promised land.   CHRISTOPHER ISHERWOOD

—— Umberto Eco ——

The Suicides of the Temple

The strangest thing about the story of the People's Temple suicides is the media reaction, both in America and in Europe. Their reaction is: "Inconceivable, an inconceivable event." In other words, it seems inconceivable that a person long considered respectable, like Jim Jones (all those who knew him over these past years, who contributed to his charitable activities or exploited him for garnering votes, have unanimously defined him as an altruistic preacher, a fascinating personality, a convinced integrationist, a good democrat, or as we Italians would say, an "antifascist"), could then go mad, turn into a bloodthirsty autocrat, a kind of Bokassa who stole the savings of his faithful followers, used drugs, indulged in the most promiscuous sex, hetero and homo, and commended the slaughter of those who attempted to escape his rule. It seems incredible that so many nice people followed him blindly, and to the point of suicide. It seems incredible that a neo-Christian sect, gentle, mystical-communist in its inspiration, should end up transformed into a gang of killers, driving its escapees to seek police protection against the menace of murder. It seems incredible that respectable pensioners, students, blacks eager for social integration, should abandon beautiful, pleasant California, all green lawns and spring breezes, to go and bury themselves in the equatorial jungle, teeming with piranhas and poisonous snakes. It is incredible that the families of the brainwashed young could not make the government intervene strongly, and that only at the end poor Congressman Ryan started an inquiry, which cost him his life. All, all incredible, in other words, unheard of, what's the world coming to, what next?

We remain stunned not by Jim Jones but by the unconscious hypocrisy of "normal" people. Normal people try desperately to repress a reality that has been before their eyes for at least two thousand years. For the story of the People's Temple is old, a matter of flux and reflux, of eternal returns. Refusal to remember these things leads us then to see in terrorist phenomena the hand of the CIA or the Czechs. If only evil really did come always from across the border. The trouble is that it comes not from horizontal distances but from vertical. Certain answers, that is, must be sought from Freud and Lacan, not from the secret services.

What's more, American politicians and journalists didn't even have to go and read the sacred texts on the history of millenarian sects or the classics of psychoanalysis. The story of the People's Temple is told in one of the latest books of that sly operator Harold Robbins (sly because he always concocts his novels with bits of reality, whether it's the story of Hefner or Porfirio Rubirosa or some Arab magnate). The book in question is *Dreams Die First*. There is the Reverend Sam (who happens to bear a very close resemblance to the Reverend Sun Myung Moon), who has founded a laboratory to which the young initiates bring all their money; he then invests it in shrewd financial speculations. Sam preaches peace and harmony, introduces his young people to the most complete sexual promiscuity, sets up a mystical retreat in the jungle, where he imposes rigid discipline, initiation through drugs, with torture and persecution for those attempting escape, until finally the borderlines between worship, criminality, and rites à la Manson family become very faint. This is the Robbins novel. But Robbins invents nothing, not even at the level of fictional translation of real-life events.

Some decades ahead of him, in *The Dain Curse*, the great Dashiell Hammett portrays a Holy Grail cult, naturally set in California—where else?—which begins by enrolling rich members and taking their money. The cult is not at all violent, even if the initiations (here, too) involve drugs and sleight of hand (among other things, the staging recalls that of the Eleusinian mysteries). The prophet, according to Hammett, was an impressive man: When he looked at you, you felt all confused. Then he went crazy and believed he could do and achieve anything. . . . He dreamed of convincing the whole world of his divinity. . . . He was a madman who would see no limit to his power.

You can almost think you are hearing the interviews published during the past few days in the *New York Times*: He was a wonderfully sweet and kind person, a magnetic personality, he made you feel you belonged to a community.

And the lawyer Mark Lane tries to clarify how Jones was seized with paranoia, by thirst for absolute power. And if we now reread the book, *The Family*, that Ed Sanders wrote about Charles Manson's California cult and its degeneration, we find everything already there.

So why do these things happen, and why in California? The second half of the question is fairly ingenuous. There are certain reasons why California is specially fertile in producing cults, but the basic scenario is far older. In brief, Jones's cult, the People's Temple, had all the characteristics of the millenarian movements throughout Western history from the first centuries of Christianity down to the present. (And I speak only of these because there would be no room to talk about Jewish millenarianism or analogous cults in the Orient, or various corybantisms in the classical age, or similar manifestations on the African continent, found, unchanged, today in Brazil.)

The Christian series probably begins in the third century A.D. with the extreme wing of the Donatists, the Circoncellions, who went around armed with clubs, attacking the imperial troops, assassinating their sworn enemies, those loyal to the Church of Rome. They blinded their theological adversaries with mixtures of lime and vinegar; thirsting for martyrdom, they would stop wayfarers and threaten death if they refused to martyr them; they organized sumptuous funeral banquets and then killed themselves by jumping off cliffs. In the wake of the various interpretations of the Apocalypse, tense with expectation of the millennium, the various medieval movements arose, the fraticelli and the apostolics of Gherardo Segarelli, from which was born the revolt of Fra Dolcino, the brothers of the free spirit, the swindlers suspected of satanism, the various Catharist groups who sometimes committed suicide by starving themselves (the "endura"). In the twelfth century, Tanchelm, endowed with impressive charisma, had his followers give him all their wealth and he scoured Flanders; Eudes de l'Etoile dragged his followers through the forests of Brittany until they all ended on the pyre; during the Crusades the bands of Tafurs, all hairy and dirty, took to sacking, cannibalism, the massacre of the Jews; insuperable in battle, these Tafurs were feared by the Saracens; later the sixteenth-century Revolutionary of the Upper Rhine fiercely pursued the massacre of ecclesiastics; in the thirteenth century flagellant movements spread (the Crucifers, Brothers of the Cross, the secret Flagellants of Thuringia), moving from one village to another, lashing themselves until they bled. The Reformation period witnessed the mystical communism of the city of Münster, where followers of Thomas Münzer, under John of Leyden, set up a theocratic state, sustained by violence and persecution. Believers had to renounce all worldly goods, were forced into sexual promiscuity, while the leader increasingly assumed divine and imperial attributes, and any recalcitrants were locked in church for days and days until they were all prostrate, bowing before the will of the prophet; then finally everything was purified in an immense massacre in which all the faithful lost their lives.

It could be observed that suicide is not the rule in all these movements, but violent death—bloodbath, destruction on the pyre—certainly is. And it is easy to understand why the theme of suicide (for that matter present among the Circoncellions) seems to become popular only today; the reason is that for those past movements the desire for martyrdom, death, and purification was satisfied by the authorities in power. You have only to read a masterpiece of our Italian medieval literature, the story of Fra Michele the Minorite, to see how the promise of the stake had a sure, uplifting fascination for the martyr, who could moreover hold others responsible for that death which he nevertheless so ardently desired. Naturally in today's California, where even a mass murderer like Manson lives quietly in prison and applies for parole, where, in other words, authority refuses to administer death, the desire for martyrdom must take on more active forms: *Do it yourself*, in short.

The historical parallels are endless (the eighteenth-century *camisards*, for example, the Cevenne prophets in the seventeenth, the Convulsionarians of San Medardo, down to the various Shakers, Pentecostals, and Glossolalics now invading Italy and in many places absorbed into the Catholic Church). But if you simply compare the characteristics of the Jim Jones cult with a synthetic model of the various millenarian cults (overlooking the various differences) you will find some constant elements. The cult is born in a moment of crisis (spiritual, social, economic), attracting on the one hand the truly poor and on the other some "rich" with a self-punishing syndrome; it announces the end of the world and the coming of the Antichrist (Jones expected a fascist coup d'état and nuclear holocaust). It starts with a program of common ownership of property and convinces the initiates that they are the elect. As such they become more at home with their bodies, and after a strict phase they progress to practices of extreme sexual freedom. The leader, endowed with charisma, subjects everyone to his own psychological power and, for the common good, exploits both the material donations and the willingness of the faithful to be mystically possessed. Not infrequently drugs or forms of self-hypnosis are employed to create a psychological cohesion for the group. The leader proceeds through successive stages of divinization. The group goes from self-flagellation to violence against the unfaithful and then to violence against themselves, in their desire for martyrdom. On the one hand, a persecution delirium rages, and on the other the group's oddness actually unleashes genuine persecution, which accuses the group of crimes it hasn't even committed.

In Jones's case, the liberal attitude of American society drove him to invent a plot (the congressman coming to destroy them) and then the self-destructive occasion. Obviously, the theme of the flight through the forest is also present. In other words, the church of the People's Temple is only one of many examples of a revival of the millenarian cults in which at the end (after a start justified by situations of social crisis, pauperism, injustice, protest against authority and the immorality of the times), the elect are overwhelmed by the temptation, gnostic in origin, which asserts that to free themselves from the rule of the angels, lords of the cosmos, they have to pass through all the forms of perversion and cross the swamp of evil.

So then, why today? Why in the United States to such an extent, why in California? If millenarianism is born out of social insecurity and explodes in moments of historical crisis, in other countries it can take on socially positive forms (revolution, conquest, struggle against the tyrant, even nonviolent pursuit of martyrdom, as for the early Christians; and in all these cases it is supported by solid theory, which allows the social justification of one's own sacrifice); or it can imitate the historically positive forms, while rejecting social justification (as happens with the Red Brigades). In America, where there is now no central object against which to join battle as there was during the war in Vietnam, where the society allows even aliens to receive unemployment compensation, but where loneliness and the mechanization of life drive people to drugs or to talking to themselves in the street, the search for the alternative cult becomes frantic. California is a paradise cut off from the world, where all is allowed and all is inspired by an obligatory model of "happiness" (there isn't even the filth of New York or Detroit; you are condemned to be happy). Any promise of community life, of a "new deal," of regeneration is therefore good. It can come through jogging, satanic cults, new Christianities. The threat of the "fault" which will one day tear California from the mainland and cast her adrift exerts a mythical pressure on minds made unstable by all the artificiality. Why not Jones and the good death he promises?

The truth is that, in this sense, there is no difference between the destructive madness of the Khmers, who wipe out the populations of cities and create a mystical republic of revolutionaries dedicated to death, and the destructive madness of someone who contributes a hundred thousand dollars to the prophet. America takes a negative view of Chinese austerity, of the sense of permanent campaign among the Cubans, the sinister madness of the Cambodians. But then when it finds itself facing the appearance of the same desire for millenarian renewal, and sees it distorted in the asocial form of mass suicide, it cannot understand that the promise to reach Saturn one day is not enough. And so it says something "inconceivable" has happened.

Ravishing
Hyperrealism

The microwave, the waste disposal, the orgasmic elasticity of the carpets: this soft, resort-style civilization irresistibly evokes the end of the world. All their activities here have a surreptitious end-of-the-world feel to them: these Californian scholars with monomaniacal passions for things French or Marxist, the various sects obsessively concerned with chastity or crime, these joggers sleepwalking in the mist like shadows that have escaped from Plato's cave, the very real mental defectives or mongols let out of the psychiatric hospitals (this letting loose of the mad into the city seems a sure sign of the end of the world, the loosing of the seals of the Apocalypse), these obese individuals who have escaped from the hormone laboratories of their own bodies, and these drilling platforms—"oil sanctuaries"—keeping watch in the night, like grand casinos, or extraterrestrial spacecraft.

Ravishing hyperrealism / Ecstatic asceticism / Multi-process tracking shot /
Interactive multi-dimensionality / Mind-blowing / *Western Digitals* /
Body Building Incorporated / *Mileage unlimited* / *Channel Zero*

Eternity

. . . *this great crystal of light, whose base is as large as Europe and whose height for all practical purposes is infinite.*   ALDOUS HUXLEY

Aldous Huxley

The Desert

Boundlessness and emptiness—these are the two most expressive symbols of that attributeless Godhead, of whom all that can be said is St. Bernard's *Nescio nescio* or the Vedantist's "not this, not this." The Godhead, says Meister Eckhart, must be loved "as not-God, not-Spirit, not-person, not-image, must be loved as He is, a sheer pure absolute One, sundered from all twoness, and in whom we must eternally sink from nothingness to nothingness." In the scriptures of Northern and Far Eastern Buddhism the spatial metaphors recur again and again. At the moment of death, writes the author of *Bardo Thodol*, "all things are like the cloudless sky; and the naked immaculate Intellect is like unto a translucent void without circumference or center." "The great Way," in Sosan's words, "is perfect, like unto vast space, with nothing wanting, nothing superfluous." "Mind," says Hui-neng (and he is speaking of that universal ground of consciousness, from which all beings, the unenlightened no less than the enlightened, take their source), "mind is like emptiness of space. . . . Space contains sun, moon, stars, the great earth, with its mountains and rivers. . . . Good men and bad men, good things and bad things, heaven and hell—they are all in empty space. The emptiness of Self-nature is in all people just like this." The theologians argue, the dogmatists declaim their credos; but their propositions "stand in no intrinsic relation to my inner light.

This Inner Light" (I quote from Yoka Dashi's "Song of Enlightenment") "can be likened to space; it knows no boundaries; yet it is always here, is always with us, always retains its serenity and fullness. . . . You cannot take hold of it, and you cannot get rid of it; it goes on its own way. You speak and it is silent; you remain silent, and it speaks."

Silence is the cloudless heaven perceived by another sense. Like space and emptiness, it is a natural symbol of the divine. In the Mithraic mysteries, the candidate for initiation was told to lay a finger to his lips and whisper: "Silence! Silence! Silence—symbol of the living imperishable God!" And long before the coming of Christianity to the Thebaid, there had been Egyptian mystery religions, for whose followers God was a well of life, "closed to him who speaks, but open to the silent." The Hebrew scriptures are eloquent almost to excess; but even here, among the splendid rumblings of prophetic praise and impetration and anathema, there are occasional references to the spiritual meaning and the therapeutic virtues of silence. "Be still, and know that I am God." "The Lord is in his holy temple; let all the world keep silence before him." "Keep thou silence at the presence of the Lord God." The desert, after all, began within a few miles of the gates of Jerusalem.

The facts of silence and emptiness are traditionally the symbols of divine immanence—but not, of course, for everyone, and not in all circumstances. "Until one has crossed a barren desert, without food or water, under a burning tropical sun, at three miles an hour, one can form no conception of what misery is." These are the words of a gold-seeker, who took the southern route to California in 1849. Even when one is crossing it at seventy miles an hour on a four-lane highway, the desert can seem formidable enough. To the forty-niners it was unmitigated hell. Men and women who are at her mercy find it hard to see in Nature and her works any symbols but those of brute power at the best and, at the worst, of an obscure and mindless malice. The desert's emptiness and the desert's silence reveal what we may call their spiritual meanings only to those who enjoy some measure of physiological security. The security may amount to no more than St. Anthony's hut and daily ration of bread and vegetables, no more than Milarepa's cave and barley meal and boiled nettles—less than what any sane economist would regard as the indispensable minimum, but still security, still a guarantee of organic life and, along with life, of the possibility of spiritual liberty and transcendental happiness.

But even for those who enjoy security against the assaults of the environment, the desert does not always or inevitably reveal its spiritual meanings. The early Christian hermits retired to the Thebaid because its air was purer, because there were fewer distractions, because God seemed nearer there than in the world of men. But, alas, dry places are notoriously the abode of unclean spirits, seeking rest and finding it not. If the immanence of God was sometimes more easily discoverable in the desert, so also, and all too frequently, was the immanence of the devil. St. Anthony's temptations have become a legend, and Cassian speaks of "the tempests of imagination" through which every new-comer to the eremitic life had to pass. Solitude, he writes, makes men feel "the many-winged folly of their souls . . . ; they find the perpetual silence intol-erable, and those whom no labor on the land could weary, are vanquished by doing nothing and worn out by the long duration of their peace." *Be still, and know that I am God;* be still, and know that *you* are the delinquent imbecile who snarls and gibbers in the basement of every human mind. The desert can drive men mad, but it can also help them to become supremely sane.

The enormous drafts of emptiness and silence prescribed by the eremites are safe medicine only for a few exceptional souls. By the majority the desert should be taken either dilute or, if at full strength, in small doses. Used in this way, it acts as a spiritual restorative, as an anti-hallucinant, as a de-tensioner and alterative.

In his book *The Next Million Years*, Sir Charles Darwin looks forward to thirty thousand generations of ever more humans pressing ever more heavily on ever-dwindling resources and being killed off in ever increasing numbers by famine, pestilence, and war. He may be right. Alternatively, human inge-nuity may somehow falsify his predictions. But even human ingenuity will find it hard to circumvent arithmetic. On a planet of limited area, the more people there are, the less vacant space there is bound to be. Over and above the mate-rial and sociological problems of increasing population, there is a serious psy-chological problem. In a completely home-made environment, such as is pro-vided by any great metropolis, it is as hard to remain sane as it is in a completely natural environment such as the desert or the forest. O Solitude, where are thy charms? But, O Multitude, where are *thine*? The most wonderful thing about America is that, even in these middle years of the twentieth century, there are so few Americans. By taking a certain amount of trouble you might still be able to get yourself eaten by a bear in the state of New York. And without any trouble at all you can get bitten by a rattler in the Hollywood hills, or die of thirst, while wandering through an uninhabited desert, within a hundred and fifty miles of Los Angeles. A short generation ago you might have wandered and died within only a hundred miles of Los Angeles. Today the mounting tide of humanity has oozed through the intervening canyons and spilled out into the wide Mojave. Solitude is receding at the rate of four and a half kilometers per annum.

And yet, in spite of it all, the silence persists. For this silence of the desert is such that casual sounds, and even the systematic noise of civilization, cannot abolish it. They coexist with it—as small irrelevances at right angles to an enormous meaning, as veins of something analogous to darkness within an enduring transparency. From the irrigated land come the dark gross sounds of lowing cattle, and above them the plovers trail their vanishing threads of shrillness. Suddenly, startlingly, out of the sleeping sagebrush there bursts the shrieking of coyotes—Trio for Ghoul and Two Damned Souls. On the trunks of cottonwood trees, on the wooden walls of barns and houses, the woodpeckers rattle away like pneumatic drills. Picking one's way between the cactuses and the creosote bushes one hears, like some tiny whirring clockwork, the soliloquies of invisible wrens, the calling, at dusk, of the nightjays and even occasionally the voice of Homo sapiens—six of the species in a parked Chevrolet, listening to the broadcast of a prize fight, or else in pairs necking to the delicious accompaniment of Crosby. But the light forgives, the distances forget, and this great crystal of silence, whose base is as large as Europe and whose height, for all practical purposes, is infinite, can coexist with things of a far higher order of discrepancy than canned sentiment or vicarious sport. Jet planes, for example—the stillness is so massive that it can absorb even jet planes. The screaming crash mounts to its intolerable climax and fades again, mounts as another of the monsters rips through the air, and once more diminishes and is gone. But even at the height of the outrage the mind can still remain aware of that which surrounds it, that which preceded and will outlast it.

Progress, however, is on the march. Jet planes are already as characteristic of the desert as are Joshua trees or burrowing owls; they will soon be almost as numerous. The wilderness has entered the armament race, and will be in it to the end. In its multimillion-acred emptiness there is room enough to explode atomic bombs and experiment with guided missiles. The weather, so far as flying is concerned, is uniformly excellent, and in the plains lie the flat beds of many lakes, dry since the last Ice Age, and manifestly intended by Providence for hot-rod racing and jets. Huge airfields have already been constructed. Factories are going up. Oases are turning into industrial towns. In brand-new Reservations, surrounded by barbed wire and the FBI, not Indians but tribes of physicists, chemists, metallurgists, communication engineers, and mechanics are working with the coordinated frenzy of termites. From their air-conditioned laboratories and machine shops there flows a steady stream of marvels, each one more expensive and each more fiendish than the last. The desert silence is still there; but so, ever more noisily, are the scientific irrelevancies. Give the boys in the Reservations a few more years and another hundred billion dollars, and they will succeed (for with technology all things are possible) in abolishing the silence, in transforming what are now irrelevancies into the desert's fundamental meaning. Meanwhile, and luckily for us, it is noise which is exceptional; the rule is still this crystalline symbol of universal Mind.

The bulldozers roar, the concrete is mixed and poured, the jet planes go crashing through the air, the rockets soar aloft with their cargoes of white mice and electronic instruments. And yet for all this, "nature is never spent; there lives the dearest freshness deep down things."

And not merely the dearest, but the strangest, the most wonderfully unlikely. I remember, for example, a recent visit to one of the new Reservations. It was in the spring of 1952 and, after seven years of drought, the rains of the preceding winter had been copious. From end to end the Mojave was carpeted with flowers—sunflowers, and the dwarf phlox, chicory and coreopsis, wild hollyhock and all the tribe of garlics and lilies. And then, as we neared the Reservation, the flower carpet began to move. We stopped the car, we walked into the desert to take a closer look. On the bare ground, on every plant and bush innumerable caterpillars were crawling. They were of two kinds—one smooth, with green and white markings, and a horn, like that of a miniature rhinoceros, growing out of its hinder end. The caterpillar, evidently, of one of the hawk moths. Mingled with these, in millions no less uncountable, were the brown hairy offspring of (I think) the Painted Lady butterfly. They were everywhere—over hundreds of square miles of the desert. And yet, a year before, when the eggs from which these larvae had emerged were laid, California had been as dry as a bone. On what, then, had the parent insects lived? And what had been the food of their innumerable offspring? In the days when I collected butterflies and kept their young in glass jars on the window sill of my cubicle at school, no self-respecting caterpillar would feed on anything but the leaves to which its species had been predestined. Puss moths laid their eggs on poplars, spurge hawks on spurges; mulleins were frequented by the gaily piebald caterpillars of one rather rare and rigidly fastidious moth. Offered an alternative diet, my caterpillars would turn away in horror. They were like orthodox Jews confronted by pork or lobsters; they were like Brahmins at a feast of beef prepared by Untouchables. Eat? Never. They would rather die. And if the right food were not forthcoming, die they did. But these caterpillars of the desert were apparently different. Crawling into irrigated regions, they had devoured the young leaves of entire vineyards and vegetable gardens. They had broken with tradition, they had flouted the immemorial taboos. Here, near the Reservation, there was no cultivated land. These hawk moth and Painted Lady caterpillars, which were all full grown, must have fed on indigenous growths—but which, I could never discover; for when I saw them the creatures were all crawling at random, in search either of something juicier to eat or else of some place to spin their cocoons. Entering the Reservation, we found them all over the parking lot and even on the steps of the enormous building which housed the laboratories and the administrative offices. The men on guard only laughed or swore. But could they be *absolutely* sure? Biology has always been the Russians' strongest point. These innumerable crawlers—perhaps they were Soviet agents? Parachuted from the stratosphere, impenetrably disguised, and so thoroughly indoctrinated, so completely conditioned by means of post-hypnotic suggestions that even under torture it would be impossible for them to confess, even under DDT. . . .

Our party showed its pass and entered. The strangeness was no longer Nature's; it was strictly human. Nine and a half acres of floor space, nine and a half acres of the most extravagant improbability. Sagebrush and wild flowers beyond the windows; but here, within, machine tools capable of turning out anything from a tank to an electron microscope; million-volt X-ray cameras; electric furnaces; wind tunnels; refrigerated vacuum tanks; and on either side of endless passages closed doors bearing inscriptions which had obviously been taken from last year's science-fiction magazines. (This year's space ships, of course, have harnessed gravitation and magnetism.) ROCKET DEPARTMENT, we read on door after door. ROCKET AND EXPLOSIVES DEPARTMENT, ROCKET PERSONNEL DEPARTMENT. And what lay behind the unmarked doors? Rockets and Canned Tularemia? Rockets and Nuclear Fission? Rockets and Space Cadets? Rockets and Elementary Courses in Martian Language and Literature?

It was a relief to get back to the caterpillars. Ninety-nine point nine recurring percent of the poor things were going to die—but not for an ideology, not while doing their best to bring death to other caterpillars, not to the accompaniment of *Te Deums*, of *Dulce et decorums*, of "We shall not sheathe the sword, which we have not lightly drawn, until . . ." Until what? The only completely unconditional surrender will come when everybody—but *everybody*—is a corpse.

For modern man, the really blessed thing about Nature is its otherness. In their anxiety to find a cosmic basis for human values, our ancestors invented an emblematic botany, a natural history composed of allegories and fables, an astronomy that told fortunes and illustrated the dogmas of revealed religion. "In the Middle Ages," writes Emile Mâle, "the idea of a thing which a man formed for himself, was always more real than the thing itself. The study of things for their own sake held no meaning for the thoughtful man. The task for the student of nature was to discover the eternal truth which God would have each thing express." These eternal truths expressed by things were not the laws of physical and organic being—laws discoverable only by patient observation and the sacrifice of preconceived ideas and autistic urges; they were the notions and fantasies engendered in the minds of logicians, whose major premises, for the most part, were other fantasies and notions bequeathed to them by earlier writers. Against the belief that such purely verbal constructions were eternal truths, only the mystics protested; and the mystics were concerned only with that "obscure knowledge," as it was called, which comes when a man "sees all in all." But between the real but obscure knowledge of the mystic and the clear but unreal knowledge of the verbalist, lies the clearish and realish knowledge of the naturalist and the man of science. It was knowledge of a kind which most of our ancestors found completely uninteresting.

Reading the older descriptions of God's creatures, the older speculations about the ways and workings of Nature, we start by being amused. But the amusement soon turns to the most intense boredom and a kind of mental suffocation. We find ourselves gasping for breath in a world where all the windows are shut and everything "wears man's smudge and shares man's smell." Words are the greatest, the most momentous of all our inventions, and the specifically human realm is the realm of language. In the stifling universe of medieval thought, the given facts of Nature were treated as the symbols of familiar notions. Words did not stand for things; things stood for pre-existent words. This is a pitfall which, in the natural sciences, we have learned to avoid. But in other contexts than the scientific—in the context, for example, of politics— we continue to take our verbal symbols with the same disastrous seriousness as was displayed by our crusading and persecuting ancestors. For both parties, the people on the other side of the Iron Curtain are not human beings, but merely the embodiments of the pejorative phrases coined by propagandists.

Nature is blessedly nonhuman; and insofar as we belong to the natural order, we too are blessedly nonhuman. The otherness of caterpillars, as of our own bodies, is an otherness underlain by a principal identity. The nonhumanity of wild flowers, as of the deepest levels of our own minds, exists within a system which includes and transcends the human. In the given realm of the inner and outer not-self, we are all one. In the home-made realm of symbols we are separate and mutually hostile partisans. Thanks to words, we have been able to rise above the brutes; and thanks to words, we have often sunk to the level of the demons. Our statesmen have tried to come to an international agreement on the use of atomic power. They have not been successful. And even if they had, what then? No agreement on atomic power can do any lasting good, unless it be preceded by an agreement on language. If we make a wrong use of nuclear fission, it will be because we have made a wrong use of the symbols, in terms of which we think about ourselves and other people. Individually and collectively, men have always been the victims of their own words; but, except in the emotionally neutral field of science, they have never been willing to admit their linguistic ineptitude, and correct their mistakes. Taken too seriously, symbols have motivated and justified all the horrors of recorded history. On every level from the personal to the international, the letter kills. Theoretically we know this very well. In practice, nevertheless, we continue to commit the suicidal blunders to which we have become accustomed.

The caterpillars were still on the march when we left the Reservation, and it was half an hour or more, at a mile a minute, before we were clear of them. Among the phloxes and the sunflowers, millions in the midst of hundreds of millions, they proclaimed (along with the dangers of overpopulation) the strength, the fecundity, the endless resourcefulness of life. We were in the desert, and the desert was blossoming, the desert was crawling. I had not seen anything like it since that spring day, in 1948, when we had been walking at the other end of the Mojave, near the great earthquake fault, down which the highway descends to San Bernardino and the orange groves. The elevation here is around four thousand feet and the desert is dotted with dark clumps of juniper. Suddenly, as we moved through the enormous emptiness, we became aware of an entirely unfamiliar interruption to the silence. Before, behind, to right and to left, the sound seemed to come from all directions. It was a small sharp crackling, like the ubiquitous frying of bacon, like the first flames in the kindling of innumerable bonfires. There seemed to be no explanation. And then, as we looked more closely, the riddle gave up its answer. Anchored to a stem of sagebrush, we saw the horny pupa of cicada. It had begun to split and the full-grown insect was in process of pushing its way out. Each time it struggled, its case of amber-colored chitin opened a little more widely. The continuous crackling that we heard was caused by the simultaneous emergence of thousands upon thousands of individuals. How long they had spent underground I could never discover. Dr. Edmund Jaeger, who knows as much about the fauna and flora of the Western deserts as anyone now living, tells me that the habits of this particular cicada have never been closely studied. He himself had never witnessed the mass resurrection upon which we had had the good fortune to stumble. All one can be sure of is that these creatures had spent anything from two to seventeen years in the soil, and that they had all chosen this particular May morning to climb out of the grave, burst their coffins, dry their moist wings and embark upon their life of sex and song.

Three weeks later we heard and saw another detachment of the buried army coming out into the sun among the pines and the flowering fremontias of the San Gabriel Mountains. The chill of two thousand additional feet of elevation had postponed the resurrection; but when it came, it conformed exactly to the pattern set by the insects of the desert: the risen pupa, the crackle of splitting horn, the helpless imago waiting for the sun to bake it into perfection, and then the flight, the tireless singing, so unremitting that it becomes a part of the silence. The boys in the Reservations are doing their best; and perhaps, if they are given the necessary time and money, they may really succeed in making the planet uninhabitable. Applied Science is a conjuror, whose bottomless hat yields impartially the softest of Angora rabbits and the most petrifying of Medusas. But I am still optimist enough to credit life with invincibility, I am still ready to bet that the nonhuman otherness at the root of man's being will ultimately triumph over the all too human selves who frame the ideologies and engineer the collective suicides. For our survival, if we do survive, we shall be less beholden to our common sense (the name we give to what happens when we try to think of the world in terms of the unanalyzed symbols supplied by language and the local customs) than to our caterpillar- and cicada-sense, to intelligence, in other words, as it operates on the organic level. That intelligence is at once a will to persistence and an inherited knowledge of the physiological and psychological means by which, despite all the follies of the loquacious self, persistence can be achieved. And beyond survival is transfiguration; beyond and including animal grace is the grace of that other not-self, of which the desert silence and the desert emptiness are the most expressive symbols.

Walt Whitman

Facing West from California's Shores

Facing west from California's shores,
Inquiring, tireless, seeking what is yet unfound,
I, a child, very old, over waves, towards the house of maternity, the land of
    migrations, look afar,
Look off the shores of my Western sea, the circle almost circled;
For starting westward from Hindustan, from the vales of Kashmere,
From Asia, from the north, from the God, the sage, and the hero,
From the south, from the flowery peninsulas and the spice islands,
Long having wander'd since, round the earth having wander'd,
Now I face home again, very pleas'd and joyous,
(But where is what I started for so long ago?
And why is it yet unfound?)

Acknowledgments

The editors wish to thank the following authors and publishers for their permission to reprint materials included in this volume. Every effort has been made to trace the ownership of copyrighted material and to make full acknowledgment of its use. Material in the public domain has been listed with its date of original publication for purposes of reference. If errors or omissions have occurred, they will be corrected in subsequent editions, provided that notification is submitted in writing to the publisher.

Maya Angelou: Excerpt from *I Know Why the Caged Bird Sings*. Copyright © 1969 by Maya Angelou. Reprinted by permission of Random House, Inc.

Mary Austin: "The Land" from *Stories of the Country of Lost Borders*, 1903.

Stephen Bach: Excerpt from *Final Cut*. Copyright © 1984 by Stephen Bach. Reprinted by permission of William Morrow & Company, Inc.

Jean Baudrillard: "Ideal Cosy Nook," "Los Angeles by Night" (editors' titles) from *America*, first published as *Amérique* by Bernard Grasset, Paris, 1986, translated by Chris Turner. Translation copyright © 1988 by Verso/New Left Books. Reprinted by permission of Verso.

Henry Bean: Excerpt from *False Match*. Copyright © 1982 by Henry Bean. Reprinted by permission of Poseidon Press, a division of Simon & Schuster, Inc.

Simone de Beauvoir: "Berkeley," "California," and "San Francisco" from *America Day by Day*, translated by Patrick Dudley. Copyright © 1953 by Grove Press, Inc. Reprinted by permission of Grove Press, Inc., a division of Wheatland Corporation.

Stanley Booth: "The Killing Ground" from *The True Adventures of the Rolling Stones*. Copyright © 1984 by Stanley Booth. Reprinted by permission of Random House, Inc.

Vincent Bugliosi: "Saturday, August 9, 1969" from *Helter Skelter*. Copyright © 1974 by Vincent Bugliosi and Curt Gentry. Reprinted by permission of W. W. Norton & Company, Inc.

Herb Caen: "Baghdad-by-the-Bay" from *Baghdad-by-the-Bay*. Copyright © 1949 by Herb Caen. Reprinted by permission of Doubleday, a division of Bantam, Doubleday, Dell Publishing Group, Inc.

Joan Didion: "Notes from a Native Daughter" from *Slouching Towards Bethlehem*. Copyright © 1961, 1965, 1968, by Joan Didion. Reprinted by permission of Farrar, Straus & Giroux, Inc.

Umberto Eco: "The Suicides of the Temple" from *Travels in Hyperreality*. Copyright © 1983, 1976, 1973 by Gruppo Editoriale Fabbri-Bompiani, Sonzogno, Etas S. p. A.; English translation copyright © 1986 by Harcourt Brace Jovanovich, Inc.; copyright © 1986, 1967 by Umberto Eco; reprinted by permission of Harcourt Brace Jovanovich.

Gretel Ehrlich: Excerpt from *Heart Mountain*. Copyright © 1988 by Gretel Ehrlich. All rights reserved. Reprinted by permission of Viking Penguin, a division of Penguin Books USA, Inc.

M. F. K. Fisher: "The First Oyster" from *The Gastronomical Me*. Copyright © 1953, 1954 by M. F. K. Fisher. Reprinted by permission of North Point Press.

Allen Ginsberg: "A Supermarket in California" from *Reality Sandwiches*. Copyright © 1963 by City Lights Books. Reprinted by permission of Harper & Row Publishers.

Ralph J. Gleason: "San Francisco Jazz Scene" from *Evergreen Review*, vol. 1, no. 2 (1957). Copyright © 1957 by Grove Press, Inc. Reprinted by permission of Grove Press, Inc., a division of Wheatland Corporation.

Thom Gunn: "The J Car," copyright © 1989 by Thom Gunn. Reprinted by permission of the author.

Ben Hecht: Excerpt from "Artist, Friend, and Moneymaker" in *A Child of the Century*. Copyright © 1954 by Ben Hecht. Copyright © 1985 by Donald I. Fine, Publishers. Reprinted by permission of Donald I. Fine, Publishers.

Warren Hinckle: Excerpt from "A Social History of the Hippies" in *Ramparts*. Copyright © 1967 by Warren Hinckle. Reprinted by permission of the author.

James D. Houston: "The Hip Plumber" from *The Men in My Life*. Copyright © 1987 by James D. Houston. Reprinted by permission of the author.

Aldous Huxley: "The Desert" from *Collected Essays*. Copyright © 1934 by Aldous Huxley. Reprinted by permission of Harper & Row, Publishers.

Robinson Jeffers: "November Surf" from *Selected Poetry of Robinson Jeffers*. Copyright © 1932, renewed 1960 by Robinson Jeffers. Reprinted by permission of Random House, Inc.

Jack Kerouac: Excerpt from "The Railroad Earth" in *Lonesome Traveller*. Copyright © 1960 by Jack Kerouac, copyright renewed 1988 by Jan Kerouac. Reprinted by permission of Grove Press, Inc., a division of Wheatland Corporation. Excerpt from *Big Sur* reprinted by permission of Sterling Lord Literistic, Inc.

Clarence King: "Mount Whitney" from *Mountaineering in the Sierra Nevadas*, 1872.

Maxine Hong Kingston: "Twisters and Shouters" from *Tripmaster Monkey: His Fake Book*. Copyright © 1989 by Maxine Hong Kingston. Reprinted by permission of the author.

Rudyard Kipling: Excerpt from *From Sea to Sea*, 1899.

Theodora Kroeber: Excerpt from *Ishi: The Last of His Tribe*. Copyright © 1964 Theodora Kroeber. Reprinted by permission of Houghton Mifflin Company.

Renée Lieberman: "Lies," copyright © 1988 by Renée Lieberman.

Jonathan Lieberson: "Escape from Esalen" from *Varieties*. Copyright © 1988 by Jona-

Mario Savio: "Why It Happened in Berkeley" (editors' title) from the introduction to *Berkeley: The New Student Revolt* by Hal Draper. Introduction copyright © 1965 by Mario Savio. Reprinted by permission of Grove Press, Inc., a division of Wheatland Corporation.

Raquel Scherr: "La Japonesa," copyright © 1989 by Raquel Scherr.

Randy Shilts: Excerpt from "Willkommen Castro" in *The Mayor of Castro Street: The Life and Times of Harvey Milk.* Copyright © 1982 by Randy Shilts. Reprinted by permission of St. Martin's Press, Inc.

Gary Soto: "One Thing after Another" from *Small Faces.* Copyright © 1984 by Gary Soto. Reprinted by permission of Arte Publico, University of Houston.

Gertrude Stein: Excerpt from *Everybody's Autobiography.* Copyright © 1937 by Random House, Inc. Copyright © renewed 1964 by Alice B. Toklas. Reprinted by permission of Random House, Inc.

John Steinbeck: Excerpt from *East of Eden.* Copyright © 1952 by John Steinbeck. Copyright renewed © 1980 by the Estate of John Steinbeck. All rights reserved. Reprinted by permission of Viking Penguin, a division of Penguin Books USA, Inc.

Randall Sullivan: Excerpt from "The Leader of the Pack," originally published in *Rolling Stone*, August 28, 1986. Copyright © 1986 by Straight Arrow Publishers, Inc. Reprinted by permission of Straight Arrow Publishers, Inc.

Amy Tan: "Jing-Mei Woo: The Joy Luck Club" from *The Joy Luck Club.* Copyright © 1989 by Amy Tan. Reprinted by permission of the Putnam Publishing Group.

David Thomson: "Driving in a Back Projection," revised and expanded version of the essay that originally appeared in *University Publishing* 12, Winter 1984. Copyright © 1984 by The Regents of the University of California. Reprinted by permission of the author.

Jane Vandenburgh: Excerpt from *Failure to Zigzag.* Copyright © 1989 by Jane Vandenburgh. Reprinted by permission of North Point Press.

Gore Vidal: Excerpt from *Myra Breckinridge.* Copyright © 1968 by Gore Vidal. Reprinted by permission of Random House, Inc.

Walt Whitman: "Facing West from California's Shores" from *Leaves of Grass*, 1891–1892.

Tom Wolfe: Excerpt from "The Cops and Robbers Game" in *The Electric Kool-Aid Acid Test.* Copyright © 1968 by Tom Wolfe. Excerpt from *The Pump House Gang.* Copyright © 1966 by the World Journal Tribune Corporation. Copyright © 1968 by Tom Wolfe. Both selections reprinted by permission of Farrar, Straus & Giroux, Inc.

Michael Wood: Excerpt from *America in the Movies.* Copyright © 1989 Columbia University Press. Reprinted by permission of Columbia University Press.

Design by David Bullen
Typeset in Mergenthaler Berkeley Old Style Book and Medium
with Berkeley Old Style Bold display
by Wilsted & Taylor
Printed by Maple-Vail
on acid-free paper